The Prince of the

The Epilogue to a Rc

Sydney C. Grier

Alpha Editions

This edition published in 2024

ISBN 9789362094001

Design and Setting By

Alpha Editions

www.alphaedis.com

Email - info@alphaedis.com

Contents

CHAPTER I.
BOTH SIDES OF THE QUESTION.

THERE were only a few passengers by the South Wales Express, and to one young man in a first-class carriage the fact was very welcome. He had bought a paper almost unconsciously from the boy who came to the window, but it did him good service as a shield, from behind which he could cast suspicious and hostile glances, after the manner of the travelling Briton, at any one who seemed inclined to disturb his solitude, as long as the train was in the station. But when once the dreary and dirty buff brick surroundings of the terminus had been left behind, the paper fell to the floor, and Lord Usk gazed out of the window with an expression which seemed too ecstatic to be evoked even by the busy harvest-fields and the nursery-gardens full of asters and late roses on which his bodily eyes were resting. And indeed the scene before him might still have been a brick-and-mortar desert for all that he saw of it. His mental gaze was fixed upon the face of Miss Félicia J. Steinherz, the sight of which had changed the whole course of his life.

Could it really be the case, he was wondering, that a month ago he had never seen Félicia Steinherz? Yes, it was perfectly true, and the curious thing was that though he now saw clearly that life must have been a howling wilderness in those days, it had not seemed so at the time. He had been fairly satisfied with himself and his prospects, and quite unconscious that the world was in reality empty and out of joint. It was with a scornful pity that he looked back from his vantage-point of to-day upon the Usk of a month ago. She was breathing the same air with him then, and yet he had not so much as guessed at her existence, nor even been conscious of a blank without her! Ah, but he had; for was she not the fulfilment of all his dreams, the realisation of the ideal of womanhood which had haunted him from his boyish days? Here and there, in one woman or another, he had caught, as it seemed, glimpses of this ideal, but closer acquaintance dispelled the illusion. The woman of his dreams still eluded him tantalisingly—until he met Félicia. He did not ask himself whether she corresponded in all respects with his mental picture; it was enough that she was herself.

He could recall at this moment the rapture which had thrilled him when she first flashed upon his sight. It was the most ordinary and prosaic of introductions. He had met Hicks, the American newspaper-man, unexpectedly in Fleet Street, and had accepted without much enthusiasm his invitation to come and call with him upon J. Bertram Steinherz, the great Rhode Island shipbuilder, and his daughter, familiarly known in the States as the Plate Princess. Usk was not keen on meeting Americans, especially American heiresses who were presumably visiting England in search of titled bridegrooms, but Hicks was a family friend, and he accompanied him meekly to the Hotel Bloomsbury, with a passing wonder at the millionaire's choosing such a locality. There was some excuse for the introduction, naturally; what was it? Oh, of course; Mr Steinherz was interested in a contract for the navigation of the Euphrates, and Usk had lately voyaged down that river, and could give him some tips. Blessed Euphrates! had it not floated him into paradise? He remembered Mr Hicks's caustic strictures on the decoration of the hotel as compared with that of similar buildings in America, and his own shrug of amusement as he wondered what degree of obtrusive magnificence would be required to satisfy the æsthetic sense of the representative of the 'Empire City Crier.' He had entered the over-decorated room without receiving the slightest warning that it contained the one woman in the world, and his recollections came to a sudden stop at the point when the great discovery burst upon him. Mr Steinherz was there, of course, gentlemanly and well set-up, with a pointed grey beard and drooping moustache, which gave him the look of a retired naval officer; and there was a Miss Logan, who was introduced by Mr Steinherz as "my adopted daughter," a thin, eager-looking girl, smartly dressed, and noticeable for a high, penetrating voice. Lastly, there was Miss Steinherz. She sat in her great carved oak chair like a princess receiving her court,—if ever a princess had such tiny hands and feet and such wonderful eyes,—and the draperies which floated round her were like nothing in heaven or earth but clouds. In cold blood Usk would probably have surmised that Miss Steinherz was wearing a tea-gown, although her dress had little in common with the loose and comfortable garment which his sister Philippa had been wont to don after a hard day's hunting. There was lace about it that a queen might have worn—indeed Usk gathered later that the precious fabric, only half revealed, had been forced by the pinch of poverty from the hoarded stores of a queen in exile—there was the gleam of tiny diamond buckles, but the effect of the whole was that of clouds, clouds which were neither pink nor lavender nor grey nor blue, but which in some mysterious manner were all these at once. A woman would have hinted at the dexterous mingling and superimposition of chiffon of various tints, but to Usk all was mystic, wonderful. He was not even aware that his eyes and thoughts were alike fixed upon Miss Steinherz until he found himself assuring her father that at certain points in the voyage down the Euphrates it was usual to drag the steamer a mile or two overland.

After all, no harm was done—or at least Mr Steinherz did not appear to be astonished by this remarkable piece of information. Miss Steinherz it was who pounced upon the slip like a cat upon a mouse, and made merry at Usk's expense for the rest of the visit. He could not have imagined an English girl's engrossing the conversation as she did, and few Englishmen would have followed her lead as meekly as did her father and Mr Hicks; but how delightful it was to hear her talk, even when he himself was her butt! Now she was leaning back languidly in her chair, playing with a peacock-feather fan, while the words flowed forth slowly in a delicious lingering drawl; anon she was sitting erect, with every faculty on the alert, and rattling forth in quick succession the raciest, the most daring remarks. Not for one moment was Usk allowed to forget the foolish thing he had said, and yet while he was half-wounded, he also half-pleased, and wholly fascinated. Miss Steinherz might say what she liked, if only she would say it in such an original and delightful way, and exhibit a new and more exquisite expression of face or pose of head with each sentence.

That night Usk paced his rooms until dawn. New impressions and sensations had so thronged upon him in the hour spent at the Hotel Bloomsbury that to be still was impossible, far more so to sleep. Now that he was removed from the witchery of her presence, it was borne in upon him what a pitiful figure he must have cut in her eyes. What could he do to convince her that he was not such a fool as he had appeared? To remain under such a stigma, to feel that he had deserved, not merely incurred, her contempt, was unbearable. An inspiration came to him, and day found him rummaging among the relics of his Eastern journey. Maps, photographs, scraps of his journals, geological specimens—everything that bore even remotely on the subject in which Mr Steinherz was interested—all these were looked out with the object of turning them to account. Usk was gazing at a most promising heap, when another inspiration came to him. He had made himself look a fool, there was no getting over the fact, and had deserved the raillery Miss Steinherz had poured upon him, but he would turn this defeat into a victory. These relics of travel, judiciously produced one by one, should procure him admission to the Hotel Bloomsbury not for one brief visit, but on many successive days. Perhaps he might succeed in rehabilitating himself in Miss Steinherz's eyes by his eagerness to help her father, perhaps not; at any rate he would see her.

There was no shooting for Usk that August, and the man whose party he was to have joined on the moors found himself thrown over. September came, but the Marquis of Caerleon tramped the Llandiarmid stubble-fields alone, for Usk was still, as his father remarked ruefully, glued to London. Miss Steinherz was more beautiful and adorable and generally goddess-like than ever. Her turns of speech were nothing less than exquisite; even the way that she said "Pap-pa" and "Eu-rope" had a subtle charm of its own, and the little affectation of the accent on the first syllable raised her somewhat colourless Christian name into something unutterably sweet and strange. Her tongue was as ready as ever, but Usk had begun to fancy that she was not quite so inexorable in making fun of him as she had been. She had actually allowed him once or twice to finish a sentence without instantly turning it into ridicule, and on this slight foundation Usk was joyfully ready to erect a hopeful superstructure. He knew her outward appearance so well—the perfect figure, the small head poised on the slender neck, the delicate nose, the little mouth, the masses of dark hair which curled in rings on the white forehead and were piled above it in the most marvellous waves and twists; could it be possible that he was beginning to know Félicia herself—the mind, heart, soul, which must naturally be equally faultless? Those wonderful eyes, so large and dark and clear,—not the eyes of a girl, looking out wistfully on life half in hope and half in fear, but of a woman who feels that happiness is her right and intends to have it,—were they beginning to soften for him—for him? Oh, the bliss of the thought, that those frank eyes might one day fall before his, that Félicia might own that she loved him!

There was the sound of a footstep in the corridor of the railway carriage, and Usk snatched at his paper hurriedly, and began to study it with all his might, holding it up so as to hide his face. When he thought the intruder had passed on, he ventured to lower his screen, only to meet the mocking, not unkindly gaze of a tall lank man who was leaning against the inner doorway, evidently waiting for him to look up.

"I would bet my bottom dollar that I could state right now what you are thinking of," said the newcomer slowly.

"Oh, it's you, Hicks! Didn't know you were a thought-reader."

"I don't begin to be one, sir. You gave yourself away, you see." Mr Hicks's gaze rested on the paper, and Usk flushed quickly as he perceived that it was upside-down. But there was no use in being dignified with Hicks, and he yielded the position with a laugh.

"I suppose you're on your way home by the new route?" he said lightly, seeking safety in flight from the original subject. "I'm just running down to Llandiarmid for a day or two to see my people."

"Is that so?" drawled Mr Hicks. "A rare and beautiful thing is family affection, any way! But I guess London licks the country this fall, doesn't it?"

"It has been a good deal pleasanter this year than usual," agreed Usk.

"I admire to see a young man open and candid, sir. Have you got any more acquainted with the Steinherzes yet?"

"You are nothing whatever but a good Inquisitor spoilt! I have seen a certain amount of them."

"And so far as one of the party is concerned, it's pretty generally concluded that to see her is to—you know how it goes along? But maybe you are an exception?"

"Really, a man can't call his innermost feelings his own when you're anywhere about, Hicks." Mr Hicks nodded approvingly. "But after all, it was you that introduced me to her, and I'll make you a present of the information, which you have probably guessed already, that I am going home to have a business talk with my father."

Mr Hicks nodded again, and Usk, whose tongue seemed to have been loosed by his first admission, went on—

"There are times, you know, when a man feels he has to pay rather dear for the virtues of his family. It's quite delightful, of course, to know that no landowner in South Wales does more for his tenants than my father, but the worst part of it is that it leaves so awfully little for us to live upon."

"Don't go around worrying over that," said Mr Hicks soothingly. "The good American girl regards it as her mission these days to shore up the tottering British coronet with her dollars."

"It's her father I'm thinking of," lamented Usk. "How can one go to a man and say, 'Mr Steinherz, I love your daughter, and if you are prepared to hand her over rather more millions than I have hundreds a year, I daresay we shall get on very comfortably'?" Miss Steinherz's prospective fortune was understood, be it remarked, to be of such satisfactory dimensions as to suffer no appreciable diminution even by reduction to English figures.

"If that's all," was the dry reply, "you can just go right away to J. Bertram Steinherz, and say those identical words. Why, sir, your request is real moderate. I guess an ordinary French or German count would have his father-in-law hand over that same pile of dollars, and rebuild his family castle, and take his crown out of pawn as well, before he would conclude to make a trade. Then he would invite the bride to embrace his religion, and when everything was fixed up according to his notions, he would intimate to the father-in-law that, much as he respected him as a dollar-grinding machine, he guessed he would be conscious of more real, whole-souled pleasure in the partnership if he could regard him as a fixture in the States for the future."

"I can't fancy Mr Steinherz standing that sort of thing. He's not—not——"

"Don't quite look the part of the ordinary heavy father from the States?" said Mr Hicks quickly, as Usk hesitated. "That is so, sir. He doesn't incline to play it, either." He stopped abruptly.

"That's it. He is so awfully dignified and polite that I feel as if I should sink into the ground when I think of going to him with an offer that must strike him as such arrant cheek. Do you know, Hicks, that he and Miss Steinherz came to the Duchess of Old Sarum's reception after all? I got them a card, but Mr Steinherz was so high and mighty about accepting that I felt horribly small."

"J. B. Steinherz was always real high-toned in his notions. At home he lays himself out to snub his fellow-citizens, and the smart set are ready to kiss his boots because he is 'so charmingly exclusive.' Here in England he doesn't hold with thrusting himself into intimacy with the British nobility, so he puts in his time at a down-town hotel, and scorns ducal invitations."

"Well, I got him to Sarum House, at any rate, and every one was asking who he was. There was one very old lady there, Mrs Sadleir, a great friend of my people's—knew my grandfather—who was quite smitten with him, and wanted me to tell her who was the elderly man with the *grand air*. When I said he was an American, she was really snappish, and said he reminded her of some one she had known long ago. I brought him up and introduced him, and they flirted solemnly for nearly an hour. Afterwards Mrs Sadleir said she couldn't place him exactly, but she was pretty sure he must be a Southerner, for he had just the fine manners of the men who used to come over here before the war."

"J. B. S. is a real white man," said Mr Hicks emphatically. "And you don't need to be afraid of sailing right in, sir, so far as he is concerned. You'll scarcely tell me he hasn't known why you were loafing around all the time at his hotel. No, you may bet your boots that it's Miss Maimie that's your rock ahead—honest Injun."

"Miss Logan? But why in the world should she have anything to do with it?"

"Women with a real consuming ambition on behalf of another woman are not plenty anywhere," said Mr Hicks slowly, "and maybe least of all in America, but that's how it is with Miss Maimie. She would sell her very soul to see Félicia Steinherz make a great marriage. Why, a year or so back she all but engineered her into marrying Prince Timoleon Malasorte."

"The Neustrian Pretender?"

"The same, sir. He was an attaché in the Scythian Embassy at Washington those days, but you bet he meant to be emperor, same's he does now, and with Félicia's dollars and her smartness back of him I calculate he'd have got there. But J. B. S. put his foot down, and the Embassy found itself bereaved of its brightest ornament. That's why I say, Watch out for Miss Maimie. Félicia won't marry any one below a duke if she can help it."

"You mean that the son of a very poor marquis hasn't much chance, then? But Mr Steinherz will feel that even more strongly than you do, don't you see?"

"No, sir, he will not. Mushroom coronets he has no use for, but he knows there's nothing shoddy about you. And don't have your natural modesty blind you to the show side of your family record. It's not every poor marquis that has taken his seat on a European throne, even for three months, or has seen his brother the wonder of four continents and the husband of a queen."

"You are getting positively epic," said Usk, his tone becoming unconsciously more cheerful.

"I guess my subject inspires me, sir. Any news of your uncle these days, by the way? Not worrying himself sick, I hope?"

"He seems well enough, but his brain-power doesn't return."

"Does he incline to plunge into politics again, or has he concluded to stick to his snug estate way back there?"

"He is as happy there as he would be anywhere, I think. Nothing has been said about his coming to Europe."

"Now it's a curious thing," remarked Mr Hicks meditatively, "but a whole crowd of the Jews have their eyes fixed upon him yet. They see that while he was boss, things went ahead, but when he dropped out, the outfit went to smash right away. Well, they suspicion that he was intrigued off the stage by the millionaires, so they just incline to intrigue him back there. They are plotting to fix things so's they can invite him along again. The Prince of the Captivity, they call him, after some old cuss that hung out his sign in those parts sometime, and they have passwords and ciphers, and every requisite of a properly equipped plot on the largest scale."

"I'm afraid they'll be disappointed. He won't let them thrust him into a position that he could not fill with satisfaction to himself."

"They'll just have to invite you to operate the scheme instead of him."

"Ah, I might have thought of it once," said Usk, with a seriousness which tickled Mr Hicks extremely, "but of course things will be different now, if——" he laughed, not unhappily. "A year or two ago I was mad to get out into the world and do something big. I often wish I had gone into the army, even now."

"Well, now, I thought you gave that up nobly because your mother was breaking her heart over it? But maybe you've been busy taking the shine off the sacrifice ever since—sort of 'If I mayn't do what I like, I won't do anything'?"

"Every one isn't a born social reformer, like my mother," said Usk, somewhat coldly. Then his face cleared. "But very likely I shall go into Parliament now, and that will please her tremendously."

"And you think it will please another person as well, maybe?"

"Yes, I'm sure it will. She made me feel awfully ashamed one day when she said how she envied people of our class in England, who could find any number of followers any day if only they cared to lead. She couldn't make out how we could throw away our opportunities and not lead, she said."

"Félicia Steinherz among the prophets!" said Mr Hicks drily. "And you have hoarded the remark to repeat it to Lady Caerleon, because you calculate that will please her tremendously too? Well, go ahead and get there! Ask me to the wedding. If you cable right away when you get things fixed, I'll find it waiting for me when I arrive home."

He rose to continue his exploration of the train, and Usk fished a scrap of paper out of his pocket, and devoted himself once more to the abstruse calculations with which it was covered. It was his earnest desire to be able to prove to Mr Steinherz that if he married Félicia, her fortune might be entirely reserved for her own use, but the facts were against him. Even if the family house in town, which had until lately been let on a long lease, were made over to him, it would be utterly beyond his father's power to give him enough to keep it up, even with the most rigorous carefulness. The family at Llandiarmid were accustomed to save—to pinch, Usk called it—but he was conscious of sudden disgust for his own selfishness when he pictured the further economies that would be necessary if his allowance was to be increased. And for what? To allow him to live in luxury without wounding his pride by touching Félicia's money! There would be no rigid economy in Félicia's household, he knew that well enough. If she wished for a thing, she ordered it, regardless of the cost, although a curious strain of shrewdness sometimes showed itself in the ardour with which she would pursue a discount of a few pence on a bill of many pounds. He had vivid recollections of the boxes which had accompanied her and Miss Logan on their return from a flying visit to Paris about a fortnight ago, and the calm way in which they had mentioned what seemed to him the fabulous sums paid for a single gown or toque. Decidedly, a household which included Félicia would be an expensive outfit to run, as Mr Hicks had once put it.

Usk had learnt something of this by personal experience. From the day when he first made the delightful discovery that Transatlantic etiquette permitted him to give expression to his feelings by presenting offerings at the shrine of his goddess, he had taken full advantage of his privileges. Félicia accepted the offerings with perfect calmness, but Usk felt a thrill of pride, which to an outside observer might have had something pathetic in it, in the fact that he was obliged to cut down his personal expenses in order to provide them. It was very foolish, no doubt; the sensible course would have been to obtain his gifts on credit, but with a touch of quixotry he chose rather to deny himself that he might keep his love supplied with the marvellous candies and rare flowers which she regarded as necessaries of life. She possessed a cultured palate and the eye of a wealthy connoisseur, and Usk went so far as to give up smoking when he was alone, and had even cherished thoughts of travelling third class. But in that case he could not have enjoyed in peace the delight of thinking about Félicia, and his heroism failed him when it came to the point.

It was not unnatural that Miss Steinherz should also be thinking of him this evening, for the floor of her bedroom was strewn with the leaves and stalks and petals of the last roses he had sent her. They were the very newest roses, the blossoms of a curious coppery-pink tinge, and Usk had paid a fabulous price for them on his way to the station. Miss Logan remarked slightingly on them when the maid had put them in water, and Félicia threw one at her. She returned it, and the mimic battle was continued until not a single rose remained on its stalk. Flushed and laughing, the girls desisted, and presently Félicia sent away the maid and allowed her friend to brush her hair, while she herself performed certain mysterious operations on her finger-nails, with the aid of the contents of a dainty gold-mounted morocco case.

"Is it Monday or Tuesday that we dine Lord Usk?" she asked lightly, with a sudden upward glance.

"It's Usk—Usk—all the time!" was the impatient answer.

"Not just all the time," said Félicia sweetly, "but I guess it soon will be."

"Félicia Steinherz, you make me tired!"

"Now don't get mad, Maimie. If a duke had come along, I'd have married him, as I've stated times and times, but, you see, that duke hasn't materialised, and Lord Usk is right here."

"I'd have had you marry an emperor," said Maimie Logan, through her teeth.

"And I'm real grateful to you, but the emperor didn't rise to the occasion either, did he? I admired to see his affections just wilt when pappa said he wouldn't give me a red cent if I married him. I was done with him then, but if he'd had the grace to stick to me, you bet pappa would have weakened at last. It was a pity, for I feel I have it in me to care more for an emperor than any other man, because he'd really have given me something to be grateful for."

"Well, don't accept Lord Usk in such a tearing hurry. There are dukes left yet, and princes too."

"Why, certainly, but you haven't looked all around this thing, Maimie. You had better make up your mind that pappa isn't going to give me any more chances of meeting those dukes and princes than he can help."

"I want to know! Why not?"

"Just listen to me, and ask yourself. Since I was 'most a baby, I've known that some way my folks were different from other girls' fathers and mothers. I guess it was pappa's high-toned manners, and mamma's never having more than half a voice in her own house; and you know as well as I do, though we don't have other people see it, what an icy terror pappa can be yet when he likes. Why, we wouldn't be here if he could have helped it." Maimie smiled grimly at this allusion to the circumstances attending their departure for England. Mr Steinherz, summoned suddenly to London on the business of his Euphrates Syndicate, had telegraphed to his daughter that he was leaving New York by the next day's boat. Félicia, who had for years demanded a visit to Europe in vain, was touched in her tenderest point. Telegrams flashed backwards and forwards, and when Mr Steinherz went on board, the first person he saw was his daughter, holding a farewell reception of her fashionable friends, with Maimie and a maid and a marvellous pile of luggage in the background.

"Yes, we fixed things pretty smartly that time," pursued Félicia; "but he has played it awfully low down on us since, Maimie. I think it's real mean of him to bring us along to this hotel, where there are only dowdy English people, and not let us go to the Continent at all, except that two days in Paris. And to have us decline all of those invitations that Lord Usk would have got us!"

"But he hasn't been ugly, Fay, as he might have been. And when you think of some girls' folks——"

"Oh, I know. Why, there's Sadie van Zyl, in the smartest set here and the very toniest society everywhere—what she must suffer when she has to produce either her husband or her father! I don't wonder she has a nerve-attack most times, and goes off to some cure or other."

"Well, now, you need never feel badly like that, you know."

"That's so, but then I never have the chance of exhibiting pappa. I should admire to have him go with us to all sorts of places, but he won't. Now, Maimie, if those Van Rensselaer girls knew just this, what would they say? Why, that there was some reason why he didn't care to show himself in Europe. That may be so, or it may not; I don't choose to inquire, but I incline to think that he settled in the States because he had taken a hand in some political game, and it didn't eventuate just the way he hoped it would. Whatever the mystery was, your mother was in it, but not your father." Maimie nodded. "Then we'll take that as understood, and you'll see I have to hoe my own row. Now Lord Usk is real nice to pappa, and from all we hear I don't see but pappa will think his folks just lovely. So I'm on."

"Wait, just wait!" entreated Maimie. "Don't go ahead so fast."

"Now, Maimie, you're going to give up all of this foolishness—see? I'm watching out for an investment in real estate, and here's Lord Usk just hungering to be developed. I shall have him run for Parliament—it's quite a toney thing to do here—and then I'll push him up step by step."

"He'll turn ugly," prophesied Maimie. "He just loves the country——"

"Maimie Logan, are you going to tell me I don't know how to fix things any way I want them? He will stay in town when I choose, and take me abroad when I choose, and go way down into the country when I let him. Say, Maimie, don't yank all of my hair right out!"

"You are forgetting his folks. I don't see but you'll have trouble with them."

"They won't trouble me any. The old lord and lady won't be encouraged to come around much in town. I guess their influence wouldn't be helpful."

"Why, Fay Steinherz, I'm sure they're real good, from what he says—church members and all that."

"I'm not running him for church elder, Maimie. Lord Caerleon is just a Temperance crank, and the old lady never put on a Paris gown nor attended a smart function in her life. And they're not smiled upon in the really good set because of those Eastern adventures they have on hand all the time. I have some use for the uncle Mr Hicks talks about, that married some queen or other, but that's different. Of course I'll visit at the Castle, and ask people there for shooting-parties and that. One must be in the country some time, I suppose. I wonder if there's a dower-house, or whatever they call it in books? If there is, I guess the old folks might be brought to see the propriety of retiring to it, and leaving the Castle to us."

"You seem to have got everything fixed up pretty nicely."

"That is so. This outfit will be run on strict business lines, you'll see. Pappa has me start under a disadvantage by his unfatherly conduct, but I wipe that out by marrying Usk. Then all depends on myself, and I can't afford to have sentiment spoil my plans. I'll see myself a duchess or *vicereine* of India yet."

CHAPTER II.
BORN IN THE PURPLE.

USK was late in keeping his dinner engagement with the Steinherzes. It was not his fault, as he explained eagerly when he arrived; he had left Llandiarmid at an unearthly hour in the morning, to make sure of catching the early train from Aberkerran, and had got up to town in excellent time. It was when he was driving from his rooms to the hotel that the delay occurred. The Archduke Ferdinand Joachim, cousin to the Emperor of Pannonia, who had just arrived on a visit to England, was being conducted in state to Buckingham Palace, and the British public had turned out in full force to welcome him. The royal carriages and liveries, and the fact that a popular Prince had gone to meet the traveller, made it evident that this was an occasion for cheering, and accordingly dense crowds lined the route, to the dire interruption of the traffic at all the cross-roads, in one of which Usk sat fuming in his hansom.

"Well, you must have had a pretty good view of the royalties, any way," said Maimie Logan.

"Oh yes, but I had no particular yearning for that. I have seen the Prince so often, you know, and I didn't care about the other chap. But I wished you and Miss Steinherz had been there. It's a chance you don't often get at this time of year."

"What is the Archduke like, now?" asked Mr Steinherz suddenly. "You would be able to see him distinctly?"

"Quite." Usk turned to his host with ready deference. "A fair-sized man, I should say—looks as though he had been born in uniform, as all those Germans do. Hair brushed straight back, rather *à la* scrubbing-brush, as far as I could see, big pince-nez, a sort of nondescript brown moustache, with the points turned up fiercely. I think that must have been dyed, though, for his hair was grey behind."

"Yes," said Mr Steinherz meditatively, "he is pretty well along—older than I am. He was in Venetia in the 'Sixties—made his name there. And it wasn't a particularly sweet name, either. I guess a good few Italians have unfulfilled vows of vengeance out against him yet."

"Say, pappa!" broke in Félicia; "how did you get to know that much about a no-account German prince?"

"Well, daughter, I don't see but I must have heard it from the Italian clerk I had once," was the leisurely reply, which silenced Félicia for the time, since she knew well enough that the clerk in question had been dismissed for falling in love with his employer's daughter. Maimie, always watchful on her friend's behalf, changed the subject, and it was not until the meal was over that her efforts to keep the peace failed. Usk had been anxious to escort the ladies this evening to a concert at which some bright particular star was announced to appear, but Mr Steinherz vetoed the proposal rather summarily, regardless of his daughter's rebellious looks. Most unjustly Félicia made Usk suffer for her disappointment, sitting bored and silent all evening, and sweeping Maimie off to bed at a ridiculously early hour, on the plea of a headache. Maimie offered no objection to the imperious summons, but took occasion to drop her handkerchief just outside the sitting-room door. Returning to fetch it as soon as Félicia was safe in her own room, she heard Usk taking his leave.

"May I call upon you in the morning?" he asked of Mr Steinherz. "I should like—— There is—— I want to ask you something."

"State it right now," was the unexpected answer. "I am having a vacation this evening, thanks to Félicia's nervous attack."

Maimie shook with silent laughter, for she guessed that Usk found some difficulty in unfolding his request now that the opportunity was thus suddenly thrust upon him. He muttered something about "Very important," to which Mr Steinherz responded by a cordial invitation to discuss the matter in his office, where they would be safe from interruption. The room was a small one, with one door from the corridor into which all the apartments of the Steinherzes' suite opened, and another from the sitting-room, and in it Mr Steinherz spent most of his time, and received all his business visitors, in an atmosphere of smoke. Maimie reviewed the position swiftly, as she heard the door between the study and the sitting-room close with a decisive slam. Félicia was fortunately in the hands of her maid by this time, and the brushing of her hair alone might be relied upon to keep her occupied for an hour at least, but it was out of the question to listen at the door in the corridor, for the hotel servants were constantly passing. Moreover, if the discussion were to be conducted in lower tones, it would be very difficult to hear it through the door. The only hope was the balcony, upon which the windows of both rooms looked, and Maimie opened the sitting-room door very softly, leaving it slightly ajar so as to afford a way of escape, and crossing the room on tiptoe, put her head out cautiously. As she had expected, the warmth and beauty of the night had tempted the two men to sit at the open window of the office, and she could see the tip of one of Mr Steinherz's shoes. The odour of his cigar reached her as she sat crouched inside her own window, leaning forward as far as she dared, and she heard him chaffing Usk upon the length of time it took an Englishman to strike a match. Apparently the match refused to strike at all, and Usk laid down his cigar in despair, for presently Mr Steinherz said "Well?" in a half-authoritative, half-humorous tone which rejoiced the listener exceedingly.

"Mr Steinherz," returned Usk with a sudden burst of frankness, "I love your daughter. May I ask her to marry me?"

Maimie thought she could imagine the quizzical glance under which the unhappy suitor would be writhing, but she was electrified by the words which answered him.

"Stop right there!" said Mr Steinherz decisively. "We will take those words as unsaid, if you please. I was not expecting them until a later stage of the proceedings, and there are some circumstances with which I guess you ought to get acquainted before you utter them."

Maimie held her breath. Her only idea had been to observe Mr Steinherz's treatment of this new suitor, and especially to see whether he really favoured him, as it had struck her he did. But was she unintentionally, and all in a moment, on the point of dispelling the mystery upon which she and Félicia had touched in their confidential talk? She heard Mr Steinherz rise and unlock a table-drawer, then return, apparently with something in his hand.

"Do you seem to know any of those faces?" she heard him ask.

"I don't think so," said Usk. "Wait a minute, though. It's an old photograph of the Emperor of Pannonia, isn't it?—and his brothers, I suppose?"

"No; his cousins, the Archduke Ferdinand Joachim and—myself."

From her own sensations, Maimie could imagine the bewilderment on Usk's face as he gazed blankly at the speaker.

"You don't see the likeness?" Mr Steinherz went on; "but the folks used often mistake us three for one another. Look right in my face; I just brush my hair back some; I turn up my moustache and hide my beard, showing the Hohenstaufen mouth. Now do you perceive no likeness to the Archduke as you saw him three hours back?"

"I see! I see!" cried Usk. "But," he added, rising and walking round his host, "from behind you need no alteration at all. If you were in uniform I should take you for him."

"Is that so?" said Mr Steinherz. "Well, you will excuse me if I resume my usual appearance? I apprehend that if it got around there was a double of the Archduke staying at the Hotel Bloomsbury, it might cause some inconvenience. And now, do you incline to hear the circumstances, or not?"

"There's nothing I should like better. I don't know whether I'm standing on my head or my heels."

Maimie could picture Mr Steinherz's grim smile. "Did you ever hear of Prince Joseph of Arragon?" he asked.

"I seem to know the name," said Usk meditatively. "Yes, wasn't it the man who ran off with an—a lady and was lost at sea, twenty or thirty years ago?"

"Who was supposed to have been lost at sea," corrected Mr Steinherz impressively. "As a matter of fact, he is sitting opposite you now."

"Oh—er—I beg your pardon," stammered Usk.

"Your remark was natural. There is now only one other person besides yourself who knows the truth. In the Schlosskirche at Vindobona I understand there is a cenotaph to the memory of José Maria Beltran, Prince of Arragon, drowned off the Australian coast in the wreck of his yacht, the Claudine, but Joseph Bertram Steinherz could give the lie to that statement if he chose."

"You escaped from the wreck, I suppose, and took advantage of the general belief to disappear—sir?" hazarded Usk.

"Not just exactly; but I will tell you all of the story. But, first, remember that you are on your honour not to breathe a word of what I tell you to any living creature, especially to my daughter; and again, don't make a prince of me. I have turned my back on all of that for ever."

Usk bowed uneasily, as Maimie could just distinguish from where she crouched. She was completely shielded from the sight of Mr Steinherz, although she had ventured to creep out on the balcony, and was now close to them, her black gown indistinguishable in the darkness. Even if Usk should chance to turn his head, she believed that she was quite safe, and could retreat into her own window in a moment.

"You will know," said Mr Steinherz, "that my father, King Paul X. of Cantabria, was driven from his throne in '48. When I was born he was already an exile at the Court of Vindobona. His mother was a Pannonian archduchess, and the two houses had always been united by the closest bonds. He received at the hands of his cousin the Emperor the honours due to a reigning monarch, and on his death it was only at Vindobona and the Vatican that my brother Ramon was recognised as titular King of Cantabria. Ramon is a man of science and a philosopher, however, and in daily life he contents himself with the older and undisputed title of Prince of Arragon. My mother was a princess of Weldart—an aunt of the lady who has already linked your family and mine by marrying your uncle Count Mortimer." Maimie saw Usk move uncomfortably, and guessed that he was trying, in a dazed kind of way, to discover whether the connection thus disclosed between himself and Félicia need be any bar to their marriage. The same idea had come to herself with a thrill of hope, but she saw its absurdity in a moment. Mr Steinherz had risen from his chair and was walking about.

"I cannot speak calmly when I think of my mother," he went on. "For political reasons, which means, in plain English, her brother's need of money, she was married to my father as a child of seventeen, after being summarily converted for the purpose. Needless to say, her consent was not asked to either process. She made him an excellent wife, and if he had taken her advice, it would, I believe, have averted the revolution which cost him his throne; but on account of her German and Protestant upbringing she was always looked upon with distrust, and my father himself shared it. So strongly did she disapprove of the perpetual intrigues by which he sought to regain his kingdom after losing it, that soon after my birth an amicable separation was arranged, without giving rise to any scandal. My mother retired with me to an estate on the Adriatic, where my father and brothers visited us occasionally, and I was sometimes conducted, much against my will, to Vindobona, which my mother, on the plea of ill-health, always avoided, and from which I always returned to her with increasing joy. As I grew older her one fear was that I might be taken from her, and to escape this she proposed that I should be entered as a student at the naval academy of the great dockyard and arsenal which lay not far from us. Though all my training hitherto had been military, it was the sea to which my own heart turned, and I don't know whether my mother or I was the more rejoiced when I was allowed to follow my bent. For several happy years I worked hard at the mysteries of shipbuilding—much harder than suited my superiors and companions, who would have preferred to see me placed in some post of nominal authority, where I should not trouble them. Several times it was suggested that I should be appointed to a sea-going ship, and sent on a long cruise, but my mother's piteous entreaties—she humbled herself to my father and the Emperor in her agony at the thought of losing me—and my own absorption in my work, which seemed likely to be productive of great advantage to the navy in future, gained me a respite. One of the complaints against me was that I withdrew myself from the society of companions of my own age. It did not occur to my accusers that in my leisure hours I had the constant society of a woman who had read widely, thought deeply, and suffered much, and that this had quite spoiled me for the company of the class of men I met every day. I always look back to my twenty-third year as the period of my greatest happiness—perhaps in contrast with the dark time which followed. A legacy had come to me from a godfather when I was twenty-one, and I spent the greater part of it in building a large steam-yacht from my own designs. Some of my relations looked askance at such waste of money, but the Emperor, finding that the yacht was intended to test various inventions of my own in naval matters, was pleased with my interest in my profession, and encouraged me. I called the yacht the Claudine, after my mother, and spared no pains to make her the smartest and most seaworthy craft of her size afloat. When she was finished we tested her in all weathers. I had a crew enrolled from among the fishermen with whom I had made friends as a boy, and my mother was always my passenger. Only one of her ladies cared for the sea, and she made her her constant companion on these trips. Aline von Hartenweg was young, beautiful, enthusiastic, devoted to my mother, devoted to the sea— is it any wonder that an attachment sprang up between us? We were so happy, so thoroughly contented with our life, that we did not ourselves perceive the chief cause of our happiness. Others saw it before we did, notably the chaplain at the Castle, whom my mother always suspected of being placed as a spy upon her. Presently a furious letter from my father announced that he was coming to put an end to this foolishness, and to send me off on a three years' cruise. My mother had long been suffering from a mortal disease, but I shall never believe that she might not have lived for years, if she had been left in peace. As it was, the shock, and the realisation of the truth, were too much for her, and when the King arrived he found her on her deathbed. She had poured out her soul to me on the subject of Aline, assuring me that the marriage would never be allowed, that our attachment could only cause misery and contention, and adjuring me to go abroad as my father wished, unless I felt that my life's happiness was bound up in Aline. I assured her that it was, and her last words to my father, who could not in decency refuse to hear them, were a petition that we might be allowed to marry. Then she died."

Mr Steinherz came to a standstill at the window, and stood looking with unseeing eyes at the starry sky overhead, the rustling black plane-trees in the square far below, surrounded by their ring of lamps, the low dark houses beyond. Maimie hid her face lest its whiteness should betray her.

"My father was less angry than his letter had prepared me to expect," Mr Steinherz went on. "He could not but disapprove most strongly of my choice, he said, and would promise nothing as to the future, but if I would consent to make a voyage round the world at once, giving my word not to hold any communication with the Countess Aline while I was away, he would see what could be done on my return. I murmured at the harshness of the stipulation, reminding him that my brother Florian had been permitted to marry Princess Erzsebet Mohacsy, who was not of royal blood; to which he replied, with the cynical brutality he sometimes affected, that she brought a princedom as the price of the alliance, whereas my poor Aline's father could barely give her a dress-allowance. I yielded. My mother's entreaties to me not to come to an open breach with my father were still in my ears, and I could not see anything better to do. I was appointed to one of the largest Pannonian men-of-war, and I did not dislike the cruise. When I had been away two years, the news of my brother Florian's death recalled me hastily to Vindobona, and I found Aline—married. What pressure they had brought to bear on her, what lies they had told her about me, I do not know and did not ask; but she was married to a rough fellow called Baron Radniky—a noble, it is true, but the very type of a churlish, bigoted reactionary. I had a terrible scene with my father when I learned the truth, and I swore I would remain in Pannonia no longer. I would cast aside my rank, as I had intended to do if I married Aline, and go out into the world a free man. He laughed in my face when I said this, and as soon as I was outside the room I found myself under arrest. For weeks I was a State prisoner inside the palace,—I, who was accustomed to freedom and an active life,—and at the end of that time my relations thought they could deal with me. The Emperor patched up a reconciliation with my father, and I was allowed my personal liberty, but forbidden to leave Vindobona. All the people round me were spies—my cousins the Archdukes, the servants, the gay young men who were set on to divert my mind. I saw there was no hope of escape at present, and I allowed myself to seem resigned. Aline lived far away in the country. She had passed out of my life, and for that I was thankful. But the vicious idleness of my surroundings I could not endure, and at last I obtained leave to set up a laboratory in my father's gardens, at a safe distance from the palace, in order to continue my scientific experiments. Here again the Emperor stood my friend, and even allowed me to send for my foster-brother, Martin Richter, and install him as my assistant. It was supposed that he did all the menial work of the laboratory; but my relations would indeed have been astonished if they had seen prince and peasant labouring together, for he knew as much of the theoretical part of the work as I did, and in the practical part we relieved one another."

"And this was all a blind?" Usk ventured to ask, as a smile, called up by his recollections, crept over Mr Steinherz's face.

"It was all done with a purpose, and when by-and-by I was allowed to run down to the Adriatic for more important experiments on board the Claudine, though the limit of my stay was strictly fixed, I knew my time was at hand. But before it arrived something happened which changed the whole character of my flight. In her lifetime my mother had befriended a young girl, the last descendant of a noble, but poverty-stricken, family of Weldart. As a child, Konstantia von Lilienkranz had shown extraordinary talent in several directions, and her own intense desire was to go upon the stage. My mother dissuaded her from this, but sent her, at her own expense, to a famous conservatorium, where her musical gifts might be cultivated, intending to find her a post as Court pianist when she grew up. Her death left the poor girl friendless, for she knew too well the light in which her patroness had been regarded by the members of the Imperial family to seek help from them. The variety of her talents had created quite a sensation at the conservatorium, and admiring professors and fellow-students had done so much to spread her fame that she was actually offered an engagement to play *ingénue* parts at a leading Vindobona theatre, while a great *maestro* volunteered to train her to sing in grand opera. Remembering the wishes of her patroness, she refused both offers, and had the courage to strike out for herself in a new line—as a society entertainer, you would call it, I suppose. She gave a series of concerts at which she herself, either as singer, reciter, or instrumentalist, supplied all the items, and the idea was so new and daring that she was the sensation of the moment in the capital. This was soon after I had been allowed a little more freedom. I was anxious to show an interest in my mother's *protégée*, and went to hear her play several times. I sent her bouquets, and asked to be presented to her, the girl receiving the attentions, as they were offered, purely as marks of kindness from the son of her patroness. But the censorious world thought otherwise, as I ought to have remembered would be only too likely in the case of a woman in her position. My cousins met me with meaning looks, and congratulated me on my conquest. 'The stony-hearted Stanzerl,' as the gilded youth of Vindobona called her, had stepped down from her pedestal, so they hinted. The cessation of my attentions might have ended the scandal as regarded myself, but the whispers had reached her. One day the old woman, half-attendant, half-duenna, who lived with her, came to me privately to beg me not to show any further interest in her charge, who was in the deepest distress owing to the reports spread concerning her. I was horrified and disgusted. That I should have brought this anguish upon my mother's favourite! Impulsively I wrote off to my brother Florian's widow, whom I knew to have the kindest heart in the world, telling her what I had reason to belief was the case, that Fräulein von Lilienkranz found the strain and publicity of her life very trying, and would be most thankful to exchange it for a more sheltered one. Would not my sister-in-law find room for her in her household, even if only as instructor in music to her year-old daughter? I waited impatiently for the answer. Princess Florian wrote in evident distress of mind. She would have been delighted to befriend any one in whom my mother had been interested, but in this case she had been *warned*—deeply underlined—that it would be *wiser* not to take any step, and she *could* not disregard the warning. I was perplexed and disappointed, but I could not give up my plan so easily. I ran down to my sister-in-law's estates on a visit—having duly obtained leave—and asked her point-blank why she would not help Fräulein von Lilienkranz. With the utmost difficulty I extracted from her that in view of the rumours connecting the young lady's name with mine, she could not admit her into her household. In vain I pointed out to her that if I had unwittingly compromised the girl, my relations might at least do what they could to clear her name, but she was afraid of offending my father, and would do nothing. Then I saw that there was method in what had been done. I was to be entangled in an ordinary vulgar scandal, to keep me from rushing into an unequal marriage. There and then I determined to turn the tables upon my friends, and I waylaid the old duenna the next day, and with all possible frankness took her into my confidence. I told her it was my desire to marry Fräulein von Lilienkranz, and intrusted her with a letter asking for an interview. The adventure pleased me; there was something chivalrous in the idea that made me half in love with the girl already, and when I saw her, her resistance to the notion determined me to persist in it. She was horrified at the thought of injuring the son of her patroness, but she was lonely and troubled, and had learnt that a public life is not the easiest one in the world for a good woman. I told her that I was resolved upon escaping from Pannonia, and that if she would give up her career for my sake, we would make a home together in the New World. I had not foreseen her adoring gratitude, and it made me ashamed, but she consented, and I laid my plans—quickly, you may guess, for whether I attended her concerts or stayed away from them, tongues wagged afresh, and Konstantia suffered a new martyrdom. I needn't waste time in telling you of the different failures and disappointments I had to face; let us go on to the decisive moment. It was a cold spring evening. I had ordered a special train to be in readiness to take me southwards at eleven o'clock, and I had also invited a number of friends to supper at ten, on the understanding that we were to make a night of it. You observe that the arrangements sound slightly inconsistent?"

"I was just thinking so," said Usk.

"Precisely; but then my friends knew nothing about the train, you see. I had hinted to one of them when I invited him that after supper 'das Stanzerl' would recite, and they had all got to know of it. The meeting-place was my laboratory, suitably decorated, of course, for the occasion, and my friends enjoyed themselves thoroughly. I was one of themselves now, they all assured me. Even my old enemy the chaplain, who I had insisted should be present, smiled benignantly upon me. Konstantia, her maid, and myself were alone ill at ease, all knowing what was at hand. When the servants had left, Konstantia gave the promised recitation. It was a scene from some classical drama, but I can't tell you what it was, for I never heard a word of it. The girl's nerve was magnificent. She did not falter once, and at the close I advanced towards her with the usual compliments, as if to lead her to a seat. She placed her hand in mine, we turned and faced the company—the priest was exactly opposite us. 'Father,' I said, 'in your presence and that of these witnesses I take this woman to be my wife.' All sprang up. I silenced them with a gesture, and Konstantia repeated clearly and without hurry, 'Before God and these witnesses, I take this man to be my husband.' We exchanged rings before they could stop us, then, 'Gentlemen,' I said, 'the Princess wishes to retire.' As I made no attempt to reach the door, they did not prevent Konstantia and the maid from leaving the room. Furious at having been tricked into acting as witnesses of a marriage ceremony, my cousins and the rest stormed at me. They vowed they would keep me prisoner until I swore that the whole thing was a joke; they even threatened to kill me there and then. As for the priest, he menaced me with the direst wrath of the Church, both here and hereafter. I listened to all that they had to say, then silently revealed to them that my hand was upon an electric button. 'You may not be aware, gentlemen,' I said, 'that the vaults under this building are packed with explosives. Here is an electric wire,' I traced its course along the wall towards the door, 'communicating with them.' There was an instantaneous, almost mechanical movement from the neighbourhood of the door as I approached it. 'I am a desperate man,' I said, with my hand on the door, 'and if I am interfered with, I set the current in motion. The result you can probably imagine. Any attempt to force the door from within will explode the mine. I wish you a very good night,' and I was outside, and making the door fast, before any of them had recovered from their surprise."

"But was it true about the dynamite and the wire?" asked Usk.

"There were certainly explosives in the cellar, and there was an electric light wire which led down to it. There was also a slight tincture of what I have since learnt to call bluff." Mr Steinherz smiled genially.

"You must have been an awfully cool hand!"

"Coolness was needed in our circumstances. I calculated that we had nine hours' grace at the outside. The laboratory was in a secluded part of the garden, the servants had been sent to bed, and the walls and door were strong. The only windows were in the roof. Unless any accident happened, my friends were safe until they were missed in the morning, and then it would take some little time to release them, and organise a pursuit. But, you will say, there was the train, which could be stopped at any point by telegraph. True, but it was Martin Richter, disguised in my fur coat and cap, who travelled by the train, and with him was the old nurse. We had calculated with the greatest nicety how far he could hope to get before the telegraph was set at work, and just before that point was reached he was to have the train stop at a wayside station, where horses were ready. We had arranged every imaginable expedient for baffling pursuit, and from thence he and the old woman were to travel by unfrequented routes to a quiet bay on my own estate, where the yacht was to be lying, having slipped out of harbour in the night. The train was merely a blind. For Konstantia, her maid and myself, I had procured English passports and circular tickets— money can do much—and we joined a large personally conducted party of returning tourists which was leaving Vindobona that night. The two girls had gone straight to the station as soon as they left the laboratory. The conductor was watching out for them, and added them to his flock without the slightest fuss or mystery. I followed, after making such changes in my personal appearance as might prevent a chance recognition—nothing theatrical, merely precautionary touches. We did not venture to show that we knew one another, and those hours of terror, which were bound to elapse before the frontier was reached, we spent in separate compartments. We crossed the frontier safely. So far my *ruse* was unsuspected, but I can't describe to you the excitement that beset me all through that journey. The approach of an official gave me a bad half-second, for my dash for freedom might be brought to an ignominious end at any moment. But we reached Calais, crossed the Channel, and arrived safely at Charing Cross, without having exchanged a word since we left Vindobona. I would not trust even the conductor, who might afterwards put two and two together. Konstantia knew what she had to do. We took tickets for Bradcross, a decayed riverside suburb which had once been a great shipbuilding centre. I knew it well, for I had explored it thoroughly on a former visit to England—the same visit, by the way, in which I danced with your friend Mrs Sadleir, whose husband was then in the Government, at a ball at Trentham House—since to me its historical associations were even more attractive than the great modern dockyards elsewhere which had supplanted it. In that train we ventured at last to meet and speak, to discuss our future. You will ask, perhaps, why I had not made straight for Hamburg and America. There were two reasons. First, if the trick with regard to the special train should be discovered, that would be the route on which we should be looked for; and again, I was anxious to make assurance doubly sure by being married a second time. The ceremony in the laboratory, such as it was, though absolutely irregular, was so far valid that nothing short of an appeal to Rome could dissolve the marriage; but we had nothing to show for it, and if all the witnesses conspired to deny it, we were powerless. Moreover, Konstantia was a Protestant, and I, of course, had been brought up a Catholic. My idea was to throw ourselves upon the mercy of some English clergyman, explaining to him as much of our story as was necessary, no more, and ask his advice. At Bradcross, I thought, I could find quiet lodgings, where we might lie *perdus* while the hunt for us went on, for the three weeks' residence which I understood was required by the English law before a marriage could be solemnised. We had to find a clergyman, a lodging, everything, and all without exciting suspicion. Fortunately, I spoke English as travelled princes are wont to do, fluently and without accent, and Konstantia with readiness, while the maid, Julie Schlesinger, her foster-sister, had picked up enough of it to find her way about. But we were a very forlorn trio as we descended the narrow flight of filthy steps that led down into the street from the Bradcross railroad platform, the girls carrying their satchels, and I the cloaks of the party."

Mr Steinherz paused, and the slow smile crept over his face once more as he thought of that first day of freedom. From far below came the dull roll of traffic in the side-streets, with an occasional sharp scraping sound as a horse stumbled on the granite roadway, while in the square itself the approach of a hansom smote upon the ear like a dropping fire, becoming more and more insistent, only to be lost again suddenly in the general rumble. Maimie was listening with the intensest interest for what was to come. She knew that her mother's maiden name had been Julia Slazenger, and she felt she was on the eve of further discoveries.

CHAPTER III.
THE BURDEN OF A SECRET.

PRESENTLY Mr Steinherz went on with his story, and Usk noticed a subtle change in his manner of speech. Hitherto, he had spoken "fluently and without accent," as he had said himself, but with a certain precision of phrase that betrayed the man to whom English was not his native tongue; now he became by degrees the American once more.

"I knew Bradcross well enough to feel sure that the old parts of the town, which had been the goal of my former rambles, were not likely to afford any decent lodging for the girls, and as we reached the street, I turned to the right, intending to try our fortune in the newer and more respectable portion. But almost next door to the station there was a lecture-room or mechanics' institute of some sort, and a placard on the notice-board caught my eye. It was the announcement of a Protestant lecture the following week, the chair to be taken by the Rev. Mr Cotton, Vicar of St Mary Windicotes. I knew the church well and had visited it often—it was the oldest in Bradcross—and this active controversialist promised to be the very man I needed, any way. We retraced our steps, Konstantia and the maid following uncomplainingly where I led, though it was evident they shrank from the narrow squalid streets through which we had to pass to reach the church. I knew where the clerk lived, and requested his wife to show the ladies the building while I called on the Vicar. The good man was at home, but at first I thought I had backed the wrong horse. He grew stiffer and stonier at every word as I explained my position. I learned afterwards that he had been victimised time and time again by persons representing themselves as Catholics desirous of embracing Protestantism, and deprived, naturally, of their former means of livelihood. But I persevered. I was a Catholic, I told him, and had married a Protestant against the wishes of my relations, who were certain to have the marriage declared invalid in order to separate us. Would he recommend us suitable lodgings, and give us his countenance until we could be married afresh according to English law? It makes me laugh yet when I remember how suspicious that good man was, and yet how completely I hoodwinked him. He was clearly relieved when he discovered that I was not in need of money, for I had been careful to furnish myself with several hundred pounds in English gold and notes; but he cross-questioned me most severely in order to ascertain whether there was any other impediment to our marriage than that of religion. Since the real state of affairs never occurred to him, naturally enough, I was able to satisfy him, but he had the prudence to consult his wife before surrendering finally, and she assured him that he was being had once more. However, they concluded to interview Konstantia, and we adjourned to the church, where we found the two poor girls, both of them tired clean out, sitting in one of the pews while the clerk's wife related in a loud whisper the history of the place—of which, as she told it, they could hardly understand a word. Our story sounded suspicious, no doubt, but the Vicar's wife forgot all of her suspicions the moment she saw Konstantia. The girl looked so very young and tired that the excellent lady was convinced of her truthfulness on the spot, and she hadn't talked to her but a few minutes before she astonished us by insisting that she and Julie should take up their quarters at the Vicarage, while a lodging would be found for me elsewhere. Pursuit was to be baffled by the simple device of anglicising our names, so that Konstantia became Miss Constance Lily Garland, and I Mr Joseph Bertram (Mr Cotton advised me unhesitatingly to drop the 'Maria' as a badge of Popery, and I did so right away). There was more kindness yet in store for us. Mrs Cotton did not think it well for betrothed people to see too much of one another, and her husband, after inquiring into my tastes, got me a temporary post as foreign correspondence clerk to a great shipbuilding firm in the parish. Here I gave so much satisfaction that the firm were good enough to offer me a permanent appointment, and when I declined that, gave me a letter of recommendation to their correspondents in America, which I never presented. That three weeks at Bradcross was quite idyllic. After my day's work, I would drop in, evenings, at the Vicarage, which lies back of the church. You approach it by a green gate in a high wall, and inside there is a little patch of grass and two or three lilac-bushes. Konstantia used to be waiting for me on the lawn, and there we would sit, never minding the smuts. If I haven't said much about Konstantia, don't think it's because there's nothing to say. She adored me in a real whole-hearted way, much more than was good for me, I am sure, and never so much as looked back regretfully at what she had given up for my sake. As for me, I was desperately in love yet with my own magnanimity in giving up so much for her, and her devotion pleased me. We really were perfectly happy those evenings, until Mrs Cotton called Konstantia in, and her husband came out to talk theology with me. I had to be stiffened up in my new Protestant principles, you see, and if I met that good man again, I would make him happy by assuring him that since those days I have never entered a Catholic church, any way. Well, the three weeks came to an end, and we were married in our English names, Julie signing the register as Julia Slazenger, but at the Vicar's suggestion we all wrote our original names on the inside of the cover at the end of the book, with a reference to the proper page, and he pasted a piece of paper over them, so that it might be removed if there was ever any question as to our identity. I have been sorry all the time since that prudence obliged me to break off all relations with these good people as soon as we left Bradcross. You see, any accident would have enabled my family to trace us that far, so it was necessary to start a fresh trail, and I took our passages for New York in the name of Mr and Mrs Steinherz, without telling the Cottons of the change. Moreover, that we might be thoroughly *demokratisch*, as suited the country to which we were going, Julie became my wife's friend, not her maid. We met with no difficulty in our second journey, and I expected none, for at my Bradcross employer's I had read in a Pannonian paper the interesting news that 'Prince Joseph of Arragon has sailed in his yacht Claudine on a foreign cruise. A vessel of the Imperial Navy has been detailed to escort his Royal Highness.' That meant, I knew, that Martin Richter had done his work so well that I was believed to be on board the yacht, and a man-of-war had been sent in chase of her. On our voyage I fell in with a man named Logan, a shipbuilder in a small way in Rhode Island. Community of tastes drew us together, and I agreed to put in a week or two in his neighbourhood before settling down elsewhere. The truth was, I was waiting for Richter, with whom I had arranged a method of communication. As soon as I let him know where I was, he was to dispose of the yacht, either by firing her or running her ashore, and join me, bringing Konstantia's old nurse with him. But instead of Martin came the news that the yacht was really lost with all hands. He had handled her with the most consummate skill, baffling the pursuing warship half round the world, but through some accident she got him cornered inside a reef in the Australian seas, with a gale coming on. He was staunch to the end, and actually tried to take the ship out by a passage that was practicable only for the native canoes, and that in fine weather. She struck, of course, and was beaten to pieces in the surf, and not a soul escaped. Our safety was secured—at that price. For days I could settle to nothing. In all my dreams Martin and I had worked together, and I could not feel able to do without him. Then my wife suggested that I should pay some attention to the hints Logan was continually throwing out. He wanted to have me join him in the business, for he was smart enough to see that I knew where I was when ships were in question. Besides, he wanted to marry Julie—she was a good-looking woman, and had picked up a lot from Konstantia—and he thought it would be pleasant if I bought the next lot to his, and built a house on it, that our wives might not be separated. The comicality of the idea took my fancy, and I went into business with him. I made things hum in that shipyard, and poor old Logan got frightened. I would go ahead in spite of all his forebodings, and at last, at his desire, I bought him out. We were just as friendly as ever. He was free of the yard yet, and loafed around all day, prophesying that my ships would go to the bottom as soon as they were off the slips; but they didn't, and when he died he left me his daughter's guardian. His wife had died before that, and

Maimie became our child 'most the same as Félicia. I went on inventing and improving, and making a pile—not because I wanted it, but because the thing just happened. We had a boy, and he died, and when Félicia was six years old my wife died, and I have gone on making money and fighting to keep out of society. And now I guess I'm through," and Mr Steinherz laughed to see Usk's start of surprise at this complete and startling return to his ordinary mode of speech.

"Then your family have actually no idea that you are alive?"

"Not the slightest. They advertised their undying grief at my loss, and boomed that shipwreck all it was worth, for it cleared off a scandal in the most satisfactory way. The surprise wedding was buried in oblivion, and when a whisper of the truth got around, it was promptly silenced. Naturally, you couldn't expect them allude to it on the tablet at Vindobona, though all of the other remarks proper to the occasion are there."

"And no one in America ever penetrated the secret?"

"Just one man, and I was in deadly fear when I found it out. It was our mutual friend Hicks. He got it in his head that I was a Hamburg shipping clerk that the police were watching out for, who had forged his employer's name and eloped with his daughter, and he set to work to trace my movements right back to my starting-point. Pretty soon he found he was on the wrong track, and then a chance word from a friend in Vindobona sent him flying along. The scandal, the rumoured marriage, the escaped Prince—there it all was, and if a mysterious hint in his paper hadn't suddenly shown me what he was aiming at, so that I took Konstantia along, and we just threw ourselves on his mercy, he would have made his own fortune and the 'Crier's' by revealing all of the story. He took pity upon us and kept his mouth shut, and he and I have been friends ever since. I have appointed him Félicia's trustee in case of my death."

"And you don't intend to be reconciled to your family?"

"Why should I? They are all thoroughly happy, believing me dead, and enjoying my property. If my son had lived—well, I don't know, but I guess I would have laid things before him when he came of age, and given him his choice. Florian left only a daughter behind him, and Ramon has three, and no sons. There seems a fate against us Albrets. If he had concluded to claim such rights as will be mine on Ramon's death, I daresay we could have fixed it. With the pile I can show, there wouldn't be much difficulty in having them recognise my marriage. The Emperor could do it, with Ramon's consent, and if I greased the wheels a bit, Félicia would pretty soon be a Princess of Arragon."

Maimie drew in her breath sharply. Usk spoke with some hesitation.

"Please don't think me officious, sir—it's quite against myself, you know—but do you think it is fair to keep her in ignorance—the Princess, I mean?"

"Miss Félicia Steinherz, you mean," corrected Félicia's father. "I think it so far fair that if the Emperor, and my brother Ramon, and all of my family, were to kneel to me to-morrow, and entreat me to come along back, I would refuse, and forbid them to mention the subject to her."

"Then you feel that your experiment was a success?"

"I don't pretend that I never felt the difference between the gayest and most polite society in Europe and that of a one-horse American coast-town, and the smart people in New York who would have liked to welcome me with open arms as a multi-millionaire haven't compensated me much. But I made a determined break out of that elegant prison of mine, just to lead my own life,—a better life, I may fairly say, than that old one,—and if it was to do, I would do it again. A succession of such marriages as mine might yet save the great houses with which I have the honour to be connected; but they won't see it so. I am glad to have cut myself off from them."

"But should not Miss Steinherz know the truth?"

"No, sir, she should not." The words came crisply. "If I told Félicia in the morning all of what I have told you, by the evening, prompted by that little firebrand Maimie, she would have cabled to Vindobona, 'What price full recognition?' I did my best to make her as democratic as we thought ourselves, sent her to the most typical American school and college I could find, and she comes back with the most consuming ambition for social distinction that I ever saw in a woman. It comes partly from the way girls are brought up in the States—but if that was all, it might expend itself in trampling under foot every male creature that comes near her. It is mostly the Hohenstaufen blood coming out. She would a million times rather be a poor relation in Ramon's priest-ridden household than an American heiress of no particular birth—or so she thinks now. With so many needy archdukes to be provided for, it would be easy enough to fix her up with a husband, and she would be plunged back in the life from which I broke away."

"But if she preferred it?"

"I don't take any stock in her preferences. When I concluded to Americanise my family, Lord Usk, I guess I began a generation too late. I should have taken myself in hand first, for I have never acquired that subservience to my womenfolk which the true American glories in. The neighbours set my wife down as a domestic martyr, I believe; and I am free to confess that if she had thought less of the honour I had done her, we might both of us have been happier. But Félicia has grown up in full knowledge of her rights as an American woman, and a pretty strong determination to see that she gets them; and I will acknowledge to you that when we fall out the forces on either side are more evenly balanced than I care about. I give my orders and stick to them, and gain the victory that way; but the peace-offerings afterwards come expensive. Can you wonder that I have no particular use for a storm over this?"

"But supposing that she should ever find out——?"

"How'd she do it? But I have watched out for that. When she marries, her fortune will remain in the hands of trustees, though settled strictly on herself. If any other person, either her husband or any member of my family, claims to get control of the money by virtue of any family or state law, I have fixed it that all but the merest pittance will go to the Mayor of New York for the time being in trust for the beautifying of the city. I guess Tammany won't have such a chance go by, and my noble relations must just climb down."

"I think you are very wise," said Usk slowly.

"But that's only in case she marries a foreigner. What I should fairly admire would be to have her marry an Englishman. I thought of an American first; but where would I find one that wouldn't lie down and let Félicia walk over him if there were ructions? Maybe you see now why I have encouraged you to visit here?"

"Because you think I could be trusted to keep Miss Steinherz in order?"

"Now don't get mad. Your feelings were not just exactly a secret, you know, from the first day you came. The actual fact is that Hicks, knowing my wishes, brought you along that you might fall in love with Félicia, and you did, right away."

"Perhaps Miss Steinherz knows your wishes too?"

"It is my mature opinion, sir, that she does not. If she did, I incline to think they would not stand much chance of fulfilment. But you are on a different platform, and I am talking with you as a business man. I would like to marry my daughter to an Englishman of sufficiently high position to make my family think twice before they meddled with him. You seem to me to fill the bill pretty well. So far as I understand, you are a young man needing money and some one to shove you along, and in marrying Félicia you would get both. I guess that tremendous ambition of hers would justify its existence then—she would see you Premier or die. Think it over."

"What is there to think about?" demanded Usk hotly. "It's not as if you had told me anything that could change my feelings. Félicia is Félicia, and I can't say more than that. I should be proud and thankful to marry her this moment if she would have me. But supposing the truth ever comes out, how can I face her if she asks me how I dared to keep her in ignorance, when she might have made a far more splendid match?"

"How would it ever come out? You won't tell her, Hicks won't tell her, I won't tell her—and there's no other person knows the secret. It would need a series of most improbable coincidences to bring it to light, any way. As things are now, you are a most suitable match for her—rank on your side, the dollars on hers. Of course, if you are afraid to go ahead, just because the unlikely will maybe happen, I can't help it."

"I only want to act fairly by her. If I felt she could justly reproach me——"

"If she does, just go down town for an hour or so, and bring her along a bracelet when you come back," was the unsympathetic reply. "Or it might even run to a necklace, but you would better reserve that for a pretty large emergency. Well, go home and think it over."

"I don't want to think it over. If you will only give your consent on condition that I keep silence, what can I do?"

"I don't see but you'll have to give in," smiled Mr Steinherz, "being the man you are, and in your present state of high emotion."

"Unless you meant me to consult my father——?"

"Not at all. I have the highest respect for your parents, but I understand they both look at everything from a lofty moral standpoint. They would think it my duty to do about forty million things that I don't incline to do, and that would tire me. No, my first reason for telling you all of this was that it seemed playing it pretty low down to put you in a position in which some extraordinary chance might spring the family history on you without warning. And, of course, you might object to mix the Plantagenet blood you Mortimers are all so proud of with that of Albret and Hohenstaufen. You feel yourselves on a level with the royal houses of Europe, I believe— even leaving out of account the Continental adventures of your father and uncle, and the new lustre they have shed upon your name?"

"May I ask your other reasons?" asked Usk, his blood tingling at the tone of genial sarcasm. It was clear that Mr Steinherz did not share Mr Hicks's enthusiasm over Count Mortimer's marriage.

"There's only one, but I won't tell you that right now. You see this envelope? I will seal it and direct it to you, and you can open it this day six months, or at my death. The enclosure will explain itself."

Usk put the envelope into his pocket, struck by the change in his host's manner, but the momentary gloom passed quickly.

"Think things over to-night, as I said. We will meet at the club to-morrow at eleven, and you can tell me what you have concluded to do. I have been frank with you, and I look to you to be frank with me. And I'll make just this one exception to your vow of silence. You may tell all of the circumstances to your uncle, Count Mortimer, if he should be in Europe any time. Don't trust them to paper. He is a man of the world, and will fix you up with the best advice. I say this because Hicks asked me some time back to nominate him as a second trustee, if he would consent to act. And one thing yet. If by any grievous necessity you are forced to have the secret become public property, face it out boldly. You would rather marry the Yankee shipbuilder's daughter than the morganatic daughter of a Prince of Arragon, wouldn't you? So I thought. Well, remember that my marriage was not morganatic. I made it just as legal and binding every way as I could, and there is to be no half-recognition. If Félicia is not a Princess of Arragon, she is Miss Steinherz of Rhode Island. I leave her mother's name in your care. All of the proofs that you'll need are in Hicks's hands—papers, portraits, little things that belonged to my mother, the list of witnesses of the Vindobona marriage, my own sworn and attested statement of the facts—Hicks has everything in charge."

"What has Mr Hicks got in charge?" asked a voice gaily as Mr Steinherz opened the door leading into the sitting-room. Maimie stood at the side-table, pouring out a glass of iced water from the jug which was placed there in compliment to American tastes. Anxious to hear as much as she could, she had found it quite impossible to escape when the voices approached the door, and had barely succeeded in reaching the table.

"What are you doing here this time of night?" asked Mr Steinherz.

"Why, I have been sitting up," said Maimie glibly, "and I guess my book wasn't soothing enough. I don't feel the least bit like going to sleep, any way, and the water in my room is just torrid, so I remembered this pitcher here, and came to get some."

She faced her guardian boldly, with bright eyes and flushed face. "I just hope he won't have me produce the book that proved so interesting," she thought, and then became aware that the glass in her hand was shaking visibly, for the long crouching in a cramped position had left her deadly cold. "Like must cure like!" she said to herself, and drank off the water with a smile to Mr Steinherz. "I'd like to have you tell Félicia that she mustn't pass along her nerve-attacks to me," she added aloud. "What with her headache and that book, I'm so nervous I could dance."

"Unless you have a particular wish for Lord Usk as a partner, I would advise you to go right to your own room, and do it there," said Mr Steinherz, and Maimie was thankful to escape. Passing Félicia's door, she caught the monotonous tones of the weary maid, who was reading her mistress to sleep, and heard also a pettish voice say, "What nonsense you make of it, Pringle! I believe you are going right asleep. I had just lost myself, and now you have waked me up again."

"Maybe I ought to go and massage her head," said Maimie thoughtfully to herself, "but I guess I'll have Pringle go on suffering this once. I want to think. If Félicia only knew! But if I told her now, the same house wouldn't hold her and her father. And I can't tell Lord Usk about it, because he knows already, nor talk about it with Pappa Steinherz, because he would know I'd been listening, and it's no use thinking of making it public, because he would be fit to deny all of the story, and I suppose it couldn't be proved without him. When I concluded to find out why he was so set on marrying Félicia off to this lord, I didn't ever expect this. It's tremendous. For—the—land's—sake!" she spoke slowly and emphatically, "what a boom I could work up if we were back in New York! But here I don't see I can do anything with it any way. I guess I'll just have to save it up in case Prince Malasorte should show his face again. I might fix things then so's it would fall to him to charge it on Mr Steinherz. But what am I to say about my listening? I'm not ashamed of it a cent—though I did feel awfully mean when he talked about his love-affairs—but some folks would think it cast a doubt on my evidence. What I want is some queer fact that would be likely to set my wits to work until I puzzled out the thing for myself. But suppose there isn't anything really. Suppose Mr Steinherz dreamed all of the story— suppose he has lost his mind! Oh, I can't endure this! There must be something right away back that I could remember, to give me the clue I want. St Mary Windicotes! Where have I ever heard that name before?"

She sat for a while pondering the question, then sprang up, and throwing open a huge trunk in a corner, plunged her arm to the very bottom, and brought out a small old-fashioned Prayer-book. She turned to the fly-leaf. On it were written the words, "Julia Slazenger, from her sincere friend Marian Cotton. St Mary Windicotes Vicarage, May 18th, 18—."

"I knew it!" she cried, "and Aunt Connie used to tell Fay and me all about it evenings when we were babies. We thought it must be a mean sort of a place, but she seemed real fond of it, and I would know it anywhere. I'll go right there, and look up that register for myself. Charing Cross, Mr

Steinherz said—that's somewhere down town, I know—and Bradcross is a suburb, so I guess it can't be far away. I'll take that message about Félicia's shoes to the store myself, instead of having Pringle go, and then I'll go way down there without any other person's knowing. I *will* find out whether it's a dream or not."

CHAPTER IV.
HIT AND MISS.

"OH, the dear cunning things! They're just too sweet for words!"

Maimie was standing before the gate of St Mary Windicotes churchyard, contemplating, with a rapt expression of ecstasy, the two huge laurel-wreathed skulls, carved in stone, now hideously blackened with time, which crowned the high gate-posts. The clerk's wife, unaware that in seeing these skulls the visitor was fulfilling one of her dearest and creepiest early hopes, felt that the grisly objects were not being treated with proper respect.

"They ain't no figures of fun, miss. It's what we all 'ave to come to," she observed reprovingly. "Not but what old Mr Cowell opposite did say, when there was a talk of takin' of 'em down and puttin' up common stone balls like in their place, 'Never a foot do I set within the church-door again if them death's-'eads is took down,' says he. 'I've see 'em all my life as boy and man, and the church wouldn't be the church without 'em.' But there's no call for strangers to be a-lovin' of 'em, but only to remember their latter end, as may be sooner than they think."

They were now walking up the path, itself flagged with gravestones, which led to the church-door, and Maimie noticed with something of a shudder the embattled rows of monuments on either hand, of all sizes and shapes and all manner of deviation from the perpendicular, and the ranges of displaced stones which lined the churchyard walls. For the moment she felt that she hated the place. How could people in their senses have had a wedding there? It was bound to turn out badly.

"And in that very pew there, as is now cleared away"—the clerk's wife was concluding with much impressiveness a speech containing valuable historical information—"my mother see with her own eyes the great Dook of Wellington sit hevery Trinity Monday, for to 'ear the appointed sermon."

This information was generally received with bated breath by visitors to the church, and the good woman was conscious of very natural disgust when Maimie responded to it merely with a casual "Is that so, really?" They had paused in the porch while the guide pointed out the modern representative of the fateful pew, but now she led the way in with a jangle of keys and a contemptuous sniff. Maimie devoured the scene with eager eyes. The fine dark oak carving in the chancel, the small oval window representing the Nativity, and the large window above it, decorated in stripes of crude colour—she knew them all, but there was something wanting.

"There ought to be pictures of Moses and Aaron there!" she cried, pointing to the chancel, "and right high up on that wall a big shadowy picture of some old king or queen, in a great gold frame."

"Well, now, to think of you knowin' that!" the clerk's wife was somewhat mollified; "and you must 'a been rare and small when you left the parish, miss, for me not to remember you."

"I've never been here in my life before, but I heard all about the church in America," said Maimie breathlessly. "What's come to the pictures?"

"Why, Moses and Aaron is there still, miss, hid out of sight behind that there bed-furniture, as I calls it—and as like as two peas to my aunt's best bed, as lived out Earlham way," pointing to an elaborate curtain behind the communion-table. "That's the new Vicar's doin'"—Maimie felt her heart sink—"and her Majesty Queen Hann and the Royal Harms is both took down and made away with—despisin' of dignities, as we're told shall be."

"But the registers are here yet, I suppose? and I can see about this marriage, any way?" asked Maimie anxiously, for the clerk was coming up the church, unorthodox corduroys marring the effect of his professional black coat. She had discovered from a board over his door that he was an undertaker in a small way on week-days, and it had been necessary to send a boy to summon him, while his wife led the way to the church.

"Oh yes, miss. No one can't do nothing to them. Here's Clegg just a-comin'. You step this way," and Maimie was ushered into the vestry, a small room panelled throughout in dark oak. Light was admitted by two windows close under the ceiling, and the decorations were confined to a table of the Degrees of Affinity, and another, quite as long and a good deal more complicated, of burial fees. Presently the clerk arrived, and opened a huge safe built in the thickness of the wall and masked by the wainscoting.

"What might be the year of the marriage you was wishin' to find, miss?" he asked, and Maimie noticed that the woman looked suspiciously at her when she answered. She had determined that she would give no clue to her identity, in case some evil chance should lead Mr Steinherz to revisit the church, but she foresaw that it might be difficult to maintain this reticence.

"And 'ave you any idea what part of the year would be likely, miss?" asked the clerk again, selecting a volume and laying it upon the table.

"May, somewhere near the 18th," was the reply, greeted with a gasp by the clerk's wife.

"And the names, miss? There was a good few weddin's just about that time."

"Joseph Bertram to Constance Lily Garland." Maimie's voice was shaking a little, but her excitement was nothing to that of the clerk's wife.

"Now you just tell me who you are," she said resolutely, interposing her substantial person between Maimie and the register. "You ain't neither of them two foreign young ladies, that I'm certain, and you won't tell me as you're Mrs Bertram's daughter—Miss Garland as was? What have you got to do with it?"

"My mother was at the wedding, and signed the register," Maimie admitted.

"Then you ain't got nothink to do with Mr Bertram's family?—though why they should think to interfere at this time of day beats me."

"'Ere it is, miss," said the clerk. "Joseph Bertram to Constance Lily Garland, by the Vicar, May 19th. Do you wish a copy?"

Moving aside unwillingly, the woman allowed Maimie to approach the table. There was no question of a dream or hallucination here, at any rate. There was the entry, and as Maimie turned over the pages, there also was the slight discoloration of the inside of the cover which showed where a slip of paper had been pasted upon it. She ran her finger along the line, and resisted an eager desire to try and tear the slip off. When the clerk asked again whether she would like a certified copy of the entry, she was obliged to pause before answering. Without the addition which that piece of paper held concealed, the certificate was of comparatively little value; and yet, supposing that by some accident or otherwise the church should be destroyed and the register with it, might not the copy just suffice to establish the marriage? Knowing nothing of Somerset House and its requirements, Maimie saw herself the *dea ex machinâ* in the restoration of Mr Steinherz to his original position, and replied unhesitatingly that she would have a copy. While the clerk was making it out, she stood looking with a vague awe at the pile of registers remaining in the safe. Was there still among those dusty volumes with their ragged edges the one which, as Mrs Steinherz had told with bated breath, contained records of many burials distinguished by the letters "Pl.," denoting a victim of the Great Plague? But the clerk's wife was not content to waste such an opportunity, and interrupted her meditations.

"And so your ma—Miss Slazenger as she were then—signed there, did she, miss?" indicating the rudely formed letters in which a hand accustomed only to the German character had inscribed an unfamiliar name. "Mrs Cotton she took to her wonderful, just the same as to Miss Garland. It do seem a pity as you shouldn't have come before she left the parish, after all the many times she have said to me, 'Mrs Clegg,' says she, 'I would give a deal to know what become of Mr and Mrs Bertram after all, that I would.'"

"Then Mrs Cotton is not dead?" asked Maimie eagerly.

"Why, whatever give you that hidea, miss? The Vicar 'ad a stroke and give up the parish, and they lives down at Whitcliffe now. This last summer as ever was, they arsk Clegg and me down for the day, and took us for a ride in a carriage, and give us tea in the garden, just like ladies and gentlemen—though if you arsk me, I say give me an 'ouse, or even a harbour, the grass bein' damp and spiders about."

"Could you give me Mrs Cotton's direction?"

"To be sure I could, miss—Windicotes, Cavendish Road, Whitcliffe-on-Sea. But, miss, if you're lookin' for witnesses to swear to that there weddin', don't you forget that me and Clegg was there just as much as Mrs Cotton and the Vicar, him givin' the bride away and me ready with a bottle of salts in case of the ladies' bein' overcome. Why, Mrs Cotton she says to me herself that morning, 'Mrs Clegg,' says she, 'don't you let your Tommy go to school to-day, and I'll make it up to him'; and if she didn't set him to play marbles just outside the churchyard gate, sayin' that if he saw a cab drive up, or so much as any strangers comin' along, he was to run in and whisper to her at once, 'and then, Mrs Clegg,' says she, 'you and me will fasten the church-door and pile the forms against it until Mr Cotton have finished the service, sooner nor let those dear young people be separated before they're properly married, for it's in my mind as Mr Bertram's cruel relations will try to part 'em at the last.' And I was that worked up with the thought of Miss Garland bein' dragged off shriekin' to one of them convents, and that nice young gentleman her 'usband—for a fine military-lookin' gentleman he was, though a trifle 'aughty in speakin'—throwed into chains and a dungeon, that I 'id my broom be'ind the church-door, and I was ready to fight for 'em, I was. Not that anythink come of it, after all." Mrs Clegg spoke with evident disappointment.

"I'll remember," said Maimie. "But don't tell any one that I've been here, any way." She folded up the certificate and placed it in her pocket-book, gave the clerk his fee, and prepared to go. "The cruel relations may show up yet, you know."

"So they may, miss, but you may depend upon me and Clegg." The clerk's wife was now escorting her out of the church. "I see you know all about that bit of paper at the end of the book there, which I understand there's property dependin' on it. Now you'll maybe 'ardly believe it, miss, but neither me nor Clegg have ever mentioned that slip to a livin' soul, least of all to the new Vicar, as ain't ashamed to walk about the parish in petticoats, and wearin' a Roman mitre on his 'ead."

The description was startling, but Maimie recognised the object of it when she was walking past the vicarage, having rid herself of Mrs Clegg by means of a gratuity. The green door in the high wall opened, and a tall thin man came out, wearing a cassock and a curious head-dress that seemed a cross between a Tam-o'-Shanter and a mortar-board. A youthful voice from the other side of the narrow street inquired shrilly, "Where *did* you get that 'at?" and a small boy scampered away as fast as his legs would carry him, while the new Vicar, with the air of a martyr, walked rapidly towards the church. As for Maimie, she stuffed her handkerchief into her mouth to restrain a peal of hysterical laughter, and turned her steps hastily towards the station. Her experiences of the morning seemed altogether too absurd and incongruous for real life, and in spite of the strained excitement with which she had set forth on her quest, the clergyman's martyrlike aspect put the finishing touch to her helpless mirth. When she was safely in the train, and had allowed herself the luxury of a long laugh over this anti-climax to her adventure, she became suddenly serious, however.

"Now let me see," she said severely to herself; "what have I gained, any way? Well, I know that Mr Steinherz and Aunt Connie were married at that church, and that there's a slip of paper which *may* cover their secret. And I've found three witnesses certainly—four if the old Vicar's mind isn't affected by his stroke—who can testify to the marriage. I guess it's just as well that the gentleman in the 'Roman mitre' wasn't the Vicar when Pappa Steinherz went to enlist his sympathies. I don't believe he has any; he might even have assisted to drag poor Aunt Connie shrieking to a convent. Well, but after all, it's quite possible yet for Mr Steinherz to have made out that he was Prince Joseph of Arragon when he isn't, or even to have invented the tale just to impress Lord Usk. I don't think so, but I'm set on looking things in the face. Any way, I guess I can't do anything towards clearing up the affair without Mr Steinherz's help, or else the use of those relics that Mr Hicks has in charge. How am I to fix things? I have no pull on Pappa Steinherz, and if I make him mad he'll just take Fay right away from me, and break my heart. I'll have to wait. And yet something ought to be done right now, or some of those old folks that can swear to the marriage will be dying off. I wonder if I couldn't take their evidence. No, I'm pretty certain it would need to be sworn to before a judge, and I daren't have any other person come into the secret, even if I knew a judge to speak to. Well, I guess I must sit tight, and that's all just now."

Nevertheless, when she left the train at Charing Cross, and took a hansom mechanically to drive to the hotel, her brain busied itself with a fresh problem, which was yet an old one, the question of preventing an engagement between Usk and Félicia. Such an engagement would put an end once for all to her ambitious schemes for Félicia's future, which seemed perfectly feasible in the light of the revelations of the night before. Not that either Maimie or Félicia herself would have cared much for the engagement, had there been a prospect of a more brilliant alliance, but it would give Mr Steinherz a vantage-ground of which he would make full use. Once Félicia was engaged, he would see that the engagement was fulfilled. He would hurry on the marriage, and never relax his vigilance until his daughter had become Viscountess Usk, and Félicia, in her present mood, would offer no opposition. The prospect of escaping from his tutelage, and feeling that she was her own mistress (Usk did not count), was far more attractive to her than Maimie's lofty hopes. It seemed that there was no help for it, and Maimie decided reluctantly to bow to circumstances, and make herself so agreeable to Usk that he could not but approve of her friendship with Félicia. As she came to this decision, she was startled by meeting Usk and Mr Steinherz face to face. Her driver was trying to cross Oxford Street in the direction of Bloomsbury, but there was a block in the traffic, and an inexorable policeman detained the hansom close to one of those islands of refuge on which strange groups assemble by force of circumstances. Here stood Mr Steinherz and Usk, unable to penetrate the solid phalanx of vehicles which confronted them, and waiting with what patience they might while the policeman marshalled a train of old ladies and country cousins in readiness for a break in the line. They were the last people Maimie would have chosen to meet at such a moment, when that dreadful certificate seemed to be burning in her pocket.

"You are out pretty early, Maimie," said Mr Steinherz.

"I——I came out on an errand for Félicia, way down in the City," stammered Maimie, remembering for the first time that the errand had never been performed.

"You should have mailed the order. I don't choose to have you running around for Félicia. You look just tired out."

"I wish you had been with us just now, Miss Logan," said Usk, changing the subject hastily, either on account of Maimie's evident embarrassment or because he could not bear to hear Félicia blamed. "We came across the Archduke Ferdinand Joachim and an aide-de-camp poking about Trafalgar Square in mufti. Wasn't it a good thing I had studied him so long yesterday, so that I could point him out to Mr Steinherz? But I did wish you and Miss Steinherz were there."

Usk spoke fast and somewhat nervously. Maimie read in his face that the night had made no change in his feelings. He was prepared to marry Félicia and keep her in ignorance of her father's descent, and Mr Steinherz was well pleased with his decision. Maimie felt that she hated them both.

"By the way," said Mr Steinherz, "I guess I am in Félicia's black books yet?" Maimie nodded, for she had left Félicia comfortably established in her room, with no intention of showing herself for the present. "Well, we lunch Lord Usk to-day, and he would be real sorry to miss her. Do you happen to know anything she wants right now?"

"Why, I guess one of those gold girdles with turquoise bosses would fix up her new Paris tea-gown to perfection," said Maimie slowly, adding vengefully to herself, as she saw Usk redden, "I won't let you down easy this time, Pappa Steinherz—talking that way about Fay before her best young man!"

"Then maybe you'll intimate that I'm bringing along something of the sort when you get back," said Mr Steinherz.

"Why, certainly. I guess you'll find Regent Street the best place," cried Maimie, as the cab moved on. It was some satisfaction to her to see the disappointment on Usk's face. "He's death on getting it over," she said to herself; "and now Mr Steinherz will have him trail half-way round London before coming in."

But her satisfaction was dashed with dismay when she remembered again the pair of dainty high-heeled slippers still reposing in her satchel. How could she account to Félicia for the morning which was to have been devoted to changing them? If she refused to give an explanation, or offered a lame one, she knew Félicia would never rest until she had solved the mystery. And if she guessed that Maimie did not wish Mr Steinherz to know what she had been doing, she would appeal to him sooner than allow herself to be foiled. There was a relentless malevolence about Félicia on these occasions, when Maimie was trying to deceive her purely for her own good, which Maimie felt deeply.

"I don't dare go back without changing them," she sighed to herself, and standing up, began an agitated colloquy with the driver.

"Can you get back to the City from here, hackman, right away?" she asked him. "There's something I have forgotten."

The man asked where she wanted to go, and then opined that the shop could easily be reached by way of Holborn. He turned at the first opportunity, and as they approached the corner Maimie caught sight of Mr Steinherz and Usk a second time, looking at some books in a shop-window. They had not gone far towards Regent Street, and Maimie laughed to herself as she thought of Usk's impatience. When she looked round again, her attention was attracted by a man standing on the pavement at the corner, who was gazing—glaring was the word that occurred to her—across the street at the bookshop opposite. He was elderly and poorly dressed, and evidently a foreigner, with a ragged beard and unkempt hair.

"An Italian," said Maimie to herself. "How he looks! like a lion stalking his prey. What can he be staring at, any way?"

As the thought crossed her mind, the man dashed suddenly into the street in front of the hansom, and seeming not to hear the lively remonstrances of the driver, who was obliged to pull up pointblank, threaded his way through the traffic to the opposite corner. Maimie, watching him carelessly through the side-window, saw him reach the pavement. What followed was done all in a moment. He took one step forward, there was the flash of something long and shining which fell and rose and fell again, and Mr Steinherz sank heavily against Usk. That was all Maimie saw, for her wild scream sent the horse, already startled by the sudden check, tearing down Holborn, and it seemed to her an eternity before the driver succeeded in stopping it, and turning back again at her frenzied entreaty. The irate policemen whose orders they had disregarded in their wild career, and the other drivers whose destruction they had sought to compass, took no notice of them as they returned; every one was running or looking in one direction. Even at that moment Maimie was conscious of a feeling of wonder as the crowd gathered. People came hurrying out of shops, pouring down side streets, rushing up from behind, and very soon the hansom could go no farther. Maimie waited in agony while the driver tried to force his horse through the crowd, and found herself the recipient of the confidence bestowed on a friend by a boy with a baker's basket.

"I see 'im come runnin' like mad, brandishin' 'is drippin' knife—as good as a theatre. 'E run strite into the middle of the street, all among the 'orses, rarght in front of the dray. Blowed if 'e didn't 'it out at the 'orses with the knife as 'e went down. 'E *was* gyme!"

"Say, who is it? what has happened?" gasped Maimie to a policeman, who found even his authority insufficient to clear a passage for him into the midst of the crowd, and was forced to content himself with ordering the people on its outskirts to move on. He answered civilly, and with obvious self-importance.

"An Eye-talian, miss, supposed to be a lunatic, that stabbed an American gentleman, and then threw himself under the 'orses' feet."

"But Mr Steinherz—the gentleman who was stabbed?" she cried. "I saw it all. What about him? He is my guardian."

"You saw it, miss? Then I must trouble you for your name and address. You'll be wanted at the inquest. They're takin' him to the 'orspital."

"Oh, where is it? You'll show me, officer, won't you? But I guess I ought to go and fetch his daughter. You'll let the hack through?"

"It's no good, miss. I doubt myself if he'll live to reach the gate. You had better send the cab away, and I'll take you to the 'orspital."

"Tell me about it, any way. What did you see?" Maimie asked feverishly, as the policeman pushed a way for her through the crowd, after she had dismissed the cab.

"All I saw as I come along Oxford Street was ten or twelve people round an old party as I thought was preachin' on the pavement. I went to move 'em on, and a lady bursts out and ketches 'old of me that tight I couldn't move. 'Oh, policeman, policeman!' she says; 'murder! save him! fetch a doctor, quick!' and 'olds me tight all the time, while the old chap goes on jawin' to the crowd about a righteous vengeance and the task of his 'ole life, and his father bein' shot and his mother turned out of doors in a winter's night, and defyin' anybody to arrest him, though he'd thrown down his knife. And then, all of a sudden, while I was strugglin' to get free from the lady, he give a great yell and cried out, 'It's the wrong man—not the Archduke!' and caught up a long knife with blood drippin' from it off of the pavement, and went for the people. They made room for him pretty quick, I can tell you, and he rushed across into 'Olborn, and me after him. You'd have said he was mad if you'd seen him charge the traffic just like an army, as I did, and he'd near got through when he was knocked down by a dray. And there's no need to take *him* to 'orspital. And what was it you saw, miss?"

"I just saw him standing on the side-walk and watching, and then he ran across and pulled out something, and struck—and struck—and then———" Maimie's voice failed her.

"Case of mistaken hidentity," remarked the policeman complacently, "but it's not often those foreigners make mistakes. Now it's a curious thing———"

But Maimie was not destined to receive further enlightenment from his stores of wisdom, for they had arrived at the hospital gate by this time, and Usk was coming out of it, looking like a man who was going to be hanged.

"He's gone!" he said heavily, in answer to Maimie's gasp of inquiry— "died just as they carried him in. But you're here—and you know all about it—you'll be able to tell Félicia. I didn't know how to break it to her. I was trying to think what I should say if I had to tell Phil that our father was dead. But you're a woman, you know how to put things, you can soften it to her——"

"Oh, I can't! I daren't!" cried Maimie, shrinking back. Then she remembered in a flash that if she threw the burden of the disclosure upon Usk, it would be a tacit recognition of his position with regard to Félicia. No, he was not engaged to her yet, and if Maimie could help it, the engagement should not take place.

"I guess I'll have to do it," she said resolutely.

"I'll take you back to the hotel," said Usk. "The policeman will call a hansom, for I'm sure you can't walk."

"Tell me just what happened. Who was the man?" asked Maimie breathlessly, when they were in the cab.

"I can't tell you. It was all so awfully sudden. We were looking in at a shop-window, when suddenly some one shouted out something in Italian behind us—about his father and mother, I think—and I heard two blows struck, and Mr Steinherz gave a kind of gasp, and fell against me. I tried to lift him up and stop the bleeding, and people were standing round staring, and the man who had done it kept talking, talking, in English. But when I got Mr Steinherz's head on my shoulder, so that his face showed, the man gave a yell and dashed away. They say there's no doubt he mistook him for the Archduke Ferdinand Joachim, and it's curious that last night I noticed there was a distinct likeness between them from behind, but not the very least in front."

"I would just love to tell you that I know exactly as much as you do!" thought Maimie enviously. Aloud she merely said, "And Mr Steinherz?"

"A doctor came up, and said he was stabbed in the lungs, and couldn't possibly live. He tried to speak, though the doctor told him not, but he could only get out a few disjointed words. And just as they got him into the receiving-room he died."

They had reached the hotel now, and Usk waited in the sitting-room while Maimie went to look for Félicia. It was more than an hour before she came back, and in the interval Usk was a prey to all kinds of interruptions. In order to spare the girls, he made all the arrangements he could without direct authority from them; other matters he put aside resolutely, refusing to allow Miss Steinherz to be troubled at present. When Maimie returned she looked so old and harassed that he was shocked.

"How is she?" he asked anxiously.

"Quieter now; I've given her a sleeping-draught. But it's been terrible. Her nerves are pretty highly strung, and she screamed fit to make your blood run cold. And I know there are millions of things to do, and I can't tell the way they fix them over here. Say, Lord Usk, you oughtn't to be here, any way; people will talk, you know they will. Folks in England are so censorious. Do, please, go right away. It makes me nervous to see you there."

Usk obeyed, with apparent willingness, for a splendid idea had entered his head. He went straight to the nearest post-office, and telegraphed to the Marchioness of Caerleon at Llandiarmid Castle.

"'Terrible accident to Mr Steinherz. Daughter quite prostrate. Can you come?'" He read over the message. "That'll bring her," he muttered. "And I never knew the people yet that the mater couldn't comfort when they were in trouble."

As he put the change into his pocket he felt a paper there. Taking it out, he found it was the envelope Mr Steinherz had given him the night before, to be opened after his death. The time had come already, he realised with awe. Stepping aside, he opened the envelope, and drew out a cutting from a newspaper.

"Great consternation has been caused in august circles in Vindobona by the reported reappearance of the Grey Lady of the Hohenstaufens. The scene of the apparition was the portion of the Imperial Schloss known as the Arragon-Palast, which is occupied by the Prince of Arragon, titular King of Cantabria, and his family, when the Court is at Vindobona, and it is alleged that the ghost-seer, a sentinel on duty, is absolutely convinced of the reality of the sight, which is believed to portend an approaching death in the House of Hohenstaufen. The last recorded appearance of the Grey Lady in this portion of the Schloss took place prior to the death of the late King Paul of Cantabria, which occurred at an advanced age ten years ago. The king was connected with the Hohenstaufens through his mother, who was a Pannonian archduchess."

CHAPTER V.
MANŒUVRES.

SO confident was Usk in his mother's kindness of heart that when Lord and Lady Caerleon arrived in London late that evening, he was waiting for them at the terminus, eager to conduct them at once to the Hotel Bloomsbury. Having seen the evening papers in the course of their journey, they were acquainted with the details of the tragedy, and did not need to be assured by him of the desolate state of the two girls.

"I knew you would come," he said.

"How could we do anything else?" asked his mother. "Poor Félicia! one's heart bleeds for her. Only just engaged, and her joy clouded in this terrible way——!"

"Oh, but—— we aren't exactly engaged yet," said Usk uncomfortably. "You see, Mr Steinherz had given his consent all right, but I hadn't spoken to Félicia, and there has been no opportunity since."

"No, of course not. But this makes it rather awkward, Usk. It seemed only natural to come and look after the poor girl when I thought she was engaged to you, but now she may consider it a liberty."

"Not she, mater! She'll think it just too sweet for words, as she and Miss Logan are always saying. They stand in tremendous awe of you."

"There, Nadia!" said Lord Caerleon, "that settles it. You have somehow managed to inspire these unknown Americans with awe, and it's your bounden duty to go and put things right—your duty, mind."

"I will go and ask if I can do anything for them, certainly, as soon as we get there, but that's different from having the right to go and mother them, as it were."

"No; that's just what they want," said Usk. "Think of it, mater—two girls alone in a strange country in such terrible circumstances! Of course they want mothering."

Lady Caerleon never allowed herself to shrink from a duty when it was once set plainly before her, and half an hour later she knocked at the door of the Steinherzes' sitting-room. Maimie, who was sitting alone, worn out by innumerable harassing interviews with reporters, police inspectors, officials from the Pannonian and United States Embassies, and various tradesmen, thought wearily that here was another caller.

"Come right in," she answered with resignation, but stood up astonished when she saw that the visitor was a stately and very handsome middle-aged lady. The surprise did not last more than a moment.

"You are the Marchioness of Caerleon," she said, and again her tone spoke of hopeless resignation. "I sort of felt you would come."

"My son told me of your sad trouble, and Lord Caerleon and I thought we might perhaps be some help to you," said Lady Caerleon, almost timidly. She was trying to assure herself that Maimie's words bespoke nothing but confidence, but she had an uncomfortable suspicion that they covered dislike, even defiance.

"Lord Usk is real considerate, but Miss Steinherz and I have no claim on the kindness of his relations," said Maimie icily. Lady Caerleon mistook her meaning, and thought she had penetrated the secret of this cool reception.

"I assure you," she said with a touch of *hauteur*, "I know perfectly well how things stand between Miss Steinherz and my son. She need have no fear that Usk will intrude himself and his wishes upon her at such a time. Pray believe that I have merely come to offer you such help as I can."

"You are real good," said Maimie, blushing as she realised what her words had implied to Usk's mother; "but I'm so awfully tired to-night, I just can't seem to say things right. I don't know what way they fix anything over here, or what to say to the people that have been coming around all day."

"My husband will undertake to see any one who comes on business, and he will advise you in any way he can," said Lady Caerleon, touched by the confession. "I really think you will find it an advantage to have a man to represent you," she added gently. "People here like it better."

"And in England it's just as well to have a lord back of one all the time?" Maimie spoke quite seriously, but it struck her at once that the words sounded like an ill-timed joke.

"I won't ask to see Miss Steinherz to-night," said Lady Caerleon, with some coldness; "but if she feels well enough in the morning——"

"If you please, miss," said Félicia's maid, entering the room, "Miss Steinherz have woke up all of a tremble, and she says will her ladyship go and see her for a moment, if she would be so kind?"

"I'll just speak to her," said Maimie quickly, and she hastened to Félicia's room. "Fay," she whispered hurriedly, "you won't have Lady Caerleon see you to-night, will you? I didn't want to bring her along till to-morrow, when I've got things fixed. I've planned it all out for us to go right back home at once, so's you won't have to come to any conclusion yet, and then in the spring we'll cross to Europe just by ourselves and have an elegant time."

"You make me tired—you and your plans and plots!" cried Félicia vehemently. "I'm so nervous I could fly, and I want to see somebody quiet and restful. That's what I feel all the time with Usk. He's not smart, but he's real good. Just bring his mother right along in."

Warned by the shrill voice and gleaming eyes, Maimie obeyed without a word, wondering maliciously what Lady Caerleon would think of the unconventional greeting she would probably receive. But Félicia made her way to her visitor's heart at once. After one look at the calm beautiful face bent over her, she rose impulsively and threw herself into Lady Caerleon's arms.

"Oh, love me!" she cried. "Pet me, just as if I was a baby again!"

"Oh, my darling!" cried Lady Caerleon, taken by storm. "Are you come to me instead of my Phil? I have lost her, you know; she was married last year, and I have wanted a daughter so much."

She held the quivering form in her arms, stilled the sobs which broke forth, murmured tender names, until Félicia consented to lie down again, and then sat by her until she fell asleep, Maimie watching in the background, with bitter jealousy gnawing at her heart. She, who had mothered Félicia since she was nine and Félicia six, was nothing to her now that this Englishwoman had come on the scene. Then she remembered certain previous experiences of the kind, and was comforted. Félicia had turned from her before, in transient fits of virtue or of friendship, but she had always come back.

"She is the dearest girl!" Lady Caerleon said to her husband, with tears in her eyes, when she was at length free to seek her own room; "very unconventional—quite a child of nature, but my heart went out to her. It seemed as if she had always felt the want of a mother so terribly, and to-night, of course, worse than ever."

During the days that followed, not only Félicia, but Maimie, learned to be thankful for the presence and countenance of Usk's parents. The reporters had been inclined to invent scandalous stories on the strength of the supposed likeness between the murdered American millionaire and the Pannonian Archduke, but when Lord Caerleon, backed by the police and the hospital officials, assured them that the likeness was purely a delusion of the murderer's, they were forced to restrain their exuberant fancy. As for Usk, he stood uneasily aloof when discussions of this kind were taking place, wondering at the blindness of the experts. With his mind's eye he saw continually one of the chief treasures of Llandiarmid, a snuff-box presented to his great-grandfather when a young soldier by the aged Emperor Matthias of Pannonia, the great-grandfather alike of the present Emperor and of Mr Steinherz, in recognition of a gallant deed of arms done under his own eye. The monarch's portrait, set in diamonds, ornamented the lid of the box, and it seemed almost incredible to Usk that his father could look at the face of the murdered man and not recall at once the miniature which was so familiar to him.

In the absence of the clue which Usk possessed, public interest, though keenly excited by the tragedy, failed to seize upon its details with the wolfish eagerness which would have been aroused by any hint of the truth. It was made clear at the inquest that the murderer, who was identified as an Italian violinist named Marco Farinelli, had been known to the police for some time as an associate of foreign Republicans in London. He had lived many years in England, having just escaped the consequences of complicity in a plot against the Pannonian occupation of Venetia. His father, who had helped him to leave the country, and forcibly resisted the Pannonian soldiers sent to arrest him, had been summarily shot, and his mother, who was ill in bed, turned out in a winter night on the roadside, where she died. For nearly forty years Farinelli had cherished the memory of his wrongs, and it was shown that he was greatly excited by the news of the approaching visit to England of the Archduke Ferdinand Joachim, who had been in military command of the district in which his parents lived. It was proved that he had tried to form a band of assassins, who were to see that the Archduke did not leave London alive; but his friends had other work on hand, or preferred not to bring themselves into public notice, and he had evidently determined to accomplish his vengeance alone. In the breast-pocket of his coat was found a paper which aroused much curiosity—a kind of itinerary of London, duly mapped out into days. "Wednesday, Trafalgar Square and British Museum; Thursday, Houses of Parliament and Government Offices ..." it ran, but the Scotland Yard officials charged with the protection of the Archduke during his visit were able to explain it. Having learnt, with considerable dismay, that the distinguished visitor proposed to devote his mornings while in London to wandering about *incognito*, they arranged with much care a false time-table, which was allowed to circulate freely in his household. The expected leakage occurred, and the whole arrangement became known in some mysterious way to Farinelli, but while he was keeping his eager watch in the neighbourhood of the Museum, the Archduke was being conducted over the Horse-Guards. The mistake which had occurred was now perfectly clear to the jury, who had heard Usk acknowledge that there was from one point of view a certain likeness between the Archduke and Mr Steinherz, and they returned a verdict of wilful murder against the Italian, adding an expression of their sympathy with the family of the victim. In Farinelli's case the verdict was one of accidental death, although there was some attempt to bring it in as suicide, and the jury were discharged, and the nine days' wonder was at an end.

Maimie had found Lord Caerleon a tower of strength while the inquest was going on. He made a point of accompanying her backwards and forwards each day, and sitting beside her in court, and he was so quiet and so impassive that her restless impatience seemed to be calmed perforce. She did not fret over the fact that Lady Caerleon and Félicia were continually together; and she received with outward resignation the news which was awaiting her when the inquest ended, and which she had, indeed, foreseen. It fell to Lady Caerleon to communicate it, which she prepared to do with some anxiety, and Maimie's lip curled when she realised what was coming. It was quite like Félicia to depute another person to make an announcement that might prove disagreeable.

"Félicia and I have been talking things over," said Lady Caerleon, "and we think we have arranged a very pleasant plan. But of course we could not decide upon it without you."

"I guess not, indeed. Félicia and I don't *ever* act independently of one another," returned Maimie, with sarcastic emphasis.

Lady Caerleon went on hastily. She thought she understood perfectly well the soreness which filled the heart of the girl who found herself set aside for the lover and his relations, and she was very sorry for Maimie. "It is very touching," she said, "how stringently Mr Steinherz in his will expressed his desire to be buried in America by the side of his wife. I can quite sympathise with Félicia's natural desire to take his body home herself, which she tells me you suggested she should do. But she is really not fit for it. I never saw any one so completely a creature of nerves. The least excitement seems to throw her into a fever, and the strain of such a journey at this time of year would be enough to kill her."

"In other words, Fay don't choose to risk a voyage in the fall," said Maimie to herself, even while she was listening with polite interest to Lady Caerleon.

"And so our idea—of course I suggested it—was that Usk should cross to America with—the body, and superintend the funeral, and see that everything was done as you and Félicia would wish, and that you should both come home with us to Llandiarmid for the winter. The quiet country life would be sure to do Félicia good, and it would be the greatest pleasure to my husband and me to have young people about us again. I can't tell you how I was dreading another winter without my daughter."

"Lady Caerleon—" Maimie was looking at her with searching eyes—"I'd like to ask you just one question—does this bind Félicia to anything when Lord Usk comes home?"

Lady Caerleon looked surprised and somewhat annoyed. "I see nothing binding in what I have said," she answered.

"There won't be any doubt that Lord Usk goes as Mr Steinherz's friend, not as Félicia's lover—that his kindness gives him no claim on her? People look at things so differently over here."

"I should have thought gentlemanly conduct was the same on both sides of the Atlantic. A gentleman does not consider that he has established a claim upon a woman when he does her a service."

"Now I have made you mad," said Maimie sorrowfully, "and I'm real grieved. It's just for Félicia's sake I'm speaking. I don't want to see her engage herself right now, when she's naturally thinking more of her father's wish, and of all your sweet love and kindness to her, than of her own feelings."

Lady Caerleon wished in vain that there was some means of knowing whether this girl was laughing at her or not. "You seem to suggest that nothing but pressure from her father would have induced Félicia to accept Usk," she said. "If you have any reason to believe this, I think it is your duty to tell me."

"Why, that's just what I can't tell you," said Maimie, with the most engaging frankness. "I don't see anything of Félicia these days, and I can't seem to find out what she feels like. Only I had my misgivings before all of this happened, and I don't want to see her rushed into anything."

"You may feel quite happy. No one will put the slightest pressure upon Félicia to do anything but please herself," said Lady Caerleon stiffly. "Usk won't even try to come to an understanding with her before he sails."

"And when he comes back, he'll just begin over again from the beginning?" cried Maimie ecstatically. "Dear Lady Caerleon, you have taken a weight off my mind!"

"What a curious person Miss Logan is!" said Lady Caerleon afterwards to her son. "I can never make her out. She always seems to suspect us in some way."

Usk's private opinion was that Maimie suspected the Caerleon family, generally and individually, of anxiety to lay hold upon Félicia's fortune, but he would not suggest this to his mother, lest in the shock of such an accusation she should insist upon washing her hands of both girls forthwith.

"Oh, I don't think she likes me much," he said lightly; "but one can't wonder at it, when she's so devoted to Félicia. You won't let her turn Félicia against me while I am away, will you?"

But Maimie had no thought of doing anything so crude. One of her reasons for wishing to return to America had been the hope of obtaining from Mr Hicks some clue to the nature of the proofs Mr Steinherz had left in his charge; but since she was foiled in this, she had decided to keep her secret to herself for the present. As things were, Félicia's claim upon her father's relations would meet only with ridicule if it was brought to their notice. The house of Albret-Arragon would be likely to entertain it only if it offered some advantage, Mr Steinherz had said, and so far there was nothing but money to offer. But time might bring other opportunities, and it was time that Maimie had gained. Still, she did not think it well to let Félicia see that she was tolerably satisfied.

"I wonder just how long you'll find Llandiarmid endurable!" she said to her. "You're to have Phil's room, you know, and sort of take her place."

"I don't care," was the irritating reply. "Lady Caerleon is just sweet. I do love to have her sit by me and talk nicely about poor Pappa. It don't remind me the least of what he was, but it's real soothing to hear."

There was a touch of the old Félicia in this speech, and Maimie saw in a flash why Lady Caerleon's society had been preferred to her own of late. Félicia felt more at her ease with a stranger, who would naturally credit her with possessing all the feelings suitable to the occasion, than with one who knew as well as Maimie had done the lack of sympathy between her father and herself.

There was now no need to remain longer in London, and after a funeral service at a neighbouring church, which was attended by the American Ambassador, and to which the Archduke Ferdinand Joachim sent a representative, Usk started on his mournful journey. His farewell was clouded by the dismay which seized upon Félicia at the sight of the funeral arrangements. They were so poor, so shabby, she lamented; it would be said all over America that she had economised on her father's funeral. It was in vain that Lord Caerleon assured her everything had been done without regard to expense; she was plunged in woe for a whole day, recounting to Lady Caerleon at intervals the extraordinary sums which had been spent on costly "caskets" and other accessories at the funerals of different acquaintances, not heeding that her auditor thought the expenditure a wicked waste, and the publication of the cost ostentation of the worst kind.

The next day the two girls travelled to Llandiarmid with Lord and Lady Caerleon. It was a long journey, and the autumn dusk was already gathering when they arrived, but just before the lamps were lighted, Maimie, who was helping the maid to unpack for Félicia, happened to glance out of the window, and laughed gently. Félicia, who was lying exhausted on the couch, recovered sufficiently to come and look out as well, and saw Lord and Lady Caerleon setting out together for a ramble in the twilight. He had already routed out and put on an old Norfolk jacket and tweed cap, and Lady Caerleon's long skirt was gathered up to a serviceable length. Her hand was tucked into her husband's arm, and they were stealing out like two children bent on a frolic, talking happily.

"Can you see yourself and Usk going out together that way?" asked Maimie, in a low voice.

"I guess not," was Félicia's emphatic answer.

"But why not? It's just awfully charming. Why, they're not even stout— Lord Caerleon is too active, and she worries too much over other folks— they're just nice, solid, comfortable, middle-aged people. Oh, you'll get like them, Fay. You're going to be put in training for that now, and don't you forget it."

Félicia answered by an apprehensive glance round the room. Lady Philippa Mortimer had not been by any means a luxurious young person, and her favourite decorations appeared to have been hunting trophies. Her room had seemed to her the very acme of comfort, but she had never cared to stay indoors when she could possibly be out, and to the two American girls the place looked woefully bare. But there was a gleam of triumph in Maimie's eye, and Félicia hid her dismay manfully. Maimie scolded herself for that involuntary glance, and waited.

For the first two or three days all went well. It was natural that Félicia should be considered an invalid after the journey, and she was pursued everywhere by Lady Caerleon or her maid, anxious to establish her on the most comfortable sofa that could be found. There was the Castle to explore, too—a small portion at a time, that she might not be fatigued; and if Lord Caerleon was wounded by her audacious and irreverent comments on the family portraits and other valued treasures, he was too hospitable to betray the fact, realising that she fully believed she was entertaining him. But the fatigue even of a six hours' railway journey is not expected to last for ever, and presently Lady Caerleon hinted to Maimie that she thought it would be far better for Félicia's health if she would exert herself a little. What was there she would like to do?

It was a shock to the busy mistress of Llandiarmid to learn that Félicia could not walk, could not sew or embroider, did not care to sing, play, or draw, and when she read, read nothing but new novels, of which the Castle was conspicuously destitute. Moreover, anything that she was invited to do happened to be one of the very things that hurt her eyes, or made her head ache, or her face flush. In her distress Lady Caerleon took counsel with Maimie, who, though well aware that Félicia would not walk lest it should make her feet large, or work lest it should spoil her hands, did not feel called upon to reveal these reasons.

"What do you do in America, if you never go for walks?" asked the perplexed hostess.

"Why, we go out riding," answered Maimie carelessly.

"Riding? Why didn't you tell me before? I never thought Félicia would ride, and it will be an excellent thing for her. There's Phil's horse——"

"Oh, I don't mean that. I meant carriage-rides and sleigh-rides."

"Oh, *driving*?" said Lady Caerleon involuntarily. "But she won't come out with me."

"I guess it's just because she's afraid you'll have her go and see poor folks. We don't do that sort of thing in America."

"If Félicia is to live here after me, I hope she will be known as a friend in every house on the estate," said Lady Caerleon seriously.

Maimie was silent. The suggestion was too absurd to need argument. Then a happy idea occurred to her. "But Félicia has learnt riding, Lady Caerleon, and if you have a well-mannered horse——"

"My husband trained Philippa's horse himself," said Lady Caerleon, and Maimie undertook to suggest the idea to Félicia. Félicia thought it sounded promising, especially since it involved Lord Caerleon's escort, and she appeared in an exquisitely cut habit, perfect down to the minutest detail.

"She looks very well on horseback, but she sits a little stiffly," remarked Lady Caerleon to Maimie, as they watched the riders start. "Has she ridden much across country?"

"Lady Caerleon!" shrieked Maimie in horror; "don't tell me your husband's going to take her 'cross lots. We don't ride that way in America—not in the East, any way—only on the roads. She'll be killed."

"You may be quite sure my husband won't take her anywhere dangerous," said Lady Caerleon; but Maimie waited in agony until Félicia returned, more dishevelled-looking than she had ever seen her. Lord

Caerleon's good-humoured face was somewhat clouded as he helped her to dismount.

"You have a very good seat—for the Park," was the only comment he allowed himself to make upon the ride, but Félicia was less reticent when she had reached her room.

"Maimie Logan," she said emphatically, "I call you to witness that I won't ever again go riding with an Englishman anywhere outside of London. When I had declined all the tempting fences and ditches Lord Caerleon showed me, I thought I was through; but suddenly we came out upon a piece of waste land, and he said, 'This is Phil's favourite bit of common. Shall we canter?' and the horse flew off before I could refuse. I was shaken to death, and the wind was ahead of us, so I haven't a scrap of skin left on my face, and I guess my bang won't ever curl again."

Maimie received this information with a shriek of unfeigned dismay, and for the next two days Félicia remained invisible to the rest of the household, submitting to many unpleasant and infallible remedies warranted to restore a damaged complexion. Lord and Lady Caerleon were overwhelmed with self-reproach, and Maimie assured Félicia that she would never be asked to ride again. This seemed to her quite satisfactory; but on the evening of the second day, when she rushed upstairs after dinner, she found her friend dissolved in tears.

"Why, Fay, your eyes!" she cried, and Félicia applied a handkerchief delicately, then wept again.

"Oh, it's killing me!" was her moan. "Everything here's just horrid. There isn't any place to lounge—not even a rocker!"

It was quite true. There was an old-fashioned sofa, on which it was possible to lie at full length, but certainly not to lounge, and a low basket-chair, which Philippa, who had upholstered it herself, had thought the most restful thing in the world. The photograph of herself and her husband, which hung over the mantelpiece, in the place where she had always kept her family photographs, seemed to smile maliciously upon the present occupier of the room, as she sat curled-up in a nest of cushions. Maimie came gallantly to the rescue.

"Say, Fay, we're fixed here for the winter, and I guess we must stick the time out. But I'll have them give you a different room if you won't spoil your eyes crying."

"How?" asked Félicia, with some interest.

"Oh, I'll fix things," said Maimie, mysteriously but with secret satisfaction. Félicia was returning to her allegiance very fast. It was another reason for contentment that Félicia asked no questions as to the way in which she secured success. This was very simple. Maimie told Lady Caerleon that Félicia slept badly, which was true, and suggested that she ought not to sleep alone. Before Lady Caerleon, somewhat puzzled, had time to propose that Maimie should move into the same room, Maimie added that she felt sure the easterly aspect of Lady Philippa's room was not good for Félicia. Informed that it was the outlook which Philippa had specially loved, Maimie retorted that that might be so, but Félicia was just perished with cold. Lady Caerleon remarked that she was sure to be cold in the winter if she would not go out; to which Maimie replied that in America the houses were heated, and people had not to go outdoors to get warm. Lady Caerleon was horrified by the implied reproach. She had meant the girl Usk loved to be so much to her, but in some mysterious way they seemed to be fast drifting apart. And now it was suggested that Félicia was suffering heroically in silence, fearing to wound her hostess by the suggestion that Philippa's room was too cold for her! Always ready to accuse herself, Lady Caerleon blamed her own lack of sympathy and insight, and entreated Maimie to say what she thought it would be best to do. Maimie was quite prepared for this. There were two rooms opening into one another, and facing south-west, which she thought would be just right. And might she look about in the unoccupied rooms of the Castle, and choose the furniture that Félicia would probably like? In her compunction, Lady Caerleon would have given leave for anything, and in due time Maimie introduced Félicia to a kind of fairy bower. There were quaint tables and cabinets belonging to the Castle, but the draperies and ornaments came from Maimie's own stores. She had foreseen this crisis, and provided against it.

Lady Caerleon found that her dream of having two young companions and helpers always with her this winter instead of one was doomed to disappointment. The two girls spent their time almost exclusively in their own rooms, and what they did there was a mystery. Maimie had American books and papers sent her by post, and sometimes her voice could be heard as she read aloud to Félicia; but Félicia's activities seemed to be confined to the eating of bonbons. When there were visitors, however, both the girls made their appearance as soon as they were sent for, and took all the burden of entertaining off Lady Caerleon's shoulders. About each of them would gather a circle of worthy squires and parsons, whose honest laughter over Transatlantic audacities of speech made the great hall ring. The country ladies, sitting silent and astonished and a little shocked, had yet eyes to note the Parisian elegance of the deep mourning gowns, even if they remarked afterwards that it was just like Americans to dress with such uncalled for smartness every day. In any case, an impression was made.

CHAPTER VI.
TOTÂ QUOD MENTE PETISTI.

"HOW did Phil stand it, any way?" said Félicia.

She and Maimie were sitting over the fire in her room, discussing the Rector's daughters, whom they had just been interviewing at tea. There is no other word to describe the intercourse between the American and the English girls, for Félicia, in a wonderful Empire tea-gown, which revealed her white arms and shoulders through clouds of black chiffon, had set herself deliberately to catechise the Misses Jones on the occupations and pleasures—particularly the pleasures—of their daily life. The Rector was a good Welshman, and his daughters, who were rosy, healthy, country girls, rejoiced in the names of Gwladys and Myfanwy. Now that Philippa was married, they were Lady Caerleon's right hand in all her schemes for the good of the parish, and their multifarious duties had hitherto left them no time to cultivate the acquaintance of the two Americans, whose clothes they had regarded admiringly from a distance. Christmas was now over, however, and in the short breathing-space at the end of the holidays Lady Caerleon had insisted on making her young friends known to one another, and with some misgivings had left the four girls together.

The conversation that ensued was not entirely devoid of friction. Something in the tone of Félicia's questions and comments seemed to rouse the two Welsh girls, and the sedate Gwladys took refuge in assuring her calmly that she could not possibly understand the pleasures and interests of a life so far removed from her own, and therefore there was no use in telling her about them. The livelier Myfanwy, on the other hand, was anxious to justify her contentment with things as they were. She and Gwladys were so busy, she said, that they really had no time to go about hunting for amusement; but when they wanted it there was plenty of one kind or another. They had their bicycles, and they took turns in driving their parents in the pony-cart, and they belonged to a harmonic society, and this winter there were University Extension Lectures in Aberkerran, and Lady Caerleon had given them tickets. They took turns, also, in going to dinner-parties, and in the summer there was tennis—which still lingered on in this remote corner of the world—and croquet (Gwladys was a crack player), and picnics, and choir excursions—the last form of dissipation was included somewhat doubtfully.

"But don't you ever have any frolics?" demanded Félicia.

Both girls looked rather offended at being asked such a question, but inquired forbearingly what in the world she meant. Félicia, racking her memory to recall the amusements of country girls in America, mentioned candy-pulls, corn-huskings, apple-bees, clam-suppers, and church-socials, to which they replied with marked coolness that in England it was only the farmers and the Dissenters who went in for that sort of thing.

"Maybe this is a frolic?" suggested Maimie, with a wave of her hand, which included the room and the tea-table.

"It is a great pleasure," answered Gwladys calmly; and Myfanwy added with effusion that they loved coming to the Castle, and wasn't Lady Caerleon sweet? Lady Caerleon returned to the drawing-room at this moment, and carried off the Jones girls to her boudoir, to show them a new photograph of Philippa, which had just arrived.

"And I know just as well as anything what she said to them when she had them alone," said Félicia. "'My dears, in your simple useful lives you are far happier than those two selfish creatures in the parlour, who do nothing all the time.'"

"And the girl with the queer name just threw her arms round her neck, and said, '*Dear* Lady Caerleon!'" mimicked Maimie.

"But how did Phil stand it, any way?" said Félicia again. "That was a real sweet letter she wrote me this morning, or I'd have thought she was trying to get at me. 'I do envy you in my dear old room. Do please ride Brownie, and use any of my things as much as you like. I wish I was at home to show you round.' How could she want to be back home? No bouquets—no bonbons—no gentlemen—no sleigh-rides—no dancing—and yet she lived!"

"Why, she was a real outdoor girl," said Maimie; "hunting and wheeling, and taking long walks, and thankful to get a day's golf at Colfton now and then. You'll act that way, Fay, before they're done with you. You're to be made over, you know, and as soon as Usk arrives home they'll set at work. Wait until you change your mourning and the dinner-parties begin. Think of putting in a whole day on horseback, and dining the Jones family in the evening!"

"I know you're trying to have me say I'll break off with Usk," said Félicia calmly, "and I would if there was anything better in sight. But there isn't. At least we are sure of getting right into society here. I know it's only the nice people Lady Caerleon visits with, not the smart people, but that I can fix for myself once I'm presented and have prospected around a bit. Lady Caerleon is best friends with the Dowager Duchess of Old Sarum and the rest of the religious aristocratic cranks, and once we break with the

Caerleons all of their doors will be shut in our faces. As I say, that's nothing if we can do better, but you've got to show me just how."

"But if I can help you to do far better?" demanded Maimie.

"Why, I'd like to hear about it first."

"That's just what you can't do. You must be quite innocent. But you'll have to fire Usk out if I give you the word."

"Well, I won't fire him out definitely until this other plan of yours works. I can do with him well enough if it should peter out. You needn't conclude I'm going to be made over to suit Lady Caerleon. I guess I can make Usk over to suit myself. But I'm open to other offers."

"If I can't fix things right away, she'll accept him with effusion just as soon as ever he comes back," said Maimie to herself; and she plotted and planned until, as she reflected ruefully, her hair must be turning grey. It was part of her scheme that Usk's family, and not herself, should take the first step towards breaking off the understanding; and she saw her chance one day when Lady Caerleon, speaking with obvious nervousness, seized the opportunity of a rare *tête-à-tête* with her to say—

"Miss Logan, I wish I could enlist your help with Félicia. I quite hoped that the winter here would make her strong, but she gives herself no chance to get well."

The implied reproach to Félicia aroused Maimie at once. "It's just that there isn't anything to do here," she replied. "If we were at home you'd soon see she wasn't sick. She would be going along from one function to another all the time."

"Kept up by excitement? Still, that shows she can do a great deal if she likes. But I want to see her able to work and play in moderation without needing a perpetual stimulus. Of course I know her father's death was a terrible shock, but the invalid life she leads at present is the worst possible thing for her. Always on the sofa, in that hot room, eating sweets or sucking that horrible gum——"

"We call it chewing gum, not sucking it," interrupted Maimie, listening apprehensively for the next words. Had Lady Caerleon found out about the cigarettes smuggled in under the guise of bonbons?

"It makes no difference. And she scarcely eats anything at meals, and seems by some instinct to choose what is most unwholesome."

"That is so," said Maimie cordially. It was clear that Lady Caerleon had discovered nothing. "I'd just give anything to get her to think of her complexion, and she doesn't begin to do it."

"Her complexion!" There were scorn and disgust, deep if involuntary, in Lady Caerleon's tones. "I am talking about her health. A more natural life and plenty of exercise—not simply creeping backwards and forwards on the terrace for a few minutes when it happens to be warm—would do more for her complexion than anything else. What I think of is the future. Miss Logan, can't you see what I feel? My boy loves Félicia, and I hope they will have a long and happy married life together. But how can they, if she divides her time between spasms of excitement and helpless invalidism? I can't help thinking of the poor unfortunate women one meets so often in travelling—rushing from place to place in search of some new sensation, never happy, never contented, always bored and yet eager, with tired eyes and all sorts of nervous complaints. And their children—their poor little children—grown-up men and women already, living and talking, and almost feeling like their elders, wizened and old before they have ever been young. Generally they are Americans, these poor people, but of late there have been more English among them. I speak in Usk's interests, I can't deny it, but I do entreat you, for Félicia's own sake, to try and help me to save her from falling into a life of that sort."

"I don't see but you'll have to leave Félicia alone," was the reply, as Lady Caerleon, with tears in her eyes, paused suddenly. "We are not made like you English people, nor brought up like you, either. I know you are not English yourself," Maimie added hastily, "but you have grown into English ways. We must move around, we must have interest and excitement, and if an American woman don't find that sort of thing ready for her, she just starts right out and provides it for herself. If we have smarter brains and more active bodies than you, it's not our fault, and you won't do any good punishing us for it. If you leave Félicia and Lord Usk to fix things for themselves, I guess they'll shake down all right."

"I am afraid not. I remember all my own troubles when I first settled here, and I should like to save Félicia as much as I can. And my husband is the calmest and most reasonable of men. Nothing but deliberate wrong-doing would make him angry, and he bore with my mistakes, and listened to my complaints, and helped me to begin afresh, in the most wonderful way. But Usk is more like me. He gets worried and irritable when he is tried beyond a certain point, and his wife ought to be able to calm him, and not irritate him further. And surely, if she loves him, Félicia would delight to do anything she can to make herself a better wife for him? Think what a joy it would be to him to find her strong and well and able to go about with him when he comes back!"

"*If* she loves him!" repeated Maimie thoughtfully. "Why, certainly—but does she love him, Lady Caerleon?"

She seized the opportunity afforded by the entrance of a servant with a note to slip away, leaving her question to do its work. The interruption could not have occurred more suitably for her purpose, and during the next two or three days she managed to avoid all private conversation with Lady Caerleon. At the same time, she was obliged to keep constant watch lest her hostess should seek an interview with Félicia herself. Her manœuvres had hitherto been successful in keeping them apart without Lady Caerleon's perceiving either the method or the reason; but now, stung by the doubt cast into her mind, she might insist upon a definite explanation. Then, if. Félicia made another scene, and succumbed to Lady Caerleon's motherly kindness, all was lost, and this was likely enough. The monotony of her indoor life, which she obstinately refused to vary by any exercise out of doors, was really telling on her nerves, and she would alarm Maimie by wild outbursts of impatience. She wanted to dance, to flirt, to go to the theatre and lose herself in a play, she wanted to run away—in fact, she was in a state in which she would respond to any stimulus applied to her emotions. Maimie knew very well that the contraband cigarettes were slightly narcotised, and by this means she tried to quiet Félicia's nerves for the moment, while still keeping her mind on the stretch by vague promises and prophecies, the fulfilment of which depended upon the success of her "plan."

As Maimie had expected, Lady Caerleon came to her, after two or three days of anxiety, for an explanation of her mysterious warning as to Félicia's feelings. The mother was determined to know the worst.

"If Félicia doesn't care for Usk, you ought to tell me," she said, "that I may prepare his mind, and not let him go on hoping in vain."

"Well, now, Lady Caerleon," said Maimie, with the frankness which her hostess found almost more trying than reserve, "I'll tell you just what I think. I don't believe Félicia loves your son—at present, but I guess if he came home and asked her, she would marry him right away."

"But why?" cried Lady Caerleon, aghast.

"Why? Can you ask? Because of all your kindness and of all Lord Usk has done. She says to herself, 'If I can repay and please them by sacrificing my own feelings, why, I'll just do it!'"

"This is terrible!" murmured Lady Caerleon. "I must speak to Félicia, and if that is really her state of mind, I will write to Usk at once."

"No, please!" entreated Maimie. "Didn't you remark that I said 'at present'? I would like to have her fall in love with him really. I thought it was real kind of you and Lord Caerleon to tell him to go and visit Niagara, and the South, and not be back until February, so's he wouldn't embarrass

Félicia by arriving home so soon. Well, now, if he didn't come back until the end of March, I guess it would be better yet. Won't you have him go and see the Pacific slope, and the Yosemite in winter? By the middle of March Félicia will be changing her mourning, and I thought we might pay a visit to her best friend, Mrs van Zyl, at Nice. She's set on having us, and it would be just lovely for Félicia. Then your son could come out and see us there, and Félicia would be able to compare him with other men. You do think he would stand a good chance then, don't you?"

This was a master-stroke. Even if Lady Caerleon could have brought herself to distrust Usk's power of attraction, she could not confess the feeling, and she had no wish whatever to do so. Indeed, she was conscious of an unaccountable sensation of relief, which she attributed to the fact that Usk would at last be able to stand on his own merits, and take his chance in a fair field, unhampered by the dubious advantage of Mr Steinherz's favour. She fell in with Maimie's proposal at once.

"I think it is an excellent idea," she said. "All the gaieties will be over on the Riviera, and Félicia will enjoy a quiet restful time." Maimie could have told her differently, but held her peace. "I will speak to my husband at once, and if he agrees with me, I will write to Usk to-day."

The idea did not approve itself quite so strongly to Lord Caerleon as to his wife, and his comments opened her eyes to a truth which she had successfully hidden from herself hitherto. Her relief sprang chiefly from the hope that, after all, Félicia might not marry Usk. With Lady Caerleon, to discover such a piece of self-deception was instantly to impose punishment, and while she still suggested to Usk that he should extend his travels, she confessed plainly that the idea was inspired by Maimie, and sprang from a suspicion that Félicia did not really care for him. She added also that his father and she left the matter entirely to his own discretion, and this intimation had the unlooked-for result that Usk promptly cancelled his remaining engagements in America, and sailed for home by the very first steamer. It was with the greatest reluctance that he had left Félicia in her trouble to the care even of his mother, but it had comforted him to feel that he was doing something for her in seeing her father's body laid in the grave he had chosen. The extension of his exile he had accepted with some unwillingness, feeling that he could trust himself to be near Félicia without forcing his hopes upon her in her time of grief. However, if his presence would embarrass her, if she did not know him well enough to trust him, he was content to stay away. But this last menace to his happiness was too much. He must know the worst. If Félicia did not love him, it was better to hear it from her own lips, and bear it like a man, than wander about the American continent tortured with uncertainty, and murmuring, "She loves me—loves me not," like a girl pulling a daisy to pieces.

It was a sunny afternoon in early February when Usk arrived at the little wayside station near Llandiarmid. No one was expecting him, for the letter he had posted in New York, announcing his return, had travelled by the same vessel as himself, and had only reached the Castle that morning. At this moment it was lying on Lord Caerleon's table, in company with the telegram Usk had sent from Liverpool on his arrival there; for Lord and Lady Caerleon had started at an unearthly hour in the morning on a long cold drive into Oldport, where a temperance convention was being held. Disregarding the stationmaster's eager invitation to step into his office while he sent to the nearest farm and borrowed a trap to take his lordship up to the Castle, Usk left his luggage to be fetched later, and struck off across the fields. He had a feeling that if he met Félicia now, he would win her, and he hurried on, his country-trained senses noting the springing wheat in the autumn-sown fields, the pleasant smell of the rich red plough-lands, the brown and crimson buds in the hedges, and the twittering of the birds in the mild sunshine. Everything spoke of life and love and hope, and Usk whistled gaily for sheer gladness of heart as he renewed his acquaintance with the many short cuts, less remarkable for their shortness than their complexity, which he and Philippa had long ago discovered, and definitely laid down as the quickest way home. The shrubbery gate was locked, of course, but he had climbed the wall at this point too often for that to be any obstacle, and he went on up the well-known paths. At the long wild border under the sunny wall which marked the limits of the garden proper he cast an involuntary glance. Philippa would have been there, on such an afternoon as this, looking for early violets, or gathering handfuls of snowdrops from among the grass on the opposite side of the walk, and perhaps Félicia——? But Félicia was not to be seen, and he turned to the old arched doorway leading into the garden and rattled at it vigorously, nearly frightening the wits out of a meek gardener's boy who was at work just inside, and opened the door timidly. On being questioned, however, the boy recovered his senses sufficiently to volunteer the remark that he 'see one of the young ladies, the prettiest one, on the top terrace by herself about five minutes back,' for which he received a munificent reward.

Climbing the long worn flights of steps which led from one to another of the broad terraces in front of the Castle, Usk kept purposely in the shade of the bushes which rose behind the balustrades. This was his chance, to find Félicia alone and take her by surprise. He reached the terrace next below the highest, and stopped suddenly. The steps which faced him turned sharply at a right angle, and on the small landing thus formed stood a sun-dial. Leaning against the sun-dial was Félicia, her long black robes trailing on the stones, her face almost hidden by the furs in which she was muffled.

"Félicia!" Usk had sprung up the steps and appeared at her side. She turned with a little scream, then a smile crept over her face.

"Well, do you know," she remarked deliberately, "I was just thinking about you. I sort of felt you were not far away."

"You wanted me? Oh, my darling!"

It was necessary for Félicia to free herself, which she did without undignified haste. Then she straightened her hat, and looked reproachful. "I don't know what I said to give you the notion of doing that, Lord Usk," she said severely.

"Only that you missed me." Usk's arm was round her again.

"Well, I don't know but I have felt lonesome at times. But I never said it was on your account, any way."

"Perhaps you would like me to make you say it?" suggested Usk, taking full advantage of his position.

"Do tell, now! Commend me to an Englishman for calm impudence! And what has brought you along just now?"

"I came because I couldn't stay away any longer. *You* brought me back, you know you did. I had to see you again."

"Then I guess you're going away again right now? You seem to be taking a look to last you a long time."

"If you're counting on that, you'll be disappointed. I shall look at you just as hard however long I stay. I should like to look at you for ever. Your face is never the same for two seconds together."

"I don't feel like allowing remarks on my face unless they're compliments, Lord Usk, and don't you forget it."

"And that wasn't a compliment? Then I'll show you the difference. Any man may pay you a compliment, do you see? but I may make remarks which are not compliments, because I love you."

"Then preserve me from being loved, any way! But maybe your sort of love isn't just the usual sort?"

"Isn't it? I'm so sorry. Is that better?" Félicia had laid herself open to an obvious retort in the confidence that Usk would not be quick-witted enough to seize the opportunity. "Do you believe that I love you now?" he asked, partially releasing her, "or shall I go on to prove it further?"

"I guess it's not necessary. I can quite believe it."

"And you do care for me—just a little?"

Félicia's face assumed an expression of intense thought. "Well, yes," she said at last. "I think I can maybe say that I do care for you—just a little."

She flashed a glance at Usk which intoxicated him with delight, and nothing was further from his mind than the idea that her answer might be literally true. "All right. I'll take it in instalments," he said joyously. "*Un peu—beaucoup—point*—no, that's not what I meant. What an idiot I am! You care for me, and that's enough."

"Yes, but Maimie don't," said Félicia dolorously.

"Oh, bother Maimie! No, I don't mean that either. Of course she can't bear losing you. But we'll both be awfully nice to her, won't we? Now that my mind is at rest about you, I'll cultivate her—make up to her, in fact."

"Not while I'm around, if you please."

"Now is it likely—if you were anywhere near?"

"I guess I'll go and tell her," said Félicia. "Isn't that your parents coming in from their ride? You go and have an affecting meeting with them, and break the news, and I'll do likewise."

Maimie was indoors, kept in by a bad cold, which she had caught when called out of bed one night to prescribe remedies for Félicia's headache. Nothing could possibly have been better timed than that cold, Félicia thought complacently, though she had shown a strong sense of injury when it had prevented Maimie from coming out with her. She dashed upstairs and into Maimie's room, and shot her bolt.

"Wake up, Maimie! Usk's come back, and we are engaged!"

Maimie dropped her book and turned absolutely white. Then she stood up and came slowly towards Félicia, who cowered before her.

"Félicia Steinherz, I could kill you where you stand!"

"How you look, Maimie! What do you mean?" asked Félicia feebly.

"Why have you done it, any way?" demanded Maimie.

"Why, I like Usk well enough, and I must have a man to trail me around."

"Do you know who's coming here next week?" fiercely.

"Oh, just some brother of Lord Caerleon's and his wife."

"Why, certainly. Do you know how many brothers he has?"

"Well, I guess there must be two, any way—this Lord Cyril and the Count Mortimer that Mr Hicks talks about all the time."

"I do admire to see a girl real smart! You've listened pretty well, haven't you?"

"I don't see but I've listened well enough. Lord Caerleon couldn't expect me do more than look interested, and interrupt just right."

"I'd have felt like boxing your ears if I'd been Lord Caerleon."

"No, Maimie, you wouldn't. It's real sweet of me to have him talk to me, and he knows it. You're fallen in love with him, because he cavaliers you around just the same as he does me, but that's no reason why I should." And Maimie was crushed for the time.

Now that Usk and Félicia were engaged, an impartial observer, with a mind appreciative of irony, might have enjoyed watching the attitudes assumed by the different persons concerned. Maimie, openly contemptuous for a moment, became calm and tolerant after the first shock of surprise, allowing Félicia to see that she did not take the matter at all seriously. If Félicia chose to break a country heart for pastime, it was no one's business but her own, and the owner of the heart had only himself to thank if he took for love the frame of mind induced by propinquity succeeding *ennui*. Félicia, feeling bound to justify her action in Maimie's eyes, overdid her part wofully. She raised Usk to the seventh heaven of delight by what seemed to him her utter self-surrender. He had never imagined that she could give herself up to him so unreservedly, although he had quite expected that she would monopolise his time and services, as she did. But that she should wish—nay, order him to be at her side all day, this filled him with a sense of wholly undeserved joy, since he could not tell that she was playing with one eye on Maimie.

It was not long before the engagement became known in the county, although it was not to be publicly announced until six months had elapsed after Mr Steinherz's death. Local interest in the event was tremendous, and the dwellers in the neighbourhood learned to watch almost daily for the Castle dogcart, with the 'young lord' driving, and the beautiful lady muffled in furs at his side. Félicia's neglect of her complexion was positively heroic at this time, but fortunately the weather was mild, and Maimie showed herself truly forgiving where face-washes were concerned.

"I guessed the fault was in the companion, and not the climate, when you wouldn't go out driving with me, Félicia," said Lord Caerleon, laughing, as he helped her out of the cart one day, and Félicia had the grace to blush.

"I don't see but I'm real English now, just like Phil," she answered brightly, for Maimie's benefit.

Perhaps the happiest of the onlookers at this juncture was Lady Caerleon. She forced herself to rejoice in Usk's happiness, in a way only possible to a woman whose tendency through life had been to choose the most disagreeable path that offered itself, in the conviction that it was the right one. Her husband, much as he admired Félicia's beauty, grumbled a little in private that Usk should choose an American bride, and one who took no interest in social questions, but Lady Caerleon persisted that love would set everything right. Félicia had even learnt to like the country since Usk had come home, and very soon, no doubt, she would be taking an active interest in the Temperance cause. In the kindness of her heart the mother even petted Maimie, for whom she still felt an instinctive distrust, and devised all sorts of little pleasures for her, to soften the loneliness that fell to her lot now that Félicia had forsaken her so completely.

CHAPTER VII.
A FAMILY LIKENESS.

THERE was a sense of mystery hanging over the Castle. Visitors were expected, and a whole suite of apartments, called the Queen's Rooms (of course because Queen Elizabeth had occupied them on one of her progresses), had been prepared for them, much to Félicia's astonishment and somewhat to her indignation. It seemed to her that she and her engagement had sunk into insignificance in view of this approaching visit of Lord and Lady Cyril Mortimer and the latter's son. Why on earth should such a fuss be made about them? she wished to know; and she took refuge in an insulted determination not to show any interest in their coming, although Maimie's eyes expressed abundant knowledge, and Usk was obviously willing to be questioned.

Lord Caerleon and his son drove into Aberkerran to meet the travellers, and afternoon tea was postponed until their return. This was a fresh grievance for Félicia, who declared herself as limp as a rag. In the intervals of eyeing the tea-table thirstily, she spared a little mild wonder for Lady Caerleon, who was moving nervously about the hall, altering the position of the furniture and rearranging the folds of curtains. The brougham drove up, and Lady Caerleon flew to the door to receive the white-haired lady whom her husband led up the steps. Félicia's quick eye noticed at once that the visitor was wearing the most magnificent sables she had ever beheld, but her amazement was extreme when she saw Lady Caerleon only checked in a deep reverence by the newcomer's seizing her hands and kissing her on both cheeks.

"Do tell, now!" whispered the astonished observer eagerly to Maimie. "Aren't these English people real stiff? or is it because Lady Caerleon is a foreigner?"

"Nadia, my dear sister!" the visitor was saying reproachfully, as Maimie shot a glance of scorn at Félicia, "you will astonish your young friends. Present them, please—I mean, you will introduce them, won't you?"

As Lady Caerleon complied with the request, in a curiously flurried manner, Félicia noticed that the stranger's face did not look old, in spite of her white hair, and that she had a very sweet smile. In her bearing there was something so dignified, notwithstanding the gentleness of her words and looks, that Félicia felt as if she was being presented at Court. In Lady Cyril's presence she suddenly saw herself as an outsider, and began to feel nervous about her manners and uncomfortable about her voice.

"But I'll watch and see how she fixes things," she told herself, with returning confidence. "I guess an American woman can just make herself over if she wants to, and not be beaten by any Eu-ropian court lady."

Lord Cyril's greeting restored her self-complacency. He was "just ordinary," she decided at a glance, small and grey-haired, with blue eyes and unobtrusive manners, but he expressed it as his opinion that Usk was a very lucky fellow, which showed him to be a person of discernment. He had brought a secretary with him, it appeared, and his wife a lady companion, but Lady Cyril's son, Baron von Neuburg, had been delayed on the Continent by the breakdown of a train, and would not arrive till the next day. Félicia was still oppressed by a sense of mystery. Why did Lady Caerleon seem to leave the initiative in everything to her sister-in-law, and why was Lady Cyril constantly on the point of taking the lead in another person's house, to the obvious amusement of her husband? The secretary and the lady companion, who were introduced as M. Paschics and Mlle. Mirkovics, were stiff and silent, and appeared, no doubt unintentionally, to disapprove of what was going on; and, most unpardonable of all, Usk's attention seemed to be devoted chiefly to his aunt, and not to his betrothed. It was not until tea was over, and the visitors had been shown to their rooms, that Félicia was able to mark her sense of his behaviour by refusing to come into the garden with him to see if there were any primroses out. Instead, she went upstairs with Maimie.

"Well!" she said, when they were in their own room, "I would like to know what's come to all of the folks. Lady Cyril's only a dowdy old thing after all, though her sables are too sweet for words, but they all treat her just like a queen."

"And she is a queen," said Maimie impatiently, "and her sables were given her by the Emperor of Scythia. She is Queen Ernestine of Thracia, who married Count Mortimer two years back, as Mr Hicks has told you time and time again, and her son, who comes here *incognito* to-morrow as Baron von Neuburg, is the King of Thracia. I meant you to marry him."

"Land alive!" was all that Félicia could say.

"I wanted to make you an empress, and you threw away your chance," went on Maimie bitterly. "And this time I was going to have you marry a king, and a week before he comes you conclude to get engaged to Usk!"

"Why, Maimie Logan, have you lost your mind?" cried Félicia, recovering herself. "You know we would never be let do it."

"I know you just would, then. I could fix it."

"Well, it's too late now, and I don't care, any way. Usk is a real good fellow, and his folks are just lovely. I'm on yet."

"I do wonder how you'll feel when you come to live way down in the country all of the year, and be out in the air mornings and afternoons and evenings. You'll have a nice round contented face like the Jones girls by then, rosy-cheeked and blowsy and dairymaidish."

"You needn't be nasty." Félicia went to the glass and examined her face with some anxiety, but the pure creamy pallor was not yet vulgarised by any touch of red. She laughed. "Not much harm done this far, Maimie. I'll tell you when I'm tired of Usk, any way."

"No, you won't," said Maimie calmly. "You're tired of him already. It's getting more and more of a trial to have him stick to you the way he does, but you let him do it just to make me mad. When you're tired clear out, you can let me know."

"And you can round up a few of the kings you keep on hand, and have me choose," responded Félicia.

Now that her perplexity was at an end, Félicia was prepared to take full advantage of the situation. Queen Ernestine's obvious difficulty in masquerading in the English household as a younger son's wife afforded her a malicious amusement, and she could not pardon Usk for refusing to respond to the frequent glances she flashed at him. At the same time, she watched the royal lady narrowly, hoping to discover the source of the peculiarly dignified charm of manner which characterised her. Those who knew could have told Félicia that it was the outcome of a life of sadness and self-repression, crowned at last with a tardy happiness chastened by apprehension. Her own soul, however, was not sufficiently awake to note more than that the Queen seemed to do and say the right thing by instinct, and that the grace of her bearing was only equalled by her consideration for others. Knowing little of her story, Félicia was captivated by her personality—although the attraction was no bar to the entertainment she derived from seeing her in a false position—and she felt quite virtuously indignant when Maimie, by what seemed an unpardonable piece of *gaucherie*, brought a shadow into the beautiful changeful eyes.

It appeared as though a demon of mischief had taken possession of Maimie that evening. The secretary and Mlle. Mirkovics had discreetly excused themselves after dinner, leaving the family party alone, and the four elders were gathered by the fire, talking. Usk and Félicia occupied a three-cornered settee at a little distance—it was a piece of furniture Usk liked, because the form of the seat obliged him to turn round and rest his arm on the back, if he was to face Félicia in talking to her. Between the two groups, at a little table close to the standard lamp, sat Maimie, looking through the annual volume of an illustrated paper some twenty or thirty years old, which she had disinterred from the library for reasons best known to herself. Occasionally she interjected remarks into the conversation of the party by the fire, enjoying the delightful feeling that she was outraging all etiquette, and yet that no one could rebuke her. It happened that the talk turned upon the escapade of a young member of a German princely family, who had recently disappeared from his home, and was understood to have managed to join the forces opposed to Great Britain in a little war which was then raging.

"Well, now, that's queer!" said Maimie. "Here in this old paper there's a case of the same sort. Just listen: 'In connection with the ill-fated Prince Joseph of Arragon, a view of whose yacht, the Claudine, we published a fortnight ago, a Vindobona correspondent sends us a romantic story. It is understood that the official accounts of the Prince's voyage to the South Seas were merely a blind, and that his journey was in reality a flight, in which he was accompanied by a charming young lady of noble birth, whose musical performances have been the delight of Vindobona this winter. It is even rumoured that they were privately married. However this may be, it is certain that not only Fräulein von Lilienkranz, but her duenna, Frau Schlesinger, and the latter's daughter Julie, who was her constant attendant, disappeared at the exact time that the Prince's voyage was announced. The keenest interest was felt here as to the *dénoûment* of the romance which has been so tragically ended by the Australian billows———.' Do tell, Fay!" Maimie broke off shrilly. "Julie Schlesinger! mightn't that be my mother's name? It caught my eye right away."

"See if there's a portrait," suggested Félicia. "Maybe it was your mother in disguise, though I don't just see how it works out."

"No, there isn't any. It says you couldn't buy one in Vindobona—that either the Prince or his family had snapped all of them up, both of him and the lady, and destroyed them. There's just the ship, two weeks back."

Usk sprang up, as though to look at the picture, but when he was stooping over the book he whispered hastily, "Perhaps you don't know that Prince Joseph was my aunt's cousin?"

"Oh, I'm real sorry. How could I know?" Maimie whispered back, with a face of guileless innocence touched with anguish. Aloud, she made some remark about another picture on the same page, and Usk returned to his former seat. As he did so, he was struck by a certain alert look, which he knew well, on his uncle's face. Félicia had turned her head when Maimie claimed her attention, and the lamplight fell full upon her profile, which was in a line with that of Queen Ernestine. Usk saw the two faces from one side, his uncle from the other, but at the same moment it flashed upon both of them that the profiles were extraordinarily alike. Lord Cyril cast a glance of calm scrutiny at his nephew, and resumed the conversation Maimie had interrupted. It was possible that he regarded the likeness as merely a coincidence, and Usk hoped this might be the case.

It might have seemed to strengthen this opinion that Lord Cyril made no remark to his nephew, but some hours later, when he looked into his wife's boudoir, where she was spending a few minutes in chat with the sallow-faced lady-in-waiting, it was clear that he had not forgotten what he had seen.

"And what do you think of your niece that is to be, Ernestine?" he asked.

"She is very beautiful," said the Queen, somewhat doubtfully, "but it does not seem to me that poor Usk has found her heart yet."

"Perhaps she has none to find. What does Mlle. Mirkovics think?"

"Miss Steinherz has something of the *grand air*, though there is a want of repose in her manners," was the temperate reply. "One would scarcely expect that in an American, perhaps. But she carries herself like a queen in her own right."

"Every American woman is that by right of birth," said Lord Cyril lazily. "Does Félicia's face remind you of any one, Ernestine?"

"Oh, you have noticed it, then? The likeness haunted me all evening, until I happened to see her refusing to say good night to Usk. He had offended her in some way, and she would only let him kiss her hand. Then I saw a likeness to my aunt Claudine, who married the King of Cantabria. It was not a happy marriage, you know, Cyril, and her portrait has a look of haughty resignation about it—a kind of 'scorn of scorn.' It is only in profile that there is a likeness, for none of our family have that little rosebud mouth or those surprised eyebrows, and Félicia is much prettier than my aunt ever was."

"It's a curious coincidence," said Cyril, apparently dismissing the subject as he left the room, but his mind was still busy with it. "There are more coincidences in the affair than this one, if I am not mistaken," he said to himself. "There was that story which came out at the inquest, that the girl's father was murdered by mistake for the Archduke Ferdinand Joachim. Come, this narrows it down. Weldart and Hohenstaufen! King Paul of Cantabria married a Weldart, and his mother was a Hohenstaufen. The girl shows no traces of Albret or Hohenstaufen features—happily for herself— but the Weldart look is very distinct, only fined and sharpened as European types so often are after a generation or two in America. Clearly, then, the deceased 'Mr Steinherz' was a son of Paul and Claudine. There were three of them. Ramon is still alive, as I know only too well. Florian died young— in somewhat discreditable circumstances, but he is indubitably dead. There remains the lost Joseph, and here, I think, we must look for the link. That shipwreck presents great possibilities. It looks a little fishy that Prince Joseph and his fair musician—oh, and the maid too, of course—should have contrived to escape when every one else on board was drowned. Was there collusion somewhere? I don't see how or why the thing was worked. But perhaps they had trans-shipped before the end came? That's more likely, and makes the whole thing credible. Well, Usk knows whatever there is to be known, and if I am at all acquainted with him, will make a clean breast of the whole matter to me at the earliest opportunity. Caerleon and Nadia know nothing, nor does the girl herself. She is too self-conscious to be a good actress. But the hanger-on—does she know? or was that artless discovery another coincidence? She also has possibilities. She allowed herself to be silenced by Usk, which she would hardly have done if she had been the brainless innocent she was impersonating for the moment. I am inclined to think she does know, and is keeping the thing dark for some reason of her own. What that may be is not apparent for the moment, but I think it is distinctly to the advantage of all concerned that silence should still be kept. To-morrow I shall probably hear what Usk thinks about it."

The confidence which Cyril anticipated he received the next morning, when Usk and he were walking into Aberkerran. Queen Ernestine had invited her sister-in-law and the two girls to assist at the unpacking of a box of Eastern embroideries she had brought with her from her Syrian home, and Usk seized the opportunity of obtaining a private talk with his uncle, who had some telegrams to send off, and asking his advice. He told his tale as briefly as possible, anxious to make an end of a disagreeable task, and there were several points on which Cyril was obliged to seek further information by means of questions. When it was all clear in his mind, he walked on for a short time in silence.

"Is there anything you think I ought to do?" asked Usk at last.

"Do? What can you do? You are absolutely debarred from enlightening Félicia, as I understand, or even from informing any one else of the circumstances. Obviously, then, the only thing that practically concerns you is the marriage at St Mary Windicotes. That's your starting-point. I suppose you didn't think of running down there to look up the register before you went to America?"

"No; I had no opportunity."

"Do it when you are next in town, and note especially whether there is that slip of paper pasted on the inside of the cover, or not. It is just possible that Steinherz *père* made up the whole story on the strength of his likeness to the Archduke, though I allow that would not account for Félicia's profile. That marriage once established, you are safe in England and America, at any rate, for people know better than to inquire too curiously into the pedigree of heiresses from the States. Of course it would not hold for a moment in Pannonia. There you would have to take your stand on the quasi-ceremony which Steinherz devised to spite his chaplain. If he had lived, it would almost certainly have been annulled on an appeal to Rome by his family, but as he was otherwise disposed of, no doubt they thought the less fuss made the better. As it is, you see, the sole evidence for it is the word of a dead man, for the other witnesses would know better than to testify to it unless the Emperor directed them to open their lips."

"But would it in any circumstance be valid?"

"It is the kind of marriage that may be either valid or invalid at the will of the families concerned. If it was to the advantage of the Albrets to consider it an ordinary morganatic marriage, they would condone Steinherz's defiance, and probably induce the Emperor to confer a title of nobility on Félicia. Or if there was something really important at stake—for instance, if you took it into your head to revive your father's claim to Thracia, and made yourself troublesome in the Balkans, and they found they must buy you off—they might even be brought to recognise the marriage as fully valid and regular, and declare Félicia a Princess of Arragon, just as a bribe to you to stay at home. It has been done, notably about two hundred years ago, in a case intimately connected with English history, but naturally, the consideration would have to be a large one. And on the other hand, if they see no advantage to them in the matter, they can deny the Pannonian marriage, and refuse to recognise the English one, and continue to give out officially that Prince Joseph was drowned off the Australian coast, however forcibly it may be proved to them that he wasn't."

"I'm glad to hear you say this, for I still feel sometimes as if I was keeping Félicia out of something that was her due."

"You needn't. By the bye, I suppose Hicks will come to England for your wedding, about this trustee-business? I should like to go through these proofs which he has in charge. If I am to be co-trustee, I must know where we stand. But I don't think you need be afraid the thing will ever come out. You won't haunt the Pannonian Court, I presume?"

"No, indeed!" said Usk fervently. "England for me!"

"If Félicia will allow it. Ah, that reminds me. Is the companion—the Logan girl—supposed to know all this?"

"Miss Logan? Certainly not. I don't think anything would have induced Mr Steinherz to tell her."

"Still, that is no bar to her having discovered the facts for herself. I believe she knows, but I don't quite see what use she means to make of her knowledge. I could wish that King Michael was not coming here, though. Is it necessary to warn you not to let Félicia see too much of him?"

"I wouldn't spy upon her on any account."

"Quite unnecessary, if you stick to her as closely as you do now. No one else could get a word with her. But it's just possible she may get a little tired of your constant vigilance."

"There's no vigilance in the matter," said Usk warmly; "it's simply that I like to be with her, of course. And if I didn't think she liked it as much as I do, I'd—I'd try to keep away from her a little."

"Don't imagine that I am blaming you or assailing her. I think I have mastered the art of letting people be miserable in their own way. If you prefer to be unhappy with Miss Steinherz rather than without her, far be it from me to interfere, even though your taste may surprise me as much as my own wife's does. I merely advise you to remember that Michael has a truly royal eye for a pretty face, and that Félicia may not know the exact value of compliments and asseverations from a man in his position."

"What's bringing him here?" growled Usk.

"Pecuniary difficulties, of course. The last Drakovics Ministry left the country plunged in debt, and old Mirkovics, who is as honest as the day, but no financier, made no attempt to retrench. He thought that anything spent on the army or on public works must be so much to the good, while the King felt it his duty to look after the beautifying of the capital and the formation of the public taste, and between them they've called down the thunderbolt which used to hang over our heads in the old days."

"You mean they've encroached upon the interest due on the Scythian loan?"

"Encroached? They haven't paid any interest for three years. Of course Scythia lay low and accepted their excuses with a pleased smile, and equally, of course, she is demanding the arrears now."

"But what can they do?"

"Oh, Scythia is most willing to suggest terms—and conditions also. One of the conditions is a Scythian marriage for Michael, and the others would deliver Thracia over, bound hand and foot, to Scythian influence. Pannonia and Hercynia are not much inclined to help, having seen all their warnings disregarded, but they will hardly be able to remain passive in view of such a complete surrender. The problem of the moment is to secure their moral support without requiring them to advance the corresponding cash, and King Michael is coming here in the hope of solving it."

"I see. He has got himself into difficulties, and expects you to get him out of them?"

"Quite so. As soon as he found himself in this fix, he telegraphed to request me to return and reorganise Thracia. It showed a touching faith in me; and once, no doubt, I could have done what he expects of me, but not now. All I can do is to go through his affairs, and give him the advice of an ordinary business man—no brilliant strokes at this time of day. I know he thinks I can raise the necessary money among my Jewish friends by my personal influence, but they have something else on hand."

"But do you mean," cried Usk indignantly, "that King Michael insisted on your coming back to Europe in spite of the risk, and that is why you are here?"

"You forget that he's my wife's son. It pleases his mother when he turns to me for help, and I am glad to do what I can for him. But I had other reasons for coming home. There is one of them." He pointed to two men, armed with fishing-rods and baskets, who passed at the moment, saluting Usk with marked deference.

"But those are the detectives who are down here to look after King Michael," said Usk. "The stout one comes from Scotland Yard, and is sent by our Government, and the other, who belongs to some private office, is employed by the Thracian Minister."

"He may belong to any number of private offices, but he is employed by the Scythian Secret Police, and he is here to spy upon me."

"And my father has given him free leave to go anywhere he likes on our land, and to fish, and so on, and he has taken up his quarters in the village!" cried Usk, aghast. "But we'll soon kick him out."

"I beg you won't do anything of the kind. His presence here is a testimony to my former importance, which I find very soothing. Moreover, he is to be made useful. You saw those cipher telegrams I sent off just now? They all have to do with a Zionist scheme for making me Prince of

Palestine, and while I am here I shall be continually having letters and telegrams and even visitors, all connected with the same thing."

"But this fellow will be spying about and spoil everything."

"He will see and report everything, for that is what he is meant to do, but he will spoil nothing. The whole thing is a blind, intended just to keep the spies busy, and the rank and file of the Children of Zion quiet, for fear of their doing something rash. The real plot is a very different matter. You may as well know the main idea. The United Nation Syndicate has been reconstituted, but its object is to be attained in a new way. So long as Scythia holds Jerusalem, the Jewish ideal is necessarily incapable of realisation. She cannot be dispossessed by force; can diplomacy do anything? Besides the Jews there is another very powerful body whose interest it is to get her out, and both these communities have fixed upon a certain person as able to do it if any one can. No; I am not the happy man. My part is merely to cover up his tracks."

"But the risk!" cried Usk. "Why should you run into danger for the sake of this other man?"

"To do old friends a good turn, I suppose. Or perhaps, now that I can't play the game myself, it's the next best thing to see other people doing it well. Have you guessed who the man is? It's Malasorte, the Neustrian Pretender. He is to be assisted to make himself emperor at last."

"But I don't see——How will that——?" Usk was unwontedly perturbed.

"The Jesuits will arrange things for him at home, the Jews abroad. Moral support and ready cash, the two indispensables again. In return for their help, he has promised the Jews to turn Scythia out of Palestine."

"And what has he promised the Jesuits?"

"Ah, that I don't know, and there, it seems to me, is the weak point. What if the Jesuits also want Jerusalem? If so, he may hand it over to the Jews first, and then kick them out of it for the benefit of the other lot. 'Mala sorte, buona fede' is the family motto, you know, but no one ever thinks of quoting it except as 'Buona sorte, mala fede.'"

"But why do the Jews and the Jesuits both think so much of him?"

"He is a very unusual man, no one can doubt it. His enemies are fond of asserting that he is not a genuine Malasorte, but his likeness to Timoleon I. is enough to disprove that calumny. His father was in the Scythian service, and married a Greek lady, descended, of course, from the Byzantine Emperors. That gives him a great pull with the Orthodox, and he is a personal friend of the Emperor of Scythia, who is very much under his influence. He believes he can induce him to withdraw his troops from Palestine, and Goldberg and the rest believe it too. So he is to have his chance."

"It's awfully queer how things are mixed up," said Usk. "Do you know this chap wanted to marry Félicia?"

"This same man—Timoleon Lucanor? Yes, I remember, he was military attaché at Washington. And why didn't he?"

"Her father didn't think his chances good enough, I fancy."

"No; I think the blood of the Albrets rose against the *parvenu*, even then. But this is interesting, Usk. Could Malasorte have had any idea of Mr Steinherz's secret? No, of course not. He would not have allowed himself to be choked off in that case. It was the money he was after, and he missed what would have been better to him than millions. Did Miss Logan approve of his suit, do you know?"

"Yes; Hicks said she pushed it all she knew."

"And yet she didn't tell him? It's pretty clear, then, that whatever she knows she has learnt since. My dear Usk, you may thank your stars that I am a wretched crack-brained failure, if you want to keep your Félicia. There are the makings of a most tremendous plot lying about—infinite possibilities—and I can't see how to put them together."

CHAPTER VIII.
LOVE IN IDLENESS.

THE arrival of Baron von Neuburg, otherwise King Michael of Thracia, did not add to the gaiety of the circle at the Castle. Scarcely more than a boy in years, his face was so curiously old that not only Usk but his father looked young beside him, and his manner was weary almost to the point of exhaustion.

"I don't take much stock in kings generally," Félicia remarked to Usk after the new-comer had been presented to her; "but for the sake of the rest I hope this one's a bad sample."

"He's not a particularly good specimen, certainly. Aren't his ways awfully riling?"

"Yes," agreed Félicia; "that's where the difference comes in between him and your uncle. Lord Cyril is just elegant. He has dipped into everything, and got pretty tired, but he don't advertise the fact. The Baron has done it too, and parades his weariness, and that's rude."

"I'm glad you don't care for him," said Usk honestly. "He's not—not the sort of fellow I should like to see you take to."

"Don't you know that by saying that you're just daring me to be as sweet to him as I know how?"

"Oh, I know people say that sort of thing about women, but no nice woman would go and make up to a man of bad character simply because she was warned against him."

"Then I'm a nice woman? Well, I guess you'll expect me do something for you in return for that acknowledgment, and I'd admire to teach the Baron a lesson."

"Not by way of breaking his heart, please."

"Not while you're around, any way. But I'd like to have him know what folks would think of him if he didn't just happen to be a king."

It is possible that Félicia set to work with all the more gusto that she was conscious of a personal injury at her introduction to the King. To her mind his look had expressed no recognition of the fact that he was being presented to a very beautiful woman. Maimie also had noticed this insensibility, and she commented upon it to Félicia, with a certain lack of tact.

"You see, Fay, he can just tolerate having you around as the future Lady Usk, but it's quite beyond him to show any interest in an untitled American girl. She's way down under his feet in the mud somewhere."

"Well, I guess it'll maybe interest him to know what the American girl thinks about him."

"Don't see how you're going to have him feel it, any way. Say, Fay, Usk is real devoted, isn't he? I'm glad you've taken him instead of the King now I've seen him, don't you think! He's solid good right through. He won't ever have you find out anything new and unpleasant about him. Every day of his life he'll come to meet you mornings with a flower, just as his father does to Lady Caerleon, and he'll like nothing better evenings than sit alone with you and read the 'Times' out loud."

"Guess I'll fix things differently to that."

"You'd better not. His way will save you a pretty good deal of trouble. He'll like you to be the same all the time, just as he is. And so's you're just decently civil to him, he'll never be ugly. It's only with a man like the Baron you need to be smart, for you lose him if he's away out of your sight a moment."

"Well, I incline to think the Baron will need to be smart this next week."

In all probability the Baron was of the same opinion before the week was over. He had come prepared to take the lead in the general conversation, even if he did not monopolise it, and nothing was further from his thoughts than that this little nobody of an American, whom the Caerleons had managed to pick up for Usk on account of her money, should take it upon herself to dispute his right. Young as he was, King Michael had already ruled so long that it seemed to him only natural to be the autocrat of any table at which he sat, and it was whispered that his meetings with other monarchs were few and far between, and also extremely short, by reason of this genial habit of mind. It was a tremendous shock to find himself called upon for explanations, laughed at for his choice of words, even contradicted, and all by a radiant being who flashed provoking glances at him from magnificent eyes, and having annihilated him, turned with irritating nonchalance to engage Usk in a low-toned conversation punctuated with soft looks.

To Usk himself these favours, thus publicly conferred, were the reverse of delightful. His hospitable soul was wounded by the treatment meted out to the guest, and he could not help feeling that it was bad form in Félicia to emphasise his own happier position at every opportunity. When he ventured to remonstrate, however, his only reward was a severe snubbing in private, for Félicia was not to be turned from her prey. Lord Cyril, to whom

Lady Caerleon appealed in distress, laughed at the whole thing, and declared that Félicia's scorn was the best possible tonic for his stepson. To have met her would be a liberal education for him, provided she continued the treatment to the end of his visit, and did not soften towards him for a moment. But there was no need for her to do this. It was enough for King Michael to notice the difference in her manner when she turned to Usk. When a rarely beautiful woman treats one man to nothing but gibes, and lavishes tenderness upon another who looks rather uncomfortable under the process, it is not in human nature not to wish to be in the other man's place for once.

Maimie had been watching eagerly for the King to reach this point, but here she found herself at a standstill. All this time she had been cultivating the acquaintance of the aide-de-camp, Captain Andreivics, who had accompanied King Michael, and was introduced as his "friend." She had picked his brains to such good purpose that she knew as much as he did of the King's circumstances, and had gone far beyond him in the deductions she drew. He could not tell her exactly how the long hours were spent when the King and his stepfather were closeted every morning with vast piles of papers, but she knew. She could picture Cyril exposing pitilessly the extravagance, laxity, and corruption which had spread through every department of State since he had left Thracia, and indicating reforms and economies which would put matters straight if the present crisis could be tided over, but performing no miracle to provide the money urgently needed at the moment. It was from the aide-de-camp, however, that she heard how one morning the King dashed away the papers with the pettish remark, "Really, Count, your brain seems as strong as ever for all these absurd trivialities. Why is it that you refuse to return to Thracia and get me out of my difficulty?" and how the incisive answer flashed forth, "If my brain was as strong as ever, sir, I should not be busy with these trivialities. I should be holding the balance of power in Europe." She knew that both Cyril and the King had reluctantly come to the conclusion that, failing the much-needed miracle, there was only one thing to be done. The King must journey homewards by way of the Riviera, where the Scythian Princess who had been proposed for his acceptance was sojourning. There was a bare hope that his apparent intention of falling in with the arrangement suggested by Scythia might alarm his Pannonian and Hercynian relations into some attempt to prevent the threatened surrender.

Maimie ground her teeth, metaphorically speaking, over this deadlock. There were Félicia's millions, far more than sufficient to fill the yawning gulf, for the sum which could bring a Balkan State to bankruptcy was trivial in American eyes, and no one seemed to have thought of making use of them. The King, however much he might admire the girl of whose beauty he had at last become conscious, had not the slightest thought of marrying her, and Cyril would take no step to utilise those convenient millions, even if they ever occurred to him, because Félicia happened to be engaged to Usk. Maimie felt that she had no patience with Usk, who to the injury of existing added insult by hanging about Félicia so perpetually that the King had no opportunity of getting up a flirtation with her even if he desired it. If Usk would only run up to town for a day or two! but he remained in Félicia's near neighbourhood as persistently as if he had known of Maimie's designs and meant to thwart them. Captain Andreivics it was who returned to London two days before the time fixed for the King's departure, and with no better excuse than the stereotyped one of "urgent business," so that Maimie lost her cavalier.

At last, just when Maimie was gloomily revolving in her mind various desperate expedients for removing Usk from Félicia's side, the motive force required was suddenly imparted from without. It came in the form of a letter from Mr Forfar, the Prime Minister, to Lord Caerleon, asking whether Usk was still thinking of entering Parliament. If so, he could do a great service to the party (to which the Marquis had always lent a loyal, if discriminating support, since his own entry on public life), by allowing himself to be adopted as the future candidate for a great Northern constituency. The sitting member was old and feeble, but had stoutly refused to tolerate the mention of a successor until recently, when a severe illness had given him a fright. He was now willing to allow a suitable "under-study" to be introduced to the party managers and make himself known in the constituency; and as the supporters of the Temperance cause were well organised and powerful, what more suitable candidate could be found than the son of the life-long Temperance champion? Neither Usk nor his father hesitated a moment in accepting the offer. The great banquet, at which Sir James Morrell had reluctantly undertaken to present his successor to the association which had so often shared with him the sweets of victory, was to take place two nights after the arrival of Mr Forfar's letter, and there was no time to be lost. Usk dashed upstairs in high excitement to pack his bag, while his father went round to the stables himself to order the dogcart, and Lady Caerleon interviewed the cook on the subject of sandwiches. It never entered Usk's mind that any one could dream he would let slip this long-desired opportunity, and he sent an eager message by Maimie begging Félicia, who was breakfasting in her own room, to drive to the station with him. When he came downstairs with his bag, however, he found her still in her "wrapper," as she called the frilled and beribboned garment which Lady Caerleon always felt ought not to make its appearance outside a bedroom. Maimie had insisted on her getting up when she brought Usk's message, and she was obliged to make a very hasty toilet, much to her disgust. She did not appear to suitable advantage, she felt, unless Pringle's skilful fingers had proper time for their work.

"Why, Fay, aren't you coming, then?" cried Usk, when he saw her.

"I guess not," responded Félicia laconically.

"Well, you'll wish me joy, won't you? This is the beginning, you know."

"Of what? The beginning of the end?"

"What do you mean?" Usk was too happy and too much excited to make any attempt to understand. "Why, it's my chance at last—what we've talked of so often."

"You have," corrected Félicia. Then a transient gleam of brightness showed itself. "Canvassing, do you mean? Then I suppose we are all to trail you along?"

"Oh no, that would be a little previous," laughed Usk. "I'm only going to be introduced to the party. There's no election on at present."

"I want to know! You're leaving me this way just for an ordinary ward-meeting? and you don't so much as ask me whether I choose to have you go?"

"Why in the world should I think you'd mind? I thought you would be delighted. Why, Fay!" in utter amazement, for Félicia was weeping delicately into a lace handkerchief.

"You said you loved me, and now you're having the Baron—everybody—see how little you care for me. You just haven't the very slightest consideration for my feelings!"

Dismayed and astounded, but still utterly puzzled as to the nature of his offence, Usk knelt down hastily by her chair, and alternately entreated her forgiveness and adjured her to tell him what he had done. With him it was a matter of course that the women of a household should send forth their men to the chances of war or politics with a brave face and words of cheer, and he could not conceive Félicia's feeling hurt at not being consulted. He did not know that Maimie's triumphant "Now you see just how much he thinks about you!" was rankling in her mind, and that she had set her heart on proving her power over him. When she consented at last to remove the handkerchief from her eyes, it was merely to intimate that he might consider himself forgiven if he did not go. Usk sprang to his feet.

"And lose this chance—give Forfar a slap in the face?" he cried in astonishment. "Why, Fay, you must be mad! You're joking, aren't you? You couldn't possibly mean it."

"I guess I mean exactly what I say. You're telling me all the time how much you love me, but I can't just seem to realise it."

"You mean that you ask me in cold blood to give up this chance, disappoint my people, offend Forfar, just because—why, it's for no reason at all!"

"I don't ask you anything," said Félicia, rising regally, and throwing him a glance over her shoulder. "I just tell you to do it."

"Well, then, I won't," returned Usk, with equal candour; but as she swept towards the door he intercepted her, breaking into a laugh, "Why, Fay, for the moment I thought you meant it. What a gorgeous scene we have been making over nothing at all! Now you don't leave this room until you say you're sorry, and signify the same in the usual manner. There! I'm getting quite a public speaker already."

"It's a pity if your future audiences don't appreciate you better than the present one," said Félicia coldly. "Kindly allow me pass. If you don't choose to consult my wishes—well, you're not the only man in the world, any way."

"Now it would serve you right if I kept you here until you gave in," said Usk, "but I hear my father tramping up and down in furious anxiety about the train. I'll settle this little matter with you when I come back, but any token of penitence in the shape of a letter will receive due consideration. And—just that you mayn't make yourself miserable thinking I'm angry with you—there! and there! and as many more assurances of pardon as you like."

He ran along the corridor, still laughing, and Félicia returned angrily to her own room. It was the laughter that annoyed her. Even if Usk had refused to yield, he ought to have taken her objection seriously. He was so sure of her that he thought he could afford to laugh at her, was he? Very well; it might be advisable to show him that he need not be quite so sure.

Maimie, in the meantime, had been taking advantage of the change in the situation. After giving Usk's message to Félicia, she wandered down to the second of the terraces before the Castle, where King Michael was wont to smoke his after-breakfast cigar. It was his custom to breakfast in his own rooms, and Maimie felt comfortably certain that Usk would not have thought of hunting for him in the garden in order to bid him farewell. When she caught sight of him, he was walking up and down somewhat listlessly, as though he missed the companionship of Captain Andreivics, but she saw a change pass over his face when he heard the tap of her heels on the terrace above. As she came down the steps, she could see him before he saw her, and it gave her a keen delight to see his look of disappointment when he met her at the foot.

"Good morning, Baron!" she remarked cheerfully. "Say, we shall be left awfully lonely to-night, shan't we—what with the Captain leaving yesterday, and Lord Usk this morning, and you this evening, I suppose?"

"I leave to-morrow," said the King, looking at her with cold surprise.

"No, is that so? I guess Lord Usk don't know it, rushing off the way he has. He would never leave Félicia unguarded a whole day."

"Is Miss Steinherz supposed to be in danger from me?"

Maimie laughed mischievously. "You know your own reputation best, Baron. I don't see but Lord Usk thought it wasn't enough to warn Félicia against you, the way he has mounted guard over her."

"Oh, our friend Usk felt it necessary to warn his bride against me, did he? I think that was not playing the game, as they say here."

"Well, I guess I oughtn't to have given him away. He knows his way about, I suppose, and—yes, it was just as well he did it."

"Why? Has it produced the opposite effect, as usual, and induced the young lady to honour me with her friendly interest?"

Maimie gave him a glance of compassion. "What good would there be in that?" she asked curtly. "No; it just showed Félicia what he expected of her, so's she concluded to satisfy him at any cost to herself."

A light seemed to break upon the King. "What! you mean that all this raillery, all the contempt she has poured upon me for a whole week, was nothing but an effort to please her bridegroom?"

"Don't you try and have me say that Félicia's an angel," Maimie admonished him. "I won't tell you her secrets, any way. And I don't see but you'll have to stay till to-morrow as you've fixed it so; but I wish you were leaving sooner."

"Miss Logan's interest in my movements does me too much honour. Perhaps it will gratify her to know that it is possible I may not even be leaving to-morrow."

"Ah, I thought that 'urgent business' of the Captain's covered more folks' affairs than his own. You mean he'll be coming down with more documents for you to study with Lord Cyril?"

"I had not meant that——" the King was beginning, but as he caught the merest hint of scorn in Maimie's eye, his face assumed an expression of deep importance. "It is extremely probable. What is the good of an aide-de-camp but to make himself useful?"

"An aide-de-camp—do tell!" cried Maimie. "And you've called him your friend all the time! Why, you must be a general, then! Say, General, they promote people pretty young in your country, don't they?"

"Mademoiselle," said the King severely, "with a young lady who has contrived to discover so much of my private affairs, it is surely unnecessary to keep up this wearisome farce?"

"M. le Baron," said Maimie, making him a curtsey, "the farce was of your own providing. If you choose to throw up your part it can't hurt me, any way."

"You imply that there is another act, if I care to play it?"

"I don't imply anything. I'm not taking any risks, if you are."

"So be it. I take the risk. Andreivics shall arrive from London with important documents. Accept my compliments, mademoiselle. I sent him away because I wished to feel that a few of my secrets still remained in my own possession. You have secured his return by means of a diplomacy which my good stepfather in his best days might have envied."

Maimie looked him over with a slow gaze of infinite scorn. "I guess," she said calmly, "that you're sort of acclimatised to being despised? You seem to lay yourself out for it so naturally. Usk was pretty wise in warning Félicia against you, and she was doing the best for herself when she chilled you off. What she can see in you——"

"Permit me to observe that you are revealing an interesting secret, mademoiselle," said the King malignantly. "After what you have said it would be ungallant in me not to remain here. I telegraph to Andreivics this morning."

"Now we begin to be moving!" said Maimie to herself, as she left him in speechless contempt. "He don't even see that I'm having him go the very way I want him. And now for Fay."

She found that Félicia, having worked herself up into a high state of resentment against Usk, had determined to punish him by entering upon a flirtation with the King. Maimie shook her head when Félicia declared her intentions.

"I wouldn't, Fay," she said. "You've done elegantly this far, the way you've frozen him off. You'll only get all of your affairs into a snarl. And what's more, I don't believe he's to be had. He knows just how to take care of himself, and I can't seem to see you making any sort of impression on him."

This was all that was needed to put Félicia on her mettle.

"Maimie Logan," she said decisively, "did you ever know any man that could take care of himself when I was around? I guess Usk will be sorry that he went off this way."

"Why, what do you mean doing?" Maimie's tone was full of alarm.

"Oh, just make things uncomfortable a little—nothing more."

"But if Usk will just stay away four or five days, there'll be a good deal more," was Maimie's mental comment.

"Michael," said Queen Ernestine to her son four days later, when she had succeeded after many vain attempts in finding him alone, "don't you think you are paying rather too much attention to Miss Steinherz?"

She spoke timidly, anticipating the black frown which gathered at once upon King Michael's brow, as he bestowed a mental curse upon Félicia's methods. It was not in her nature to be content with a secret adoration. The King might waylay her in the garden if he chose, or look for her in her favourite nook in the picture-gallery, and enjoy her society until Maimie, posted judiciously near at hand, felt it her duty to interrupt them, but he must not attempt to hide his chains in public. Hence King Michael's relations had the pleasure of seeing him dancing attendance upon the whims of a languid beauty, who had vouchsafed to lay aside much of her sharpness of tongue, but still betrayed no delight in his attentions. Even Usk could not have desired more absolute unconsciousness of her conquest than Félicia exhibited.

"Have you ever known me forget my position?" King Michael asked at last, when his mother's face had grown more and more anxious.

"Never," she answered, recalling many memories at once humorous and pathetic.

"Then rest assured that I never shall."

"But, dear," urged the Queen, "in that case would it not be as well to return to London? It looks—mind, I only say it looks—as if you were taking advantage of Usk's prolonged absence to rob him of his bride's affections, and you would not wish to do that."

"Count Mortimer has already given me a pretty strong hint to go, but I will not leave my work undone."

"But he told me to-day that it was all finished."

"On the contrary, it is only half-done," was the reply, with an enigmatical smile. "Who would have thought I should become so deeply interested in a matter entered upon so lightly?"

"So lightly—when the future of your kingdom and your own happiness may depend upon the arrangements you are able to make?" cried the Queen, in surprise. "You don't take things seriously enough, Michael."

"Possibly not, but sometimes things take me seriously, quite against my will."

* * * * * * * *

"I would just love to hustle some folks a little!" Maimie was reflecting, much about the same time. "Usk will arrive home in a day or two, and I'd like to have things fixed. I never thought the Baron would have so much grit in him, but the way he fights off a definite declaration is real fine. But Fay is even with him there. What with his precious kingdom, and her engagement, they can't seem to get on at all. And until they do, I can't step in as fairy godmother to put things straight."

While the thought was still in her mind, the door opened violently, and Félicia ran in. Flinging herself upon the sofa, she began to cry, not weeping in the artistic way which had damped Usk's departure, but shedding genuine tears of disappointment and mortification.

"I'll never forgive you!" she sobbed out to Maimie. "This is the second time you've put me in just the most horrid sort of a position. You had me encourage the Malasorte man until he cooled off of his own accord, and now the King has told me in so many words that he can't ask me to marry him—after having me say I cared for him. I wouldn't mind so much but for that."

"Well, you can marry Usk yet," was the unsympathetic reply.

"After expecting to be a queen!" fresh sobs followed "He spoke so's I really concluded it was all safe. And you sit there and say nothing. I hate you!"

"Why?" asked Maimie calmly.

"How can I help it when you're so mean and ugly? You told me you could fix things, and I thought you had fixed them right away. And then you have all of this happen!"

"Now look here, Fay," Maimie grasped her shoulder. "If I operate my scheme right now, will you promise to give up Usk and marry the King? I won't go a step without knowing that."

"I don't feel like giving him up until you have got things fixed. If they should chance to go wrong, I would just find myself left."

"It may be some time before they go right, I grant that, but you must take some risks. Well, if I let you stay engaged to Usk for the present, will you break off with him when I give the word?"

"Ye-es, but you'll have to be quite sure about it."

"I'll see to that. Where did you leave the King?"

"On the second terrace. He was real sorry to have to say what he did, but I was so mad I wouldn't stop," said Félicia, with a curious kind of self-satisfaction.

"It must be real nice to be able to love folks according to what they can give you!" soliloquised Maimie, as she went in search of the King. "She would accept Usk when there was no other man in view, but now the Baron holds the winning cards—unless there should be any fascinating emperors around before we get things fixed. But here's the lucky man!"

King Michael was walking from end to end of the terrace, smoking moodily. His hands were thrust deep into his pockets, and the blackest possible frown was on his brow. He was hard hit, Maimie saw, and scarcely likely to welcome the appearance of the person to whom he might consider that he owed his present unhappy frame of mind, but she met him boldly.

"Say, Baron," she said, placing herself in his path, "is it true you've told my Félicia you love her, but can't marry her?"

"It is, mademoiselle. If you have chosen this terrace as a promenade, I will go elsewhere."

"Well, if I was a king, I guess I'd marry the woman I loved."

"Pardon me, I am not only a king. I am a son of the house of Schwarzwald-Molzau, and we do not mingle the blood of Charlemagne with that of—manufacturers."

"And so you sigh as a lover and obey as a son? But you wanted to marry Lord Usk's sister once, I know, for Mr Hicks told me."

The King's eyes flashed gloomily. "I do not understand this catechism," he said angrily. "It is intolerable! The Mortimer blood is equal to that of any semi-royal house in Europe, and there were special reasons why a marriage with Lady Philippa would have been very pleasing to my subjects."

"Well, I guess a marriage with a Princess of Arragon would about satisfy them, any way."

"Not if she were a Catholic."

"Is that so? Well, the girl you have just told that you love her and can't marry her is a Princess of Arragon and a Protestant."

"Impossible. I know the Prince of Arragon's three daughters well, and Don Florian's only daughter is married to another cousin of mine."

"You are forgetting. There was a third brother."

"Don José? But he was not married. Oh, I remember there was some talk of a morganatic marriage. But that is not to the purpose."

"Excuse me, but I guess it's very much to the purpose."

"Allow me to say that you do not know how these things are regarded— how I regard them, necessarily."

"But suppose the marriage was recognised? Wait, I'll tell you about it," and she ran through the circumstances hastily. "If the marriage was good enough for the Arragon family to accept Félicia as one of themselves, I guess it would be good enough for you?"

"Undoubtedly; but I do not see the faintest likelihood that the House of Albret would recognise the marriage."

"That's where your help would be wanted. I'd like you to lay the whole thing before Lord Cyril to-day, and have him operate it."

But the King started back, aghast. "My dear Miss Logan, do you not see that it would be fatal—suicidal—for me to appear in the matter? Count Mortimer has his nephew's interests to consider."

"That is so; we mustn't go ahead too fast," said Maimie. "Then you incline to think Félicia and I may fight all of the battle for ourselves?"

"Quite so. There can be no objection to your consulting Count Mortimer, purely on her behalf, you know; and if by any chance your efforts should be crowned with success, why—you have given me hope—I am happy again!"

"Oh no, you aren't—not yet. We shall want your help any way. I know well enough there's no hope of having Félicia's family recognise her unless some one puts pressure on them. Are you ready to intimate at the critical moment that you are real keen on marrying her, if they can fix things right?"

"That would be highly injudicious. I think I had better not appear——"

"As you please. You throw up your cards, then, and Félicia will just marry Usk."

"You place me in a most difficult position, but rather than lose Félicia——"

"I thought so. Then you would better go way back to the Riviera right now, and make a little gentle love to the Grand-Duchess Sonya, just to keep your folks sort of interested, you know. I'll let you hear when you're wanted."

CHAPTER IX.
A CHANGE OF VENUE.

"WHY, Uncle Cyril! how awfully good of you to come and meet me!" Yet Usk's eyes strayed to the dogcart waiting in the road just beyond the station fence, and the stolid groom in charge of it. "Is—is any one else here?"

"No; Félicia is not here. What do you think of putting your bag into the cart, and walking up?"

"All right. I shall be glad to stretch my legs. Félicia isn't ill, is she?"

"I saw no signs of it when I started. But why should you expect her to meet you? I understood you and she had quarrelled?"

"Quarrelled? Why, it was nothing—the most utter nonsense! She never wrote me a word for four whole days, though. But I wrote to her every day, and at last, on the fifth evening, I had a letter from her—an awfully jolly letter, but making the most tremendous fuss about the way she had behaved, calling herself names, and all sorts of things. It seemed so uncalled-for that I really thought she must be going to be ill, for she's not a bit morbid generally, is she?"

"Few people less so, I should think. The letter reached you five days after you left here, you say. It was written the day before, of course?"

"The evening before. I know she said she was writing when the house was quiet. But I'm awfully glad she's all right. She's so unexpected, isn't she? You never can tell what she'll do next."

"I used to notice the same thing about my wife in the early days of our acquaintance. There is a peculiar charm about that unexpectedness when it is introduced into politics. It quite prevents any feeling of flatness."

"Now one would have imagined"—Usk was still pursuing his own train of thought—"that she would have come to meet me after that letter."

"The unexpected again, you see."

"But how did you know anything about our——? Well, it wasn't a quarrel——"

"The suspension of friendly relations? I inferred it from what I saw after you were gone."

"And you spoke to Félicia? Very kind of you, I'm sure, but—well, you know——"

"You prefer to conduct your own love affairs? Quite so. Make your mind easy; I did not speak to Félicia. But if I remember rightly, I did send you in your mother's letter a strong hint not to stay away more than the two days you intended at first."

"Yes, I know, but you said 'unless it will damage your chances,' and it would have done, horribly. You see, it was such a piece of good luck old Morrell's taking to me so tremendously, when he had hated the very mention of a successor before, that I couldn't go and hurt his feelings. He would drag me round the constituency, and hunt up all the local organisers to introduce me to them, and we really covered an immense amount of ground. The party agent said I couldn't have made a better start."

"Don't think I want to see you less keen. It isn't that. Did Félicia tell you any news in her letter—anything that had happened?"

"No; there was nothing of that sort. But really, Uncle Cyril, I don't think she was angry with me for staying away. I wrote her awfully long letters— and sent her things, too. She couldn't think I had forgotten her."

"I never thought she did. But did she express regret for anything in particular, or merely for her general treatment of you? I have an object in asking," as Usk looked at him in surprise. "Don't think it's mere curiosity."

"She didn't mention anything definite—except just to say that if things went wrong between us, it was Maimie Logan's fault, not hers, which I could have told her myself. Oh, by the bye, that's another queer thing. I had an hour or two to spare in town, so I ran down to Bradcross and looked up Mr and Mrs Steinherz's marriage at St Mary Windicotes. It was there all right, but the queer thing is that some months ago a lady came and asked about it, and got a copy of the entry, and I'm pretty sure it was Miss Logan."

"Exactly what I thought. How did you find out?"

"There was the paper pasted on the inside of the cover, just as Mr Steinherz said, and I tried one of the corners with my nail to see if it was loose. Then the clerk's wife, who had been in a great state of excitement ever since she heard what entry I wanted to see, cried out, 'Why, that's just what the lady did as come here in the autumn!' When I said, 'What lady?' she nearly had a fit, and refused point-blank to tell me anything, saying she wished she had bitten her tongue off before the words slipped out. I tried the usual persuasive, and assured her that I had the strongest possible reasons for wishing good and not harm to Mr and Mrs Bertram, as she called them, and their descendants, and at last I got it out of her that the lady was not old, and not very young, not a regular foreigner, but not quite English, and dressed very smartly,—'fine enough for a carriage,' the old woman said, which is just what every one here says about these two girls whenever they go out walking. Then she told me what her voice was like, and I couldn't doubt for a moment that it was Miss Logan."

"This is most interesting. When did you say it happened?"

"About six months ago, as far as I could make out. Either just before or just after Mr Steinherz's death, I should think."

"When she was in London, of course. Well, I am glad to have this cleared up. She told me a lame story of having been put on the track by some writing in an old prayer-book belonging to her mother, and said she had pieced together into a coherent whole things remembered from childhood and details picked up since."

"She told you!"

"Yes; that is the piece of news I wondered whether you had heard. She knows the whole story, and has confided it to Félicia, and Félicia will be satisfied with nothing short of full rights and recognition. The story, as she told it, was less detailed than what I had heard from you, but it corresponded with it so exactly that I felt certain she could not have developed it in the way she made out. After this discovery of yours, I haven't a doubt that she was listening, either when Mr Steinherz explained things to you, or when he made Hicks Félicia's trustee—no, scarcely that, unless he read aloud to him the attested statement which was to be left in his charge. Well, we can't prove it against her, but that's the truth, I feel certain."

"And Félicia knows—the whole thing?"

"The whole thing. Now, Usk, I am going to depart for once from my invariable rule, and give you a piece of good advice. There are two ways in which you can take this. Either you could throw yourself into Félicia's view of the matter, and do everything in your power to help her press her claim—which is never likely to be established. Do you feel yourself debarred from such a course as that?"

"Absolutely, by my repeated promise to Mr Steinherz."

"I thought so. Then here's the alternative. Forbid Félicia to take any step in the matter. Let her understand that if she does, everything is over between you. Give her the choice. Otherwise, whether she wins or loses, you will infallibly drift apart, for no woman will stand seeing a man indifferent or opposed to an aim which is the breath of life to her. If she cares for you enough to give it up for your sake, it's a different thing."

"I couldn't ask it of her," said Usk. "In one way, it's almost a relief that this has come out. I have always felt as if I was defrauding her, somehow."

"Usk," said his uncle, "there's a good deal of your mother in you, and that makes it perfectly hopeless to offer you any guidance. One could generally get Caerleon to see reason, after a tremendous amount of hammering, but nothing but fanaticism would move your mother—in her young days, of course. Well, I don't envy you the next few months. I have cabled to Hicks to let me know the exact nature of the proofs he holds, and also whether the trustees are debarred like you from asserting any claim on Félicia's behalf. It was necessary to find that out, though those two girls were so impatient of delay that they were ready to set out for Vindobona there and then, and press the claim in person. I had to point out to them that Félicia would do well to remain as far from Pannonia as possible for the present. There are various approved ways of disposing of inconvenient young ladies who persist in raking up forgotten scandals, especially when there are a good many millions in question as well."

"Yes. She is safest here, if she is resolved to go on. But what I can't make out is why Miss Logan should have been silent so long, if she knew everything six months ago."

"I can't be certain, but I have my suspicions that my hopeful stepson comes in somewhere. That's why I should be glad to see you put your foot down, and end the matter one way or the other."

"You mean that he and Miss Logan are plotting that he shall marry Félicia if the claim is allowed? Rather fine from their point of view, wouldn't it be? But they are reckoning without Félicia."

"Where did you get your wide knowledge of women?" asked Cyril, with intense interest. Usk answered quite unsuspiciously—

"Oh, I don't know. I don't know many, but I know Félicia."

"And you won't even attempt to dissuade her from pressing the claim?"

"I mean to tell her how anxious her father was that she should let things alone, but I can't help it if she decides not to. It's her own concern, and she has a right to judge for herself."

It would have been well if Félicia had also been able to adopt this moderate view, and to concede to Usk the right of judging for himself. But she demanded not merely his passive permission, but his active approval, for all that she saw fit to do, and as he was not disposed to go a step beyond the line he had laid down, the relations between them became somewhat strained. The two lived in an atmosphere of argument. Even the low-toned conversations in the drawing-room at night were devoted to persistent efforts to make Usk confess that Félicia was in the right, and that her success was certain. He kept his temper admirably on the whole, but this led only to further attacks, for Félicia could not believe he was in earnest. She lost her temper somewhat frequently, but Usk understood that this was due to "nerves."

"I guess I know why you'd like to have me let things slide," she said angrily one morning on the terrace. "You're thinking of the dollars."

"The dollars! What dollars?" asked Usk.

"Mine, of course. Pappa's pile, which was to procure me the honour of admission into your noble family."

"Are you trying to see what I'm like when I'm 'riz,' as Hicks says?" asked Usk laughing. "Why, Fay, he would tell you that it was the thought of your dollars that frightened me more than anything—kept me back for ever so long."

"Then what was it made you conclude to go ahead at last?"

"Look in the glass," said Usk, and Félicia was mollified.

"I'm real glad I have the dollars, any way," she said, slipping her hand into his arm. "This place wants making over from cellar to garret."

"Does it? I suppose it seems so to other people, but it's perfect to us. By the bye, Fay, you hurt old Wright's feelings terribly the other day by depreciating his stables."

"Why, I only said I'd have those old shacks pulled down, and a real elegant range of stabling built—just like at Bagatelle."

"One may like good horses, and drive them too, without making palaces of their stables. Ours are all right."

"Well, I'll never be satisfied until they're just as good as those at Bagatelle, with all sorts of cunning little notions around everywhere. Why, even Baron von Neuburg had heard of the Bagatelle stables, and we made an excursion over there for the day, so's he might see them. But there's just everything to be done to this house and the grounds. I've an idea of a glass piazza to close in that upper terrace, but the whole front of the house wants modernising real badly."

Usk restrained himself with some difficulty. "Perhaps you don't know that the Castle is considered one of the finest houses in the country?" he said. "It would be horribly out of character to try to make an American summer hotel out of it."

"Well, I'd as lief have it that as a ruin," said Félicia indifferently. "But it don't even look old, only shabby. That's what I would just admire, to add on towers and battlements, and all that, and make it a real castle."

"A sham castle," said Usk. "And I don't think you would care to live in it."

"Oh, I'd have plate-glass windows, and electricity everywhere, of course. And inside! Why, your mother has the rooms so bare, they feel to me 'most indecent. When I fix up the picture-gallery, you'll see it'll be just elegant. All those musty old pictures and horrid suits of armour and swords and things will take a back seat. Now you feel like looking at them because there's nothing else to see, but when I've inaugurated my reforms, one of them will just be on hand here and there as a surprise."

"And how do you intend to dispose of them, then?"

"Why, instead of that horrid old dull tapestry and black panelling, I'll have silk hangings in pastel shades, each room a different colour. I'll have them weave them on purpose for me in France. And all those cute little recesses in the gallery I'll turn into cosy nooks, with French furniture and nicknacks and Japanese things, and now and then a suit of armour that'll just give you the coldest kind of a shudder. And some of the pictures can be cleaned, and the rest be hidden back of the hangings. It'll be too cunning for anything."

"Rather!" said Usk, with a short laugh. "I am only delighted to think that my father and mother will probably be supreme here for twenty or thirty years yet, happily, and that by that time you'll have learnt to be so fond of the Castle that you won't want to lay a finger on it."

"Now that's real horrid of you!" said Félicia angrily. "I don't see but Lord and Lady Caerleon would very well leave the Castle to us, and go and live some other place. I don't choose to board, especially with your folks. I want a house of my own, so's I can stamp my individuality upon it."

"That you can have in London. There's no likelihood whatever of my parents giving up the Castle to us, I am thankful to say. Why should they?"

"Why, because they've had it ever so long," cried Félicia. "I shall want to have house-parties here, when we're not in town. Say, Usk! I'll restore the Abbey, and we'll have that for our country-house."

"The Abbey!" Usk was aghast. "Do you know that all our family are buried there?"

"Oh, we'll soon fix them up somewhere else. Why, I'll have just the loveliest sort of house-parties, not like any other person's. We'll call them 'retreats,' and I'll design a cunning little nun's dress for every one to wear. The papers will just gloat over it, and all of the smart set will be fighting for invitations."

"I don't like jokes of this kind," said Usk, with forced calmness. "Of course, when you are mistress of the Castle, you can alter the arrangements as you please, provided you don't destroy or make away with the old things, but I give you fair warning that you won't touch a single stone of the walls, or do anything to desecrate the Abbey."

"Ah, I guess I'll have to burn the Castle down. Then I can build it up again as I want it!" said Félicia airily, leaving Usk with the uncomfortable conviction that she had been joking all the time, and that he had made a foolish display of strong feeling, and invoked his authority quite unnecessarily. However, it pleased Félicia so much to have made him angry at last, that she treated him better for the next few days, until the tension became acute once more under the influence of a stray piece of news from the Riviera.

In answer to Cyril's telegram, Mr Hicks had cabled that there was nothing to prevent the trustees from supporting Félicia's claim, if she did not consider her father's strongly expressed wish as binding on her, and he added such details as to the papers and other objects left in his charge by Mr Steinherz as enabled Cyril to draw up a statement at once. The relationship between his wife and the royal family of Arragon gave him the opportunity of proceeding privately, much to his satisfaction, for expecting the whole affair to end in smoke, he did not care for it to be canvassed in the European press. Félicia would have preferred publicity, for she had been looking forward confidently to becoming the heroine of the sensation-mongering American papers, and felt that she was being defrauded of the interviews and portraits that were her due. She yielded, however, to the strong pressure brought to bear on her by Maimie, who pointed out that a Steinherz boom would certainly alienate King Michael, not knowing that King Michael himself was on the verge of rendering this precaution unnecessary by carrying out too faithfully his part of the programme. It was a paragraph in a weekly society paper which made his doings known at Llandiarmid. Queen Ernestine brought the paper to her husband when it reached the Castle, and pointed out to him anxiously the "Lady's Letter from the Riviera."

"Listen to this, Cyril," she said. "'Among last week's arrivals at Nice was the young King of Thracia, travelling *incognito* as Baron von Neuburg. He may be seen every day in close attendance on the pretty Grand-Duchess

Sonya, who is making a short stay at the Conciliation with her father, the Grand-Duke Eugen of Scythia, and the announcement of their betrothal is daily expected. It is well known that the attachment between them is of long standing, but that the course of true love was interrupted by the attempt of the Dowager Queen and her English husband to marry King Michael to the latter's niece, a daughter of the Marquis of Caerleon. Happily the young lady was possessed of less ambition or more good sense than her august relations, and made a love-match with a commoner a year or two ago, so that her unwilling suitor is at liberty to return to the real object of his affections.'"

"It strikes me," said Cyril, "that there is something more than the unbridled imagination of the lady journalist at work here. I seem to recognise the touch of a well-known hand. Let me look." He turned back to the beginning of the letter, with its usual altruistic self-congratulation on the number of distinguished personages sojourning on the Riviera, and pointed out among them the name of the Princess Dowager of Dardania. "As usual!" he said. "Well, that relieves your mind a little, doesn't it? All the same, it might be as well to write and advise Michael not to play his part too seriously."

But if Cyril's acuteness, born of experience, had lessened the Queen's anxiety, there was no one to reassure Félicia in the same way. She found the paper that evening and read the paragraph, and the crown which had been merely shadowy seemed to become real and desirable in proportion as it receded from her view. She blamed Maimie for mismanaging things, blamed herself for consenting to remain at Llandiarmid and prosecute her claim by deputy, and blamed the King most of all for his inconstancy, showing a jealousy which her own equivocal position did not by any means justify. She slept little that night, and Maimie, who sat up for hours alternately arguing with and soothing her, was at her wits' end. It was her chief terror that Félicia might insist on following the King to the Riviera forthwith, but it would be almost as bad if she betrayed herself by making scenes at Llandiarmid. She tried to persuade her to remain in bed the next day, but Félicia refused pettishly, and made her appearance about an hour before lunch, looking so ghastly that Usk uttered an exclamation of horror. Unfortunately, this was a fresh grievance.

"If I am looking sick, you needn't tell me so," she complained.

"But you ought to see the doctor. Let me ride over and fetch him."

"No; I want to have you amuse me. Don't look at me that way. You make me nervous. Why don't you say something amusing? I guess you would make yourself sick worrying if you were tormented like me—not knowing whether you were a princess or just a no-account girl."

"Isn't it enough to be Miss Steinherz of the United States? Look here, Fay, why not chuck it all? It's only making you ill and miserable, and you have a capital opportunity now. Uncle Cyril asked me to tell you that Don Ramon of Arragon flatly refuses to recognise or even consider your claim, and you can accept that as final. Otherwise you'll have to approach the Emperor of Pannonia, and go through all this bother again, with just the same result."

"How do you know it would be just the same?" demanded Félicia sharply. "It's to your advantage to try and keep me out of my rights, because you don't want to lose me."

"Well, oughtn't you to be pleased at that? But I don't see why I should lose you if your claim was allowed."

"Well, I guess if I was a princess——"

"You'd throw me over? Thanks, awfully! Do you imagine that if I became a prince it would make any difference to you?"

"Ah, but you'd raise me to your level, any way. I couldn't raise you."

"No, indeed, and I'm thankful for it. But don't let us bother about such nonsense, Fay. You're no more likely to be a princess than I am to be a prince, so why not recognise the fact and withdraw gracefully, instead of wearing yourself to death worrying about it?"

"Because I don't feel like acting that way," said Félicia obstinately. "Well, supposing they did acknowledge me, and we had to break off our engagement, what would you do?"

"What other men do when they're jilted, I imagine—grin and bear it."

"Would the world become a blank to you? Would you never believe in a woman again?"

"I should never believe in you again, certainly. But other women—why, there'd be the mater and Phil just the same. Why shouldn't I believe in them?"

"Well, you might say you wouldn't, any way," pouted Félicia.

"Look here," said Usk. "You said you wanted to be amused, and I hope you are. All this sort of stuff doesn't amuse me at all. Let's come out."

"No, thanks. I'm awfully interested, analysing you. I do wish you were different—sort of imperious, you know, so's I daren't disobey you. I'd love to be made to feel that I just had to do whatever you wanted, and there was no choice about loving you or anything. It would save so much trouble."

"I'm sorry, for your sake, that I'm not that kind of man. I never met one, but I've read about them in books. Seems to me you'd have a cheerful time—especially when you wanted to disobey him, and didn't dare to."

"I guess it would be better than this, any way. I can't think why things should be so horrid. I just want to have a good time, that's all, and every single thing seems to conspire to prevent it. It's real hateful!" and Félicia broke into genuine sobs. Usk's first impulse was to walk away, but he restrained it and stood awkwardly by. His own temper was considerably ruffled by this time, and he was not disposed to blame himself for Félicia's tears, but her sobs became more and more vehement, and he cast his injured dignity to the winds.

"Don't, Fay, don't!" he entreated, kneeling down beside her. "I was a brute to say what I did. I didn't mean it—whatever it was; at least, I didn't mean you to take it like this. It was my fault, I know. What was it I said that hurt your feelings? You know I didn't mean it. Oh, do stop. Here's your Maimie coming, and she'll be sure to say I made you cry, and I don't know what I could have said."

But Félicia sobbed on, and Maimie glared at Usk as she came up.

"I do think you're real horrid," she said judicially. "Here's Fay making herself sick crying, and you teasing her all the time. I'll have her go up to town and see a nerve-specialist, now the weather's warmer. Your cars are so draughty in winter that I'd just as lief have taken her to the Arctic. But I know all this is telling upon her nerves, and it's awfully bad the way you go on exciting her. Come, Fay, darling."

She swept away the still sobbing Félicia, leaving Usk to mental abuse of himself and her in turn, and having settled her in her room, went with a grave face in search of Lady Caerleon. She felt certain that the shock and strain of the autumn and winter had been too much for Félicia's strength, and that it was imperative to take her to a London doctor at once. Grieved and startled, Lady Caerleon offered to accompany the two girls herself, but Maimie declined her escort gracefully. She and Félicia and the maid would run up to town for two nights, and see whether the complete change from her present surroundings would do anything to restore Félicia's cheerfulness. The inference was obvious, and Lady Caerleon interposed to restrain her husband when he wished to insist upon accompanying the girls. It was out of the question, he declared, for them to make the journey alone, and stay at a hotel by themselves, but his wife was strongly of opinion that it was better to leave them to take their own course. Things could not go on as they were at present, and a little reflection might show Félicia how severely she had of late tried the patience of her friends.

It is possible that there was in Lady Caerleon's mind the thought, or even the hope, that Félicia might discover that she was happier apart from Usk, and take the opportunity of breaking off her engagement, but the actual upshot of the visit to London was quite unexpected. It was announced in a letter from Maimie, brief and agitated in appearance.

"DEAR LADY CAERLEON," she wrote, "I'm in the most awful state of mind about Félicia. The doctor says it would be simply fatal for her to return to the country at this season. She must just be in a cheerful place, with lively people around, and everything bright. Most happily, the letter that arrived when we were starting was from Mrs van Zyl, repeating her former invitation to Nice, and I have wired to tell her to expect us right now. We have bought a travelling-suit each, and a waist or two, here, but we will just take a few hours in Paris as we pass through, and get some decent gowns. I am sorry to have quit Llandiarmid so suddenly, but at present I can think of nothing but Félicia. She looks awfully sick, but I hope to see her revive in the South. She will insert a note to Lord Usk if she feels able. Will you kindly send our baggage after us to the Villa Bougainvillea?"

There was no note enclosed, and this omission threw Usk into a terrible state of alarm. Félicia was ill, perhaps dying, and he was to blame. He would hear of nothing but rushing off to Nice at once, and he was throwing his things into a bag when his uncle came down the corridor and saw his preparations through the open door of his room.

"I think this is a little unnecessary," he observed gently.

"Why, she may be gone before I get there!" cried Usk.

"Scarcely. It may interest you to know that her boxes and Miss Logan's are all packed and locked. It's no good shutting your eyes to it, Usk. The visit to the doctor was a polite fiction to enable the girls to leave the Castle without interference. We will put it more kindly, and say they were bent on going, and wished to save us the trouble of dissuading them. The question now is, what are you going to do?"

"I don't know why I should do anything but go to her," said Usk doggedly.

"Are you certain you are wanted?"

Usk turned on his uncle. "If you know anything, say it, and don't keep hinting things," he cried. "Why shouldn't she want me?"

"You think you would not be *de trop* when Michael was present?"

Usk's eyes flamed, and he made a step forward, but his hands dropped suddenly to his side. "I'll see her," he said hoarsely, "and tell her she must choose once for all between that fellow and me. I won't be kept hanging on, to be made useful if she doesn't succeed in landing him. But I don't believe it's that at all. She's anxious and worried about this wretched claim of hers, as she told me herself, and it's just a chance that he happens to be at Nice."

"Very well. As you say, it's as well to see her before you judge. Your aunt and I think of going to Nice to look after Michael a little, and you may as well travel with us, and not rush off in this dramatic way. You won't want to make your differences of opinion public, I suppose, in any case?"

CHAPTER X.
A DAMSEL IN DISTRESS.

NICE was looking its loveliest, but to Usk, making his way along the Promenade des Anglais in the direction of the Villa Bougainvillea, it was not lovely at all. He was uneasy and troubled in mind, and thoroughly out of tune with his surroundings, and with the gay groups of well-dressed people he met. The palms and the sunshine, the blue sea and the white houses set in flowers and greenery, all jarred with his mood. Not another word had reached him from Félicia herself or from Maimie, but although he had only arrived the night before, there had been time to learn that the Baron von Neuburg now divided his abundant leisure and his *petits soins* between the Grand-Duchess Sonya and a beautiful American girl who was staying with the fascinating grass-widow, Mrs van Zyl. Even now, as he turned into one of the side-avenues, in order to reach the smart white house nestling in its groves of orange- and lemon-trees, he met a motor-car of the latest and most elaborate construction, and recognised in the two men who occupied it, disguised as they were by huge spectacles and mackintosh coats and caps, King Michael and Captain Andreivics. He saw a meaning glance pass between them as they returned his salute, and he walked on faster, reaching the villa quickly enough to find the two ladies who had shared the drive still lingering on the rose-hung piazza in front of the house. They wore businesslike dust-proof gowns, edged and faced with highly decorated leather, and their faces were hidden by long gauze veils crossed behind and tied, French fashion, under the chin, but Félicia's exquisite figure was unmistakable, and Usk mounted the steps without waiting for an invitation. He was received with a little shriek.

"Well, now, I was sort of expecting you!" cried Félicia. "It's just wonderful how one's friends find one out. Sadie, this is Viscount Usk, the son of the kind folks that have been boarding Maimie and me all winter."

A kind of chill ran through Usk's veins. "She hasn't even told the woman of our engagement!" he said to himself.

"Awfully good of you to come so soon!" said Mrs van Zyl, a small, sharp-featured woman with artificially bleached hair and a high voice. "I guess we must change these horrid gowns now, but maybe you'll *five o'cloquer* with us this afternoon. I know there are just about three hundred people coming."

"You are very kind," said Usk, then he turned to Félicia. "I will come at any time when it is convenient for *you* to see me," he said pointedly.

"Well, I don't see but you can do that at tea," she replied.

"Say, Lord Usk, we can't have you monopolise Miss Steinherz!" cried Mrs van Zyl. "She's just about the most popular girl in Nice, and she's getting fresh invitations all the time."

"I won't detain her long," said Usk, not offering to withdraw.

"Ah, you're bringing some message from your mother!" said Félicia. "You come this afternoon, any way, and I'll see you have a chance to deliver it."

Usk accepted his dismissal, and went away, in no wise comforted. He said nothing to his uncle or aunt of the reception he had met with, but in the afternoon he returned to the Villa Bougainvillea with absolute punctuality, determined to come to an understanding with Félicia. He was shown into a small room, which was apparently the private boudoir of the mistress of the house, so full was it of the rococo and the bizarre. Presently Félicia glided in, in a wonderful shimmering tea-gown of heliotrope shot with silver, and partly veiled with long falling scarves of filmy lace, and Usk noticed with a pang that her whole face and bearing seemed to have changed. There had been a starved look about her at Llandiarmid, as if the cold northern air and the simple life of the Castle had afflicted her with actual pinching hunger, but here she was evidently in her element. The luxury of the surroundings, the curious and costly objects which over-filled every corner, seemed only a fitting frame for her beauty. Her face was calmer and softer in outline, and her voice had lost its sharp tone as she said, laying a little hand lightly on Usk's arm—

"Are you awfully mad with me, Usk?"

It would be brutal to say that he was, and moreover, Usk was conscious that his anger seemed to have melted away. It was impossible to cherish it in the presence of those speaking eyes, that caressing hand.

"Oh, Fay, Fay!" he cried, catching her in his arms. "I knew it was all right really. I knew you didn't mean to be so horribly unkind."

"Unkind? to you? Oh, Usk!" Félicia dropped her head on his shoulder for an instant, then raised it hastily and felt surreptitiously at her hair.

"Well, you were, you know. It nearly broke my heart this morning when I saw you hadn't told Mrs van Zyl that we were engaged."

"But I did tell her, Usk, only she's real mad about it. They all beg and entreat me not to make it public just yet on account of the claim. Sadie is ready to swear that the Emperor won't ever entertain it if he thinks I'm provided for now. The only chance is to have myself appear as a wealthy heiress entirely at my own disposal."

"And so you throw me over to deceive your father's people?"

"I don't throw you over. I just ask you to wait and not announce our engagement for the present. That can't hurt you, any way."

"It does hurt me very much to see you encouraging King Michael."

"Encouraging him? because Sadie and I went for a ride on his automobile? You get one, and we'll come with you."

"It's not that. There's an idea that he will marry you if your claim is substantiated."

"Do tell! I'm real grateful to his Majesty. Well, Usk, I'm not responsible for any plans he and Maimie may have fixed up together, but I haven't ever said a single word to him about any such thing, nor he to me."

"Then you are not thinking of marrying him, even if by some miracle the Emperor should persuade your father's people to recognise you?"

"I've imagined all the time that I was thinking of marrying you. No, Usk, I won't make any pledges. I'm going to have you trust me." She laid her white arms, from which the hanging sleeves fell back, round his neck. "If you don't feel like it, say so, and I'll set you free this moment, but if you're the right kind of a man, you'll believe in me."

"I do believe in you," said Usk hoarsely, kissing first one wrist and then the other; "but don't make it harder for me than you can help, Fay."

"I'll make it just as hard as I can," laughed Félicia, stepping back, "to punish you for doubting me at all. I shall fairly admire to test your faith and see what it's worth, so just remember that when you find things in a snarl. You do trust me?"

"I do, absolutely."

"Good boy! And you'll defend me against the nasty suspicious things your uncle says? It's real kind of him to be so anxious to secure me in the family, but I don't feel like gratifying him just yet."

"But you won't encourage the King? It's that which makes him――"

"I won't promise not to go riding with him, if that's what you mean. Sadie will go around with me everywhere, you needn't be afraid. She knows what it is to be a chaperon in Europe, and she'll do her duty to the death. And now I guess we've had just about enough high-falutin'. But before we go in the *salon*, just look at these patterns for our dominos for the *corso*

Tuesday. Don't you think this shade of heliotrope is quite too sweet for anything?" She held it up to her face.

"It's a pretty colour," said Usk hesitatingly. "But, Fay——"

"And we're going to fix up the carriage with those light-purple anemones—just a mass of them. I wanted hepaticas—you can get real nice shades in them, a much pinker purple, you know—but every one says they wouldn't last above an hour. Don't you think it'll be awfully elegant?"

"But surely you aren't going? Your mourning——"

"Silly boy! don't you call this mourning?" She flourished the heliotrope silk before his eyes. "But maybe, if you are very good and unexacting beforehand, I won't go. I'd just as lief see it from a window. Now mind, I won't have you trail me around everywhere. You'll get your turn with the rest, but it don't do to be covetous."

It was with some misgivings that Usk followed her to the *salon*, which was full of people, of a type with which he had not hitherto had much acquaintance. The ladies were mostly Americans, either sojourning in Europe without their husbands, like Mrs van Zyl, or married to Continental noblemen of various nationalities. There was a sprinkling of these gentlemen present, but most of the men were unencumbered by domestic ties, and purely cosmopolitan, the product of the modern health resort. Originally French, Brazilian, or Hungarian by race, they had travelled so much in search of sport or distraction that the whole civilised world was equally dull to them, and the only place which was still able to kindle a spark of excitement in their breasts was Monte Carlo. With them the talk was of the tables or of pigeon-shooting, while the ladies preferred generally to discuss flowers and fancy dresses. Lent fell late this year, so that although it was the middle of March, the last days of the Carnival were still to come, and every one was on the alert to discover what her neighbour was going to wear.

Usk left the villa before any of the other guests, meeting King Michael on the threshold as he did so. The two young men eyed one another with unfriendly glances. Each resented the other's presence, without having the right to object to it; but Usk noticed uneasily that the King walked straight into the hall, and that Maimie, looking more eager and anxious than ever, in a sprightly black-and-white gown, fluttered out to meet him, and took him into the little boudoir whither he himself had been conducted only an hour before. His uncle's words recurred to him, but he set his teeth. "She has asked me to trust her, and I will—I do," he repeated.

It was natural, perhaps, that Cyril should not be so ready to accept this view of the case. When Usk entered the *appartement* at the Hôtel des Rois, which had been taken in the names of Lord and Lady Cyril Mortimer, he was met by the secretary Paschics, who said that his uncle wished to see him as soon as he came in. Usk was not at all anxious to see his uncle, and his misgivings returned sharply upon him as he sought him on the balcony of their sitting-room.

"Well, have you had any talk with Félicia?" asked Cyril.

"Just a little. I only had her to myself for a minute or two."

"And is she willing to have the engagement announced?"

"Well, no; not just yet. She has got some idea that it would prejudice her claim if it was known."

"Then you have broken it off?"

"Rather not. I have agreed to keep it private a little longer."

"In fact," said Cyril, with slow scorn, "you set out to end an anomalous state of things, and then agree to perpetuate it. You bind yourself and leave her free, though it's perfectly clear that she is merely keeping you on as a last resource in case she loses Michael."

"It's nothing of the kind," said Usk. "She has no thought of Michael—she told me so herself."

"You are in love with love," said Cyril bitterly, "and honour, and self-sacrifice, and all the other things of which Miss Steinherz knows no more than she does of good taste. Don't you see the girl's fooling you?"

"It may look like that to you, but you don't know her as I do. She's playing for a great stake, and she shall have her chance. I won't let her be able to say that she would have won if I had not baulked her. She won't win, of course, but at least it won't be my fault, and she will leave off thinking about it, and we shall be all right."

"She is nothing but an adventuress who can't make up her mind to burn her boats."

Usk turned very white. "You have no right to say that of the lady who has promised to marry me," he said.

"I beg your pardon; I ought not to have thought aloud. It is a bad habit that has grown on me of late. My dear Usk, if she had promised to marry you I should see daylight. As it is, she may have promised and she may not. Can you assert a promise if the lady sees fit to deny it?"

"She won't deny it. And, anyhow, it's a thing that only affects me. I am satisfied to wait until she chooses to announce our engagement, and I don't see what any one else has to do with it."

"In other words, I am to mind my own business. But, unfortunately, this is my business, though I assure you no one can regret it more than I do. I have just heard that the Grand-Duke and Duchess of Schwarzwald-Molzau are on their way here. He is Michael's uncle, and it is quite natural that he should be frightened by the reports about the Grand-Duchess Sonya, and come to find out the truth for himself, but I haven't a doubt that he is also commissioned to inquire into Félicia's affair on behalf of the Emperor of Pannonia, his brother-in-law. They have come to the conclusion that her claim is a serious one, and he is to see if she is presentable, and whether she can be bought off. Now, suppose Michael takes it into his head to say that he will marry Sonya Eugenovna unless he is allowed to marry Félicia, what am I to do? No one would expect me to help him to cut out one of my own family, but I am not allowed to say she is engaged to you. I tell you frankly I should very much prefer to eliminate you from the matter, for you and she are not in the least suited to one another; but it seems that you object to that. It's what I should like best of all to see Félicia engaged to Michael, and her fortune made useful in re-establishing Thracian credit, and yet I must invent obstacles to prevent it. Of course the usual convenient fiction of the overmastering avarice and ambition of the Mortimer family will come to the front, and I shall be accused of plotting to engineer Félicia into a marriage with you for the sake of her money, and putting her up to this preposterous claim of hers in order to strengthen my position by an alliance with royalty. Pleasant, very!"

"I'm awfully sorry, but you can hardly expect me——"

"To renounce your *fiancée* in order to spare my battered reputation a few more knocks? I quite see that. Oh, don't think I blame you. Here am I groping helplessly to try and find the thread of affairs which I could once have worked out in my sleep, and losing my temper with you over it. It's that which drives me wild."

He rose hastily, and left the balcony by the farther window, and Usk, feeling perplexed and somewhat guilty, returned into the sitting-room, where Queen Ernestine was writing at the table.

"Don't trouble your uncle more than you can help, Usk," she said, looking up. "He is very much worried just now."

"It's not my fault——" began Usk indignantly. Then he stopped, and fidgeted awkwardly with the inkstand. "I don't want to bother you, or to do anything rude," he broke out; "but if you could say a word or two to the

King! Of course it's only natural he should admire her, and that she should be pleased, but—well, you see how it is. I don't think I'm jealous generally, but it really is rather rough on a man. And it's just the uncertainty that's weighing on Uncle Cyril, too. Don't you think—is there any reason why the King shouldn't marry this Scythian Princess?"

The Queen looked almost terrified. "You don't understand," she said. "It is not that we could have any objection to Sonya herself; it is simply that the marriage is being pressed on by my cousin, the Princess of Dardania, for her own purposes. She has hated your uncle for many years, and she hates me because I am his wife. It was her influence which banished your uncle from Thracia, and led to the present troubles. To see Michael delivered over to her again—— No, I must fight to the end against that."

"I'm sorry," said Usk. "I only thought—well, if he was married to some one else, you see, there would be no excuse for these women to persuade Félicia that he was after her. That's what it is, you know. It's not her fault, it's theirs. They get round her and make her think that he really means something, and she doesn't know——"

"That he is only amusing himself?" supplied the Queen, as he paused. "Oh, Usk, I see your trouble, and I will do anything I can to help you. I fear it might not be much use to speak to Michael, but if we could only see him happily married! There is just a chance that he might take to the Schwarzwald-Molzaus' youngest daughter, who is coming here with them. But she is a mere child, only confirmed last year, and I could not wish them to marry unless they loved one another. I am afraid I have been indiscreet in speaking of it, but it would smooth your path, wouldn't it? Indeed I will help you if I can."

She held out her hand mechanically, and Usk kissed it, in the way he had learned from his uncle. The Queen laughed.

"I ought to play my part better by this time, at any rate in my own family, ought I not?" she said. "Are you going to see that poor Mr Nicholson, Usk? If there is anything he would like, flowers or fruit, or books, you will tell me, won't you? It seems sad to be so ill away from home, and all alone."

Nicholson was a college friend of Usk's, who was now at Nice as a hopeless invalid. Usk had not cared for him particularly at Cambridge, but had been startled and touched to meet him in the hall that morning, and learn that he was alone save for a servant. Nicholson himself protested that the Riviera had done him no end of good, and that he was going to join in the Carnival gaieties on Shrove Tuesday, but his appearance made the words seem a bitter mockery.

"Thanks awfully," said Usk. "I was just going to sit with him a bit, and I'm sure he'll think it tremendously kind of you. I was wondering whether I might ask him in to tea one afternoon? I thought he would like to talk to you a little. He doesn't know in the least who you are, of course, but his people don't seem to realise how ill he is, any more than he does himself, and there seems to be no one——"

"I understand. Yes, of course, ask him to come in to-morrow if he feels well enough, and we will take care not to invite any one else."

Usk took his departure, and spent an hour with his sick friend, whose society was harrowing enough, owing to the ghastly contrast between his plans and ambitions and his state of health. But there was a reward for Usk when he returned to his own room, for a tiny note was awaiting him from Félicia. It was written with purple ink upon paper of a lighter shade, and perfumed with heliotrope—all the very latest Parisian fancy of the moment—but Usk tore it open without a glance at anything but the direction.

"DEAR BOY," it ran, "Did you think me awfully mean this afternoon? This is to make up. I have told Sadie that I am just not going to the *fêtes* Tuesday, but I haven't told her that I am coming riding with you instead. I am, if you ask me nicely.—Yours,

FÉLICIA."

Naturally, the only thing to do on receiving such a letter was to hasten to secure the smartest possible vehicle for a long country drive. But Usk found to his dismay that not a single proprietor would let out a carriage of any description on the day mentioned save for use at the Carnival, and he was obliged to invite himself to tea at the villa instead. Félicia pouted when he told her of the change, and kept him for some time in anxiety as to whether she would allow him to come or not, averring that the ideal lover would have purchased a complete turn-out rather than disappoint his mistress of the drive on which she had set her heart. Usk pleaded that he had not the money, whereupon she retorted that an American would have made the purchase on credit, and resold the cart and horse at a profit immediately afterwards, thus combining business with pleasure. However, she was at last induced to promise to be at home, and Usk felt his self-respect restored. He would have Félicia to himself, without the intervention of Maimie, or Mrs van Zyl, or the King, and his uncle would be forced to see that his suspicions were unfounded.

But when the Tuesday afternoon arrived, a note was brought to Usk as he sat in Nicholson's room reading to the invalid, who had got as far as the Jardin Publique in the morning, and there discovered that his strength was at an end. This note was written with crimson ink upon rose-scented pink paper, and Usk found that it came from Mrs van Zyl. It was very short.

"DEAR LORD USK,—Félicia is real sorry to disappoint you, but she thinks it her duty not to miss such an excellent opportunity of seeing the Carnival. I wish we could have you come with us, but our carriage is full.— Yours truly,

SADIE VAN ZYL."

Usk crushed the note angrily in his hand when he had glanced at it. Of course it might mean no more than that Félicia was to view the Carnival procession from a window, but he felt almost certain that she would don fancy dress and join in all the gaiety that offered itself. And who was to occupy the fourth seat in the carriage? Only one answer suggested itself— King Michael. Usk fought against the conviction in vain. At last he stood up, and spoke hurriedly to Nicholson, who had been watching him curiously.

"I'm off. I shall go and see what all the foolery is like, anyhow."

"Disappointed of your tea-party?" laughed the invalid, his worn face elfish, almost malicious. "But you can't go down into the thick of the fun in those things. You'll be mobbed. Look here, you wear the togs I ordered for myself—we're about the same height. Ring for Jenkins, and he'll bring them. I was going as the typical Englishman of French caricature. Now then, there you are. Don't forget the whiskers, mind."

"They aren't the right colour for me," said Usk, tossing down the long Dundreary whiskers which had been selected to match Nicholson's sandy hair. "I'm sure I shall look enough of an ass without them. Where in the world did you get such checks?"

"Horse-blanket," responded Nicholson, breathlessly but proudly. "Tasty, isn't it? I thought when I chose it I should make a sensation, but now I know what the French believe about us, I'm certain it will fall flat. People will only say, 'That English fellow has no business to come in his ordinary clothes.'"

"Ordinary!" gasped Usk, from the adjoining room, where he was arraying himself rapidly in the scarlet and yellow checked knickerbockers, the orange tawny Norfolk jacket, the golf-stockings combining all the colours of the rainbow, and the aggressive sun-helmet, surrounded by a white puggaree striped with red and blue, which Nicholson considered would enable the French populace to identify the typical Englishman so dear to their hearts. Football boots and an alpenstock completed the costume, and when Usk had donned the orthodox velvet mask, Nicholson lay back upon his pillows, and laughed and coughed until the tears ran down his cheeks.

"I wouldn't have missed it for anything," he gasped. "I shouldn't have realised the effect half as well on myself. You might have stepped out of 'Le Rire,' except for your modest air of uneasiness. Swagger a bit, and grind your teeth. Walk as if the whole earth belonged to you. And do put on the whiskers. They'll look all the funnier with your dark moustache."

But this last sacrifice to appearances Usk declined to make, and after Nicholson had reminded him to provide himself with a good bag of confetti and a tin scoop, he crept downstairs, hoping fervently not to meet any one he knew, and went out by the side door of the hotel, whence he found his way easily to the Old Town and into the main stream of gaiety. His sole idea had been to look for Félicia, to convince himself that she had deliberately broken her promise to him, or perhaps to have the delight of finding that Mrs van Zyl and Maimie were joining in the fun without her. But once in the whirling, ever-changing throng, he soon recognised that there was little hope of finding any one. Strangers accosted him, rallied him on his loneliness, invited him to join them. Confetti flew about in showers, small hard bouquets hurtled through the air from the decorated carriages as they passed, and the phantasmagoria of sound and colour fleeted and shifted every moment. Overhead, against the glowing blue of the sky, were strings of fluttering flags and wreaths of evergreen; a little lower, windows and shop-fronts were garlanded and decked with bright-hued stuffs; the lofty cars which lurched past vied with one another in the richness of their colour-schemes and the *bizarrerie* of their mechanical devices; small foot-soldiers and dragoons on prancing steeds were pressed hither and thither in valiant attempts to keep a line. There were people in the road, people on the pavement, people in every door and window, people on the roofs. Bands blared, maskers hissed, cackled, hooted, neighed, yelled; imperious policemen forced their way along with the word "*circulez*" on their lips, although to obey was obviously impossible. People entangled each other in long paper streamers, banged each other with bladders, knocked off each other's headgear, poked confetti down each other's collars, all in high good-humour, and amid shrieks of laughter. Dominos of every possible colour and shade of colour, Pierrots and Pierrettes of every degree of inanity, debased national and historical costumes of every country and every era, eddied round Usk, but he tried in vain to distinguish any figure that he knew. Anxious and troubled as he was, he had soon had enough of the scene, but he kept his temper, and flung his confetti with the best, until they were exhausted. By this time he had managed to traverse almost the entire route of the procession, and he turned to retrace his steps. As he did so, he noticed a band of men with false noses, who seemed to be chaffing some one in their midst. As Usk was carried close to them by the crowd, he saw that the centre of attraction was a girl in German peasant costume. Her hair hung in two thick plaits below her waist, and in her short skirts she looked little more than a child. Her stiff little round cap had been tweaked off by one of the group surrounding her, two more had possessed themselves of the ribbons from her hair, and were announcing that they would wear them next their hearts for ever after, and another had pulled the knitting from her apron-pocket and was drawing out the pins. The girl herself was clinging with both hands to her mask, in evident though unnecessary terror that it would be the next thing torn from her, and gazing round like a hunted hare for a way of escape. With an inarticulate exclamation, Usk pushed his way into the circle. Whoever the girl might be, her terror and distress were obvious, and he could not see her tormented by this rabble. To his utter astonishment, as soon as her eyes fell on him, she darted forward and seized his arm.

"Oh, you have come at last!" she cried in English. "It has seemed so long!"

"The fair Gretchen has found a cavalier!" laughed one of the tormentors.

"May they be happy!" cried another, and in the shower of confetti which followed, Usk made his escape, the girl still clinging to his arm. She was shaking from head to foot, and he managed to drag her into a doorway, while he stood before her to protect her from the crowd. Presently a small meek voice said—

"Please forgive me. I ought not to have pretended I knew you, but I was so frightened." The tears were raining down.

"Oh, never mind," said Usk cheerfully, wondering how this child had been allowed out by herself. "They wouldn't have hurt you really, you know. Shall we wait here and watch for your people?"

"I don't know where they are, and papa will be so angry."

"Why? Did you come out without his knowing?"

"Oh no. I was with him, and I wanted to hold his arm, and he wouldn't let me. He said I made him look absurd," a sob. "But I knew we could not keep together if I let go, and we were separated in a moment."

"All right. Don't cry. I'll take you home at once if you like. Your father will guess you've gone back. Where are you staying?"

"At the Hôtel des Rois. But please don't allow me to trouble you."

"It's no trouble at all. I'm staying there too."

"Oh, are you? But I didn't see you at breakfast. It was so nice seeing all the people, and trying to guess who they were."

"I am with my uncle and aunt, and they prefer to have their meals upstairs."

"So do papa and mamma. How droll! But it is my birthday to-day, and mamma allowed me to breakfast on the terrace, for a treat. You are English, aren't you? When those horrid men all came round me, I thought, 'Oh, if only I could see a German or an Englishman!'"

"You ought to be careful," said Usk sagely. They were walking through a quiet street by this time, on their way back to the hotel. "There are a good many shady characters about."

"Shady? I don't know that word. But it means dark, dangerous—is it not so? But I could see you were not like that, of course."

"I'm glad I was labelled English and harmless to the foreign eye," said Usk. "I shouldn't have thought myself that this get-up would have inspired confidence."

"What strange words you use. One judges people by their faces, not by their get-ups—is that the word?"

"There isn't very much of my face visible to judge by."

"Ah, one can judge a good deal by the general outline," said the girl confidently. "Oh, is your uncle the poor sick Englishman I met in the gardens this morning?"

"No; that's a friend of mine."

"I was so sorry for him, because I have been ill so much myself. When I was a little girl I almost died every winter."

"But you look all right now."

"I am quite well, thank you, but mamma lived up in the mountains with me for two whole years, that I might become strong. I was her baby, you see." Usk smiled involuntarily, the remark sounded so naïve. "Franz, my next brother, was ten years old when I was born, and all the rest are much older. I am even younger than two of my nephews, the Princes of Schreckingen."

"Surely you must be the Princess of Schwarzwald-Molzau?" asked Usk diffidently.

"The little Princess they call me, or Princess Lenchen. At least they used to do that, but now papa says I am always to be called the Princess Helene.

I am grown-up, you see, but I don't feel as if I were. When I was confirmed I thought there would surely be a difference, that I should feel grown-up, but I don't, and it displeases papa. He used to laugh at the things I said, and say, 'How does the child get such things into her head?' but now he is angry, and says, 'Will that child never grow up?'"

She spoke so dolorously that Usk laughed. "You'll be grown-up quite soon enough," he said. "I don't know what to call you—your Grand-Ducal Highness?"

"I do not know yet who you are," she replied, with a quaint little air of dignity.

"Probably you'll know my uncle's name better than mine—Count Mortimer."

"Oh, then we are cousins!" she exclaimed in delight. "At least we have the same aunt. She was married first to my uncle, you know."

"And now she is married to mine. Does that make her more my aunt or yours?"

"Ah, but she is my mother's cousin as well."

"That gives you the advantage, certainly."

"But does it make Count Mortimer my uncle? I am so anxious to know that, and I am afraid to ask papa. He—he doesn't——"

"Care for the connection? None of you do, I suppose. But I think you'll like it better when you know my uncle."

"Like it? I wish him to be my uncle!" she cried. "You do not know; but since he came to Molzau for my sister Theudelinde's wedding, four years ago, and I heard all about him, I have—oh, I do not know the English word—*geschwärmt* for him. What is it that you do to a great poet, or painter, or any great man?"

"Admire him?" suggested Usk.

"Oh no, no! You admire a horse. Have you no sisters? Did they not set up some hero's photograph and place flowers in front of it, and watch for any mention of his name, and long to obtain his autograph?"

"Now you mention it, I believe Phil—that's my sister—did have a severe attack of hero-worship some years ago. It was about the time Lord Williams came home from Africa."

"Lord Williams? Oh, I know—Bills!"

"And you pretend not to understand slang!"

"I am sorry. I have heard my English cousins speak of him so much, and they told me it was considered quite wrong in England to call him anything else. Then what is the word?"

"Adore, I should think. Or I know a girl, an American"—Usk's face clouded again as he thought of Félicia—"who would say she enthused over him."

"Enthused? That is a good word. Well, then, I enthused over Count Mortimer. I found a portrait of him in an illustrated paper—one of my English cousins was staying with us, and her lady had brought it—and I cut it out, and had it framed. I put it up in my room, and made a wreath of green leaves for it on the dear Count's birthday, and no one was allowed to dust it but myself. Mamma laughed at me, but when the trouble came, and your uncle left Thracia, you know, she told me I had better take it down, lest papa should see it and be angry. So I took it down, and laid it in a drawer, and looked at it every day; but when the Count married Aunt Ernestine, I thought papa could not mind, and I put it up again. But when he saw it he was—oh, I cannot tell you how angry! and he broke the glass and tore up the portrait. But do you know what I shall do now? I shall ask Aunt Ernestine to give me a photograph of him and write my name on it herself. Papa couldn't tear that up, could he?"

"Far be it from me to say what papa couldn't or wouldn't do!" returned Usk, almost helpless with laughter, as they mounted the steps of the Hôtel des Rois. The girl turned to look at him reproachfully, so that Usk saw before she did an elderly gentleman, in a high state of excitement, standing in the middle of the hall, and apparently giving orders to the whole staff of the hotel in an imperious style, which contrasted ludicrously with his peasant dress and the mask which was pushed up on his forehead.

"Communicate with the police instantly!" he was saying, with a strong German accent. "They could do nothing, you say? But I insist upon it. What! is my daughter to be torn from my side and kidnapped with impunity?"

"I am here, dear papa," said the Princess Helene meekly. "I lost my way, and this—this kind English gentleman brought me home."

Still spluttering and choking, the Grand-Duke turned round, and glared at his daughter as if he was angry with her for being brought back. Then he turned again to wave his hand majestically, and when the waiters had fled, allowed his gaze to rest upon Usk, who became once more painfully conscious of his attire. "I am obliged to you, sir," said the Grand-Duke coldly.

"Papa," whispered his daughter, anxious to improve matters, "it is Aunt Ernestine's nephew." She shrank from the look she received as if from a blow.

"You are the nephew of Count Mortimer, sir, I understand? The Count is a worthy man, and at one time did good service to my house. I am glad you follow in his footsteps." And the Grand-Duke led his daughter away.

CHAPTER XI.
KNOWN TOO LATE.

THE Grand-Duke and Duchess of Schwarzwald-Molzau were entertaining a strictly family party at dinner in their *appartement* at the Hôtel des Rois. King Michael and his mother were naturally the chief guests, and the Queen's presence involved Cyril's. Usk had also the honour of being invited, owing to the service he had rendered to the Princess Helene, and there was a vacant place at the table, no explanation of which was at first offered. Usk felt supremely uncomfortable, and was very conscious of being an outsider, though reflection, or policy, or his wife's influence, had induced the Grand-Duke to show himself gracious, if not cordial. Cyril's help was desirable, even indispensable, in solving the problems which lay before King Michael's relations at this moment, and there was a widespread belief that it was not wise to show any discourtesy to "the Mortimer," however defenceless he might appear. Not that Cyril displayed any disposition to insist upon his rights. With the tact which always distinguished him, he claimed nothing that his hosts might not be willing to concede, and in spite of his delicate position exerted such a genial influence that before the end of the meal the Grand-Duke was addressing him with absolute friendliness. It was Queen Ernestine who was nervously on the look-out for slights offered to her husband, so that throughout the evening she was clearly ready, as he told her afterwards, to sail magnificently out of the room at a moment's notice, sweeping Usk and himself in her train. Her vigilance was not without its effect upon the Grand-Duke, beside whom she sat, and as he hoped much from her influence over the King, he took pains, in a rough and somewhat tactless fashion, to show her that her fears were unnecessary.

King Michael sat next to the Grand-Duchess, a stout, comfortable-looking lady whose sole anxiety seemed to be her husband's temper. When she had satisfied herself that he was desirous of pleasing the Queen, and exhibited no active antipathy to Cyril, she settled down to enjoy the King's society. Usk, judging by her occasional exclamations and generally shocked expression, thought that he was probably entertaining her with the recital of some of the escapades with which he daily edified the population of Nice, and that she, regarding him as a possible son-in-law, was listening indulgently, if with a certain amount of gratifying horror.

Sitting solitary, since the empty place happened to be next him, Usk had plenty of opportunity of observing his fellow-diners, and he took a special delight in watching the pair opposite him. The Princess Helene was looking very small and shy, and as young as ever, in her simple white gown, with her hair coiled round and round the small head, which seemed overweighted by the heavy plaits. She was not pretty, thought Usk, looking at her dispassionately, she was too thin and pale, but the over-abundant hair was of a warm brown, and the large eyes a deep hazel. If she was with people who were kind to her, and was not in constant fear of being snubbed or called to order, she would be a jolly little girl. To this conclusion he was led by observing her demeanour to Cyril, which reminded him of the way she had talked to himself under the protection of her mask two days before. At first she was almost too shy to speak, on finding herself in the actual presence of her idol, but the barrier was soon removed. There were few people that Cyril could not set at ease, and this little romantic girl was no exception to the rule.

"He talked to me about interesting things, as if I was quite old," she said to Usk in the drawing-room afterwards; and when Usk hinted that this would not generally be considered a compliment, she was almost angry. "People always will think that girls want compliments, and simply to talk about balls and stupid things of that kind," she cried, "instead of books, and politics, and *life*; but the dear Count is not like that. I have often thought that some day I might see him and listen to him, but I never, never dreamed that he would talk to me, and let me talk to him. And I should have lost it all if *he* had not been so rude and come in too late for dinner."

She was sitting at the piano, which was isolated from the rest of the room in a recess, and Usk was standing beside her to turn over the pages of her music. As she spoke she threw a little scornful glance in the direction of the defaulting guest, who had made his appearance, with profuse apologies, when the meal was just over. A man of uncertain age, looking young in a dim light, but considerably older when the glare of the electric lamps fell upon him, he was presented to the Queen as the Grand-Duke Ivan Petrovitch of Scythia. At first he had appeared to think it his duty to hover round Helene with talk of the very kind she despised, but when the four elders of the party drew together for conversation, he seemed to find a more congenial companion in King Michael, who had taken no notice of his little cousin save to tease her with reminiscences of their childhood which made her blush painfully. Usk, whose Welsh blood had boiled under the calmly inquiring glance turned upon him by the new-comer, was glad enough to follow Helene to the piano, where she tried over the accompaniments of various songs, and played now and then a few bars of one musical composition or another, "just to encourage conversation," as she put it.

"Don't you hate him?" she inquired presently, under cover of the music, with a turn of her head in the direction of the visitor.

"I don't much like his looks," Usk agreed.

"He may say that he lost his train from Monte Carlo, but I am quite certain that he stayed at the tables too long on purpose."

"But that seems rather aimless, doesn't it?"

"Oh, he wished to be rude. I don't know why, but I am certain it was that. He makes me—I forget the word—quake? quiver?—all over when he comes near."

"He grues you, does he? So he does me."

"I am so glad, because it shows it is not a fancy of mine. Do you know what I think it is? Look at him through the leaves of that palm; see how smooth he is, how well-brushed—is not that the phrase? Then think of him as he would look without his beard. I have seen a picture of him when he was much younger in his cousin Sonya's album, and oh! it was such a cruel face. I call him the Tartar—you know the saying, *Grattez le Scythe, et vous trouverez*——? It amuses mamma very much, but she told me not to tell papa. He would be displeased."

"I don't think I would tell the Grand-Duke either," suggested Usk, half-pityingly. Could the child be so blind as not to see what the presence of the Scythian Prince at this family gathering portended?

"Oh no, I should not think of it. And besides, when he comes near me, I can never talk at all. I feel like a mouse in a trap, and I can only say yes and no. You know that he married one of my cousins? She died before they had been married a year, and I believe"—her voice dropped, and her eyes sought Usk's with a haunting horror in them—"that he killed her."

"Oh no!" Usk felt compelled to say. "Why should he?"

"I don't mean that he murdered her with a dagger or with poison. I should think it would be enough to kill any one to see that face and that sneer always opposite them. And they wanted her to enter the Orthodox Church, and she refused; and I don't think he would be very kind if his wishes were opposed, would he? Oh, it was brave of her, poor Leopoldine! I should have surrendered, I know. I should be too frightened to hold out."

"I say, you know," said Usk awkwardly, "perhaps you're misjudging him. He mayn't be as bad as he looks."

Helene shook her head. "It is the feeling his presence gives me," she said. "Now, there is Michael. I dislike him, but I am not afraid of him. He is like a big boy who tortures flies for sport, not thinking. The Grand-Duke Ivan would do it for the sake of cruelty. And there is the Emperor Sigismund. Every one says how hard he is, but he is not cruel. He is always kind to me. He used to call me his little kitten, and I could always persuade him to do what I wanted. That was when I was a little girl, of course."

Usk was silent, lost in amazement at this new light upon the character of the Hercynian ruler. Helene was looking through a pile of music.

"Ah!" she said. "This is what you in England call the Wedding March; is it not so? Shall I startle them all by playing it in Michael's honour? It seems quite certain that he is to marry Sonya Eugenova. Cousin Ottilie was calling on mamma to-day, and told us so much about them both."

"No doubt the Princess of Dardania would know more about it than any one else," said Usk drily, "but," he added, unhappy recollections of his own coming to the surface again, "it would be a pity to congratulate the King too soon."

"Then shall I play it for you?" she asked suddenly. "Cousin Ottilie told us you were betrothed to a beautiful American girl. I hope I shall see her. Michael knows her family, does he not? Mamma said he was a good deal at their villa."

"No, please don't," said Usk hurriedly, laying his hand upon hers as she was about to begin. "As you have heard so much, I can explain things to you which I couldn't to any one else. We are not exactly engaged—at least, you know, I would give anything to be, but she won't have it. It's—it's just that she doesn't like to be bound, you know. Of course she thinks I should try to monopolise her, and she would find it awfully dull."

Helene's face, as she sat at the piano, wore an expression of disapproval. "I don't understand," she said. "She has not refused you—no? And yet she will not bind herself? But this is not treating you honourably."

"Oh, I don't mind," Usk assured her, with involuntary mendacity. "She's—she's an American, you know, and American girls like to be free above all things. I don't want her to refuse me at all. I'm quite content to wait until she is willing——"

"To be betrothed? But why should she prefer freedom to becoming your bride?" Usk felt some astonishment, until he remembered that she was using the word in the German sense. "Surely she would receive far greater consideration, besides having the right to your escort everywhere, and all the respect you would naturally show her?"

"Oh, it's not that." Usk felt helpless to explain the points involved. "An American girl gets all the consideration she wants anyhow, and that's all there is going, or she'll know the reason why. And you see she would much rather have different men to take her about than me always."

"I do not understand," said Helene coldly, rising as she spoke. "It seems to me that you ought not to allow her to treat you with such insult. She cannot be a high-minded girl."

"What next?" thought Usk in amazement, as he put out the piano-lights before following her. The party was breaking up by this time, and Helene bade him good-night with freezing coldness. He was at a loss to know how he had offended her, especially when he noticed that in saying farewell to his uncle she handed him, with a deep blush and a look of entreaty, a morocco-bound book. The Grand-Duchess laughed pleasantly.

"What, Lenchen, that absurd album of yours again?" she said. "Don't give yourself any trouble about it, Count, I beg of you. Every one spoils this child by being too kind to her."

"What is it, Cyril?" asked the Queen curiously, when they had reached their own *appartement*. Cyril flung the book on the table with a groan, and his wife and Usk laughed when they saw that it was lettered "Confession Album."

"What is there about me that impels romantic little girls to let me in for things of this sort?" he demanded. "I thought Philippa said that these wretched books had gone out years ago, but it seems some malignant cousin brought your niece this one from England, and my feelings are to be butchered to make a holiday for her."

"Poor little Lenchen!" sighed the Queen. "I am glad you were kind to her, Cyril."

"Ah, poor little girl! If Michael was her last chance of escape from Ivan Petrovitch, I'm afraid it's a bad look-out."

"He took pains to show that he was not at all attracted to her," said the Queen, in a low voice. "I suppose it was as well to make it plain, but——"

"The unfortunate parents were doubly snubbed," said Cyril. "It was quite clear that Ivan Petrovitch saw he would only be welcomed as a son-in-law if Michael disappointed them, and he showed his resentment by arriving late. I don't envy his future relations-in-law, I must say."

"The poor little girl herself hates him," said Usk.

Cyril looked up quickly. "Did she confide that to you? Confidences of that sort are dangerous. It is discreet to forget them at once."

"I'm not likely to hand it on to the Grand-Duke Ivan, at any rate. And talking of confidences, the Princess of Dardania seems to have been indulging in a good many this afternoon."

"On matrimonial matters? So we heard. Perhaps you don't know that she was asked to join the family dinner-party, and refused on account of the company she would meet—otherwise you and me?"

"No," said the Queen calmly; "she could not bring herself to meet me."

"My dear Ernestine—your own cousin! Ah, I see. Because you had degraded yourself by stooping to me—was that it?"

The Queen looked at him searchingly. "Raised myself, rather," she said. "Yes, that is no doubt the reason, Cyril."

"I see the book Nicholson wanted has come. I think I'll take it in to him and see how he is," said Usk, who felt himself slightly *de trop*. From his brother-in-law Mansfield he had gathered the idea that the Princess Dowager of Dardania would at one time not have scorned to marry Cyril herself, but he knew his uncle well enough to be certain that no word would ever pass his lips on the subject.

"Ottilie is determined that Michael shall marry Sonya," said the Queen, when he had gone out.

"Yes; it was considerate of her to call and quench any hopes that the poor Schwarzwald-Molzaus might be cherishing. I shall be curious to see if she tries anything of the kind upon Félicia."

"I don't think she would regard her as a serious rival to Sonya."

"Then she would be very much mistaken. The Grand-Duke took the hint I managed to give him far better than I expected. If his own daughter had married Michael, it would not have solved our difficulties at all, for there would still be the money to be found. Little Helene won't have more than a few thousands, at the outside, and her father sees the difficulty. He will make Michael introduce him to Félicia, and will watch her for a day or two before he takes any decided step. And Félicia is the kind of girl who will appeal to him by her very audacity. She will surprise and amuse him, and calmly ignore his prejudices when that unfortunate little Helene would be cowering in terror."

"Cyril, did it strike you? If we could get rid of Ivan Petrovitch, there is Usk. Of course, I mean if Michael insists on marrying Félicia."

"Usk marry Helene? My dear Ernestine, may I ask you to keep that idea to yourself? If it came to pass, I should never leave Europe alive."

"Cyril, what do you mean? What difference could it make?"

"Simply that I should have become too powerful. You know me as I really am, dearest, a broken-down cobbler, patching things clumsily together. But to Scythia, which means Soudaroff, I am a plotter of the most dangerous type, at the head of a widespread conspiracy for establishing myself as ruler of Palestine, and bent on strengthening my position by royal alliances. You know, and I know, that when we quit Europe it will be to return to Sitt Zeynab and not leave it again, but end our days there in peace, away from the politics which nowadays I can't touch without spoiling. But Soudaroff thinks, and very naturally too, after all the pains that have been taken to impress it upon him, that my leaving will be the sign for a desperate attempt—which he, knowing me as I was, believes will be successful—to oust the Scythian garrison from Jerusalem. If I have the additional support of the Schwarzwald-Molzau influence behind me, as he would infer if Usk was allowed to marry Helene, surely it is clear that his only chance is to put me out of the way?"

"Cyril, you terrify me. Let us leave things to settle themselves, and go back to the desert at once."

"No, no; we'll see the young folks out of the wood if we can. Though how we are to get things settled if Usk refuses to bring Félicia to book, I don't know."

Usk, in the meantime, had gone to Nicholson's rooms, and found the invalid sitting up in bed, his bright eyes looking ghastly by contrast with his hollow cheeks.

"Thought you'd be coming in," he said, "and I wouldn't lie down, for fear I should go to sleep, though Jenkins has been at me incessantly. Look here; I wanted to show you this."

He held out the page of a newspaper, which had the unfamiliar look peculiar to English printed with French type. It was one of the ephemeral society sheets which spring up once or twice a season in the larger health resorts, and after enjoying a brief *succès de scandale*, suddenly sink out of existence. Usk looked at the passage to which he pointed:—

"Tuesday's Carnival procession was quite the best and most fashionably attended of late years, and bearers of nearly every well-known name in Europe took part in it or were among the spectators. Observed of all observers were the 'Famille Pierrot en deuil,' comprising two ladies and two gentlemen attired in Pierrot costumes with deep black borders. The idea was most cleverly carried out, down to the black pompons which adorned the white sugar-loaf hats of the two Pierrettes; and universal admiration was attracted by the *abandon* with which the wearers threw themselves into all the fun of the occasion. It is whispered that one of the Pierrots was the youthful monarch of a Balkan State, whose whole-hearted gaiety has given great delight to Nice this season; and that the ladies were the fascinating

American tenants of one of the florally-named villas in the Croix de Marbre, whom he honours with a good deal of his society."

"Rather suggestive of your friends of the Villa Bougainvillea," chuckled Nicholson, coughing as he spoke.

"This thing ought to be prosecuted," said Usk wrathfully. "Or who edits it, do you know?"

"How can I tell? But you can't horsewhip a man for telling the truth."

"It's not true! Why——" Usk was happy again—"if they went, they were to go in mauve dominos. She—one of them—showed me the stuff."

"Of course she did! And what was to be under the dominos? They were only for driving. It was when your friends left their carriage that they would come out as full-blown Pierrettes."

"It's not true," repeated Usk, doggedly but hopelessly. "There's the book you wanted. Good-night."

Once more his mind was made up to force an explanation with Félicia. He had not been near the Villa Bougainvillea since receiving Mrs van Zyl's note on the day of the Carnival, for he had determined that Félicia owed him an apology, and that he would not move without it. Now, however, he felt he could rest no longer under this uncertainty. If Félicia had the smallest regard for him or his wishes, she would not have taken part in the Carnival at all; and if she had no regard for him, what prospect was there of their living happily together? It was with these thoughts in his mind that he made his way to the villa the next morning, as early as he thought Félicia would be likely to be up. To his astonishment he was ushered into the *salon*, where Mrs van Zyl greeted him with a severe expression of countenance.

"I don't know whether Félicia will receive you," she said coldly, when he had explained that he came to see Miss Steinherz, "but I will send and ask her, any way."

An awkward pause ensued, during which Usk endeavoured vainly to make conversation, wondering the while what was the reason for this treatment, and Mrs van Zyl eyed him as if he had been a convicted criminal. Presently, however, she was summoned to the door, and a whispered colloquy followed, which appeared to have a satisfactory result, for she went out, and Félicia entered the room. She seemed the embodiment of injured rectitude as she halted opposite Usk, and looked him over sternly.

"I guess you're come to apologise," she said at last.

"Nothing of the sort. I want an apology from you," broke out Usk.

"Do tell! You're the person to ask for apologies, aren't you?"

"Exactly, and I mean to have one."

"Am I to apologise because you broke your appointment, and haven't been around for two whole days?"

"Considering that you broke the appointment through Mrs van Zyl, and went to the Carnival, which you had promised you wouldn't do, I scarcely thought you would care to see me."

"And if I told you that Sadie wrote you just to test you, and that I was waiting for you here all of Tuesday afternoon, what then?"

"I should ask who the two American ladies were from this house who were at the Carnival with King Michael."

"I guess Sadie and Maimie are just as good Americans as I am," said Félicia languidly. "Well!" she cried, with sudden fire, "if I told you all that what would you do?"

"I should accept your word, of course."

"Oh, how kind! how condescending! Well, then, I just won't tell you anything of the sort. You won't have any word to accept, do you see? and you can just do as you like."

"Félicia, you are not treating me fairly!" cried Usk, torn asunder with doubts. "Tell me you were not at the Carnival, and I will make any apology you please. You had no right to test me as you say, for I think I have passed the stage for that sort of thing, but if it was a test, I failed; I acknowledge that."

"This is a test, too," said Félicia calmly. "You promised to trust me, and I mean to see what your trust is worth. I have suggested an explanation, and if you don't choose to accept it, you can just go."

"Only tell me that you were not at the Carnival."

"I won't say a word. And you make out to love me!"

"And I do. If I leave off loving you, it will be because you have killed my love with your own hands. You know I love you, Fay. Could I bear the way you treat me if I didn't? Am I to stand all the tests and you none? Give me just that one assurance, and you won't repent it. I shall be bowed down with shame."

"I don't see but I'd better ring for Jacques to show you out," remarked Félicia conversationally, moving towards the bell.

"You don't care for me! You can't care for me!" cried Usk.

Félicia turned towards him again. "Solemnly, Usk, if I care for any one, I care for you, but I won't be treated that way. I must be trusted all in all, or not at all. If you can do it, say so, and stay."

Her hand was on the bell-rope. Her beautiful eyes looked sadly, entreatingly at him. There were tears ready to fall.

"I can! I do!" he cried. "Oh, Fay, you are cruel to me!"

"Cruel only to be kind," said Mrs van Zyl, entering the room just as Usk's arms were round Félicia. "I guess you're in again, Fay? You'll stay lunch, Lord Usk? We receive this afternoon."

The last piece of information was not particularly delightful to Usk, but he stayed, and was rewarded for abandoning his private judgment by many tender looks and caressing words from Félicia. A certain amount of triumph over Maimie was visible in her glance, and Usk guessed miserably that Maimie had prophesied he would not allow himself to be cajoled. Even now he felt horribly conscious that he did not believe in Félicia's explanation. He had yielded because at the moment the fear of losing her seemed intolerable, but his submission degraded him in his own eyes. All Félicia's endeavours to hide his chain with flowers were useless; she did not love him, and he did not trust her.

Matters were no better when Mrs van Zyl's guests arrived, and he had no longer to keep up the dreary pretence which Félicia insisted on treating as solid reality. He did his duty in helping to hand round tea and cake, finding seats for elderly ladies, and making up sets for croquet, but the company was not to his taste, although it was evident that Félicia found it very much to hers. Once more he noticed the change in her. At Llandiarmid she had been merely the shadow of her real self, perversely critical or genuinely languid, but now she had recovered the health and good spirits which had been so noticeable before her father's death. The well preserved, tightly buttoned, barons and counts who owed allegiance to the other American women present crowded round her, and competed for her smiles with rival sallies of wit, and the weary cosmopolitans forgot to talk of such an one's score and some one else's bad luck. She held her court among them, listening to their deftly turned compliments with an indifference which was almost contemptuous, until the splendid eyes would all at once be lifted lazily, and a comment be uttered—sometimes only a single word—which set all her hearers laughing. She could hold her own with ease even when her indifference piqued them all to unite against her. Still reclining with half-veiled eyes in her hammock, she would annihilate half her assailants at once with a single sally, and then dispose of the rest by a few crisp sentences in succession. It was perfect, Usk saw. No wonder these fellows were attracted and amused, and yet—and yet—what was to be the outcome of it all? Was it possible for Félicia—even if she ever intended to marry him—to be happy as his wife? Morbidly awake now to her methods and aims, he found no pleasure in the fact that King Michael had not put in an appearance all day, but rather a reason for her restoration of himself to favour. In spite of his protestations to his uncle, he was occupying now the most degraded of all positions, that of a stalking-horse employed to pique the other man into renewing his attentions.

CHAPTER XII.
MURDERED FAITH.

"WE really ought to buy something at the refreshment-stall," said the Grand-Duchess; "but what is one to do with cakes in a hotel?"

"We might have tea here instead," said Queen Ernestine. "Usk, perhaps you can find us a table in a quiet corner?"

A bazaar was being held on behalf of some object connected with the English church, and the Queen, escorted by Usk, had met the Grand-Duchess of Schwarzwald-Molzau and her daughter making the round of the stalls. One of the lady members of the committee, who was hovering at the Queen's heels with the view of directing her attention to the most desirable, and expensive, articles on each stall, heard the remark about tea, and appeared suddenly in front of the party, her whole aspect eloquent of a desire to be addressed.

"Perhaps you can help us, Miss Waverley?" said the Queen, with a smile. "We should like to find a table a little more private than this one."

"I can show you the very place, Ma'am," replied Miss Waverley breathlessly. "There is a little nook here where your Majesty can see all that goes on without being seen, if your—if the gentleman will just help me to move this table."

"Which of us is anxious to see all that is to be seen?" asked the Queen, as Miss Waverley hurried away to order the tea. "I think it must be you, Helene. Sit here, dear, where you can watch the people. Do put those parcels on the floor, Usk, and sit down."

"I'm trying to decide whether Miss Waverley takes me for your equerry or your footman," said Usk. "In either case she will be very much scandalised if she catches me sitting down. I think I had better receive the things from her and present them. Does your Majesty wish to be served on the knee?"

"I wish you to sit down in the place that is left for you, and to amuse the Princess Helene while her mother and I have a talk."

"Ma'am, I obey," and Usk took the seat pointed out to him. "How will your Grand-Ducal Highness please to be amused?" he asked of Helene.

"Why are you talking in this way? It is not at all like you," she said wearily, and he noticed that the pale little face looked thinner, and that the eyes were heavy. "Why should you make this pretence?"

"Because the world is full of pretence, and we can't get away from it," he answered, bitterly enough. Her eyes sought his face in a moment.

"Oh, I am sorry," she said quickly. "I ought to have known that there was something wrong. I see it in your eyes."

"I had rather not talk about it, if you don't mind. But I might say the same thing to you. Something has gone wrong, hasn't it?"

"Ivan Petrovitch has found out that I call him the Tartar, and papa is so angry. He made me apologise to him."

"And how did he take it?"

"Oh, as one would expect. He only said smoothly, 'I hope the Princess Helene will think better of me when she has more opportunity of judging,' but his voice made me shiver. What did he mean?"

"Well, you know," said Usk, as her eyes met his again with that look of horror in them, "I told you——"

"Don't say you told me it was a foolish thing to do. I know it, but I am quite unhappy enough without that." She sat looking out between the draperies which shaded their corner, but her eyes seemed to see nothing of the gay room and the busy people. Then she turned suddenly to Usk again. "I am very rude and absent of mind," she said. "You must forgive me, please. I wanted to tell you that I saw your beautiful lady yesterday."

"Miss Steinherz?" growled Usk.

"Who else could it be? She is very, very beautiful, and her beauty is uncommon—original—how shall I say it?—witchlike?—oh no, that has a bad meaning in English, has it not? Spirit-like? ah, that is it. She is an Undine—before she had found her soul, of course."

"Why do you say 'of course'?" asked Usk. Helene started.

"Oh, I beg your pardon. What could I have been thinking of? Please forgive me, I ought not to have said such a thing. It was merely a silly thought of mine. Do forget it, please."

"I think it was the truth," said Usk bitterly. "At least, if she has a soul, I have not found it, but I don't think she has."

"Oh, don't say that. She is so beautiful."

"Judge for yourself. I have fought against it a long time, but now it is forced upon me. She does not love me, and only tolerates me near her to make another man jealous."

"Oh no, no!" Her tone was sharp with pain. "You love her, and yet you can say this to me—almost a stranger!"

"I have not dared to say it to myself before, but it's better to face it," was the stubborn reply. "I oughtn't to sadden you with it, I know, but I can't talk to my uncle and aunt about it."

"It will not sadden me, if I can help you. See, you have misunderstood Miss Steinherz, have you not? She conceals her love, perhaps, she is shy and proud? Perhaps even she coquets with you; she shows kindness to another suitor for the sake of teasing you? That is foolish, it is even wrong; but the heart is there, and loves you. You do not understand women very much, perhaps? So often they think it undignified, unwise, to let the love they truly have be seen. That is it, is it not? not—not what you say. A good woman could not act in that way, and she must be a good woman if you have chosen her to love out of all the world."

"I wish I could think so!" said Usk, in a tone of such misery that Helene's eyes filled with tears.

"Oh, if only I could help you!" she said. "I can only pray—pray that the good God will show you her heart full of love for you, that you may learn how you have misjudged her. Think how you will be obliged to humble yourself before her when you discover the truth!"

"I shouldn't mind that," said Usk, with the ghost of a smile.

"I'm afraid our tea-party won't add very largely to the profits of the refreshment-stall," said the Grand-Duchess. "I think we have eaten one cake of five centimes between us. Lenchen, darling, you are over-tired. Eat one of these cream-cakes, to please me."

"I can't, mamma. I am not hungry."

"I can give them a five-franc piece, if you like, madame," suggested Usk, "and ask them to add the change to their profits."

"Ah, that is a good idea. And if you see our *chasseur*, Lord Usk, perhaps you will kindly tell him to call up the carriage."

Neither Queen Ernestine nor Usk spoke much as they returned to the hotel, for both were thinking of the conversation at the tea-table; but as soon as Usk had put down his parcels, and betaken himself to Nicholson's rooms, the Queen turned impulsively to her husband.

"Oh, Cyril," she said, "they are going to sacrifice that poor child!"

"Little Helene? Is it all settled?"

"They have not told her yet, but I can't help thinking that she begins to perceive the truth. There is a look in her eyes——"

"But why doesn't the Grand-Duchess break it to her, and let her have time to get accustomed to the idea?"

"She is afraid. The child has such a horror of Ivan Petrovitch that Adelheid thinks it would nearly kill her. She has always been so delicate, you know."

"But it will be much worse, surely, if it comes upon her suddenly?"

"So I should think, but I can see that Adelheid is afraid both of Ivan Petrovitch and her husband. Ludwig is bent upon the marriage. He has never cared very much for Helene; she has always been her mother's child. And he thinks he sees the romantic strain coming out in her."

"No doubt of that, I should say. It is really curious how it reappears once or twice in a generation."

"Yes; and Ludwig can never forget his cousin Ernest Albrecht, who died long ago. He was originally intended to marry Adelheid, you know, but they allowed him, after years of waiting, to resign his rank and betroth himself to dear Sister Chriemhild at Brutli. Ludwig is determined never to allow anything of the kind while he is head of the family."

"Still, he might find the girl a more attractive husband of her own rank than that unspeakable Scythian. Has the Grand-Duchess pointed that out to him?"

"Ah, but Ivan Petrovitch is also determined upon the match. I hope I don't misjudge him, Cyril—or rather I hope I do, for Helene's sake—but it seems to me that he sees the child's horror of him, and enjoys it. It gives him actual pleasure to play upon her sensitive nature, and watch the torture it inflicts upon her."

"Pah! it makes one sick!" said Cyril, rising hastily, and walking up and down the room. "But what can we do, Ernestine? We can't interfere to prevent a marriage which the girl's own parents have arranged."

"I thought you might be able to think of something."

"Nothing would be any good, except to provide a more eligible suitor, and where is he to be found? You could hardly wish me to make definite proposals on Usk's behalf when he has no eyes for any one but Félicia?"

"No, certainly not. Besides, Ludwig would not think him at all eligible. I only wish he might. It is wonderful how Helene has taken to him. She seems to open out like a flower in the sunshine. Adelheid was quite delighted at first, but to-day she asked me to arrange that they should not meet much. She is afraid that Ludwig might think they were falling in love."

"Really these complications seem hopeless. I suppose Usk will see before long that Félicia is simply fooling him, but I don't in the least think he will turn to Helene for consolation. He will be very hard hit."

"And the woman who treats him in this way will marry Michael!"

"Well, if she jilts Usk for him, we must infer that she loves Michael," said Cyril drily.

"Loves his crown, perhaps. But that is uncharitable. Still, what hope can there be of her exercising a good influence over him? Oh, Cyril, isn't it terrible to see everything going wrong around one, and not to be able to put it right?"

"I thought you believed that, after all, things were better managed than you could arrange them yourself?"

"I know. I am wrong to be so faithless. But one cannot see how all this is to end."

Usk walked away from the Villa Bougainvillea with bent head and compressed lips, and crossing the Avénue de la Gare, took the direction of the Cornice Road. Félicia had befooled him once more. It was arranged that he should come to the Villa at a certain time in the afternoon, as he had done each day since their reconciliation, more with the object of asserting his rights than because he felt any special pleasure in Félicia's society. To-day, as he approached the house, he had caught a distant glimpse of a motor-car dashing off in the opposite direction, and it was hardly with surprise that he heard the servant say that madame and mademoiselle were not at home. There was a meaning look in the man's eyes, and for a moment Usk thought of asking him where the ladies were. But he rejected with disgust the idea of bribing a servant to spy upon Félicia, and moreover, there in the drive were the marks of the wheels of the automobile, conclusive evidence. Conscious that the man was watching his face with malicious interest, he remarked merely that he would look in again later, and walked slowly down the steps with head erect. But when he was out of sight of the door, he gave up the pretence, and his pace quickened insensibly. He must walk on and on until he was away from every one, and could think over this last treachery and all that it implied.

Crowded streets and close-set houses, villas in gardens, desolate building-land with straggling beginnings of avenues and terraces here and there—they were all passed at last, and he was breasting the slope of the mountain. Past the Observatory, up a farther ascent, and he came upon a quiet spot enough, though four roads met there. He left the road and plunged into the wilderness of low scented bushes, hating the perfume they gave out as he crashed through them. Mounting a hillock, he found a spot bare of bushes, and flung himself on the turf, invisible to any one passing along the road. For a time he could only lie there writhing in impotent passion, digging his feet into the ground, and tearing up handfuls of grass and tiny flowers and flinging them away. The instinct of destruction was strong upon him. He loathed the beauties round him and the beauty outspread in front—the long slopes clad in every shade of green, grey-green of olives, light-green of carob, dark-green of orange and lemon-trees, bright-green of pistachio, stretching down to the almost painful blue of the sea, from which the eye sought relief gladly in the white of the town opposite and the grey of the castle crowning the hill above the harbour. It gave him no pleasure, even when the breeze ruffled the olives suddenly into silver, and revealed gleams of gold among the orange-groves. He hated the whole prospect for its very beauty. It was like Félicia, beautiful, changeful, cruel.

After a time the keenness of the pain which possessed him became a little dulled, and he found himself resolving upon his future course. To depart at once from Nice, leaving a scathing letter of farewell for Félicia, was the plan which suggested itself first, but it was obviously incomplete. He had realised now that he had nothing to hope for from her in the way either of justice or tenderness, and it would be a mistake to allow her to declare that he had gone away in a fit of jealousy without giving her a chance of explaining matters. No, he must see her again, distasteful as the thought was. She would try, no doubt, to entangle him again in her sophistries, to wind him round with that net of cajolery into which he had walked with his eyes open, but this time it would be in vain. Never in his life had he felt so miserable, so degraded, as during the past week, when Félicia had been everything that was tender and affectionate. He had deteriorated morally since he had condoned her faithlessness for the sake of her beauty and her fascinations, but he was not the man to regard such deterioration with equanimity. He would free himself from the toils and turn his back upon Félicia for ever, returning to England wiser, if poorer, robbed, as it seemed, of one whole side of his life. He had no doubt as to his own course, but he must make it clear to Félicia that he was leaving her finally—must place the issues before her so plainly that she could not evade them or wriggle out of her responsibility.

How this was to be done was the question. The moral agony through which he had passed seemed to have blunted his mental powers. His reasonings ended abruptly, as though he had come suddenly to a blank wall or fallen from a height; and though he struggled with himself, he could not arrive at any decision. He was still lying on the turf, utterly spent, his hands gripping the clods he had torn up, when a voice behind him said, "Lord Usk!"

He turned angrily and sprang to his feet, enraged that any one should have observed him in this dark hour. Behind him stood a tall lady very elaborately dressed in black. Her face, with its strongly marked features and dark eyes, was handsome, though worn, and her abundant black hair was still without a thread of grey. Usk knew her well. She was the Princess Dowager of Dardania, who had shown a good deal of interest in his sister Philippa and himself two years since at Ludwigsbad.

"I must apologise for intruding upon you," said the Princess, as he stood speechless, "but I saw you from my windows—with a telescope,"—she pointed to a house just discernible among the trees on one of the upper slopes,—"and I ventured to follow you. Perhaps you would not mind coming a little lower down the hill? There is a spot where we can be quite sheltered from observation, and I should not like the dear young friend for whose sake I am here to know what I had done."

Usk obeyed in silence. Speech seemed to have forsaken him, and he could only follow the Princess, and sit down on the turf opposite her, as her gesture invited him to do.

"We need not beat about the bush," she said. "You, like me, have a particular interest just now in King Michael of Thracia,—I because his fickleness is breaking the heart of the dear girl who is my one comfort, you because he has chosen for the time being to set his affections upon your *fiancée*."

Usk bowed, and opened his lips to speak, but the Princess held up her hand.

"Wait, if you please. I sympathise with you sincerely, but chiefly for reasons with which you are not at present acquainted. Bad as his conduct is, Michael is not wholly to blame. He is inspired by others, who have taken advantage of his weakness of character to serve their own ends. Don't interrupt me," as Usk, who began to see whither this was tending, raised his head again, "but listen. The whole affair is the work of your uncle, Count Mortimer. I don't say that he is working for his own aggrandisement in any vulgar sense, but with his incurable instinct of intrigue, he has seen how to reap advantage from Michael's inconstancy."

"Before you go any further, madame," said Usk firmly, "I may as well tell you that nothing you can say will make me doubt my uncle's good faith."

An angry shadow crossed the Princess's face. "Perhaps you will at least have the politeness to hear what I have to say before you decline to believe it," she said. "I am doing Count Mortimer all possible justice, and distinguishing him absolutely from the common herd of adventurers, when I say that the prospect of securing Miss Steinherz's millions in his own family had no charms for him. It was much too simple and obvious. But when the preposterous claim which the young lady has chosen to put forward came to his knowledge, then he saw an opening for his peculiar talents. You do not need me to tell you that Miss Steinherz's claim is utterly hopeless, judged by the family laws of the houses both of Albret and Hohenstaufen. The marriage in London is invalid on the face of it, and of the asserted marriage at Vindobona not a single witness has come forward. Even if it could be proved to have taken place, it was invalid without the sanction of the Emperor and the King of Cantabria, as well as of the Pope. But strange things are sometimes done in the name of expediency, and your uncle thinks that for the sake of her millions Miss Steinherz might possibly be admitted into a family which is in chronic want of money, to settle a difficulty which demands large sums. Here, then, is the state of the case. Michael, engaged to my dear Sonya, whose dowry would put an end to all his difficulties, is deliberately exposed to the charms of Miss Steinherz, who is betrothed to you, and he succumbs, but cannot marry her since she is not of royal blood. Now steps in Count Mortimer. To provide Michael with a bride of German descent, and furnish the needed money without expense to the Three Powers, will give him a claim on their gratitude, which is just what he needs for the furtherance of his private ends. Your love, your interests, have no part in his scheme. He does not broach his idea until Miss Steinherz's claim has been definitely rejected by the house of Albret, and then he approaches the Emperor, his constant patron in the past. The Grand-Duke of Schwarzwald-Molzau is sent to report on the affair. You have wondered, perhaps, why King Michael has absented himself for nearly a week from the Villa Bougainvillea, while you have been received there. It was simply because the Grand-Duke was sending his report to Vindobona, and waiting for the answer. To-day it has arrived, and he is authorised to see Miss Steinherz and find out what extent of recognition will satisfy her. You have still time, but only just time, to put an end to the affair. If Miss Steinherz is satisfied with the acknowledgment that her father was morganatically married, she will receive no more, naturally, and Michael cannot marry her. If she stood alone she would not get that; but in view of her betrothal to you, I think it might be conceded. But the idea is that the marriage shall be retrospectively recognised as fully legal, and the girl raised by letters-patent to the status of a Princess of Arragon; and things have gone so far now that you can only prevent this through your uncle."

"And how is that to be worked, madame?"

"Go straight to Count Mortimer, and tell him"—her nostrils dilated, and there was something tigerish about her mouth—"that every detail of his plot for establishing himself in Palestine is in my hands. I know of everything, down to the penny subscription among the poorest of those he has deluded to purchase a crown and royal robes for the 'Prince of the Captivity,' as they call him. The whole proceedings at every meeting of the conspirators are reported to me, their agents are known and followed everywhere. If he renounces this marriage project of his I will take no further steps. When Michael marries Sonya I can afford to laugh at Count Mortimer and his puny tricks in the East. But if he goes on I will hand over all my information immediately to Prince Soudaroff, and he may guess how much hope he has of success, even of safety, after that. There is my message, which will restore happiness to you, and also to the poor girl who is breaking her heart for Michael. Will you deliver it?"

"I will deliver it to Count Mortimer, madame."

"You exhibit no superabundant gratitude, Lord Usk. Surely if I restore you your bride and her fortune, and also give you the opportunity of saving your uncle from the consequences of his own imprudence, I deserve thanks, at least?"

Usk smiled involuntarily. It did not seem to strike the Princess that he could have any hesitation in marrying Félicia, although Félicia was moving heaven and earth to enable her to marry King Michael. Probably her fortune was expected to obviate any distaste he might feel.

"Surely, madame, success and the applause of your own conscience would be reward enough?"

"Your uncle has been speaking against me!" she cried angrily.

"Indeed, madame, I have never heard him express anything but the highest possible admiration for your talents."

"You are too polite. It would be well not to imitate your uncle too closely in his cleverness, lest you should do so also in his fate. Is it allowable to ask what you intend to do about Miss Steinherz?"

"I have not made up my mind, madame. But I shall not forget to deliver your message. May I have the honour of escorting you home?"

She declined the offer with a gesture, and, descending into the road, walked slowly towards the house in the trees, while Usk turned his steps again towards Nice. This new information gave him the crowning test of which he had vaguely felt the need. After all, it was just possible that Félicia might even now care for him enough to decide in his favour rather than lose him altogether, and she should determine matters for herself. The hour of struggle on the hill-top had not been wasted, for he had made his decision. He would not be her slave any longer.

Félicia gave a little scream when he was suddenly announced at the Villa. She was in a small upstairs sitting-room, which was sacred to her and Maimie, and she was wearing a black gown with white ruffles, which gave her a most incongruously Puritan look. Usk's lip curled in spite of himself as he saw that her hair was dressed to correspond with the gown, for it was evident that she was ready to receive the Grand-Duke. Maimie, no doubt, had suggested the pose, so well carried out, of the daughter only lately bereaved, turning wistfully for consolation to her dead father's family. Usk himself knew too much to be anything but an intruder at this moment.

"I wasn't just expecting you," Félicia gasped.

"I won't stay unless you wish it," he returned. "If you will just tell me whether you intend to marry King Michael or me, I shall know whether to go or not."

"But I can't tell you right now," objected Félicia, taken aback, "because—why——"

"Because you don't know. You'll marry Michael if you can get him, and if not, then you'll put up with me. But I don't care for being put up with, and if you mean to think of Michael still, I will go."

"Well, then, you're just horrid!" cried Félicia angrily. "I guess I've told you 'most a dozen times that I like you best, but if I'm a princess I must marry according to my rank."

"Won't do, Fay. If you stick to me I'll stick to you, princess or no princess; but if not, I prefer to depart now rather than later."

There were genuine tears in Félicia's eyes. "You won't understand, Usk," she said, "and I don't see but it must seem strange to you. I don't pretend to be romantic—American girls aren't generally that, I guess—but I like you, really. If they reject my claim after all, I'll just settle down real happily with you, and you'll forget all of this."

"And if they acknowledge it, you'll settle down happily with me all the same?"

Félicia looked down. "I guess I won't just have things in my own hands then," she said.

"Oh yes, you will, if you choose. If you're engaged to me, I'll take good care that you don't marry any one else."

"You don't know the temptation of a crown, Usk," said Félicia softly.

"I know my father tried it, and was jolly glad to give it up."

"Oh, your father!" The tone was eloquent. "But for me, Usk!"

"Very well; if you prefer your crown, say so, and I'll go."

"You're real tiresome, fussing me like this. Do just wait a little."

"Not another hour," said Usk.

"Say, Fay!" Maimie burst into the room, "come right down; the Grand-Duke's here. Don't stop to prink. That gown is just distracting already."

"Now, Fay, decide," said Usk. "If you make up your mind to stick to me, it's natural for me to be with you when you receive the Grand-Duke, and to explain to him that we are engaged. If you tell me you don't want me to be there, I shall know you are giving me up."

"Do tell!" cried Maimie. "Who asked you to make conditions, Lord Usk? Send him off right away, Fay."

"You said you cared for me," urged Usk. Félicia wavered.

"Félicia Steinherz, if you give in now I'm done with you," said Maimie, and Félicia unhooked Usk's ring from her bangle, and threw it at him.

"I just hate you both!" she cried; "but I've concluded which to choose."

CHAPTER XIII.
MALA SORTE.

"Is that you, Usk? Come in. Why, what's gone wrong?"

"Félicia and I have broken it off. I thought you'd be glad to know."

"I am interested to hear it. You broke it off, I hope?"

"I suppose you would say it was done by mutual consent," said Usk drearily. "I told her to choose between the King and me, and she chose him."

"I am glad she has made a definite choice, at any rate," said his uncle. "Hard hit, Usk? What do you mean to do."

"Leave this to-morrow, unless you or Aunt Ernestine want me for anything."

"Why, where are you off to?"

"Only to London. My father will be busy with this Bill of his, and I daresay I can help him a little."

"Right. Throw yourself into it. Work as hard as you can. But don't you think such a sudden departure will seem a little marked?"

"I don't know. I can't help it." Usk wondered why his uncle was looking at him with such a curious, meditative gaze. "I couldn't stay here and meet them every day."

"I suppose not. The natural instinct is to hide yourself, no doubt. But don't give way to it more than you can help. It'll soon wear off, and you will find some one who will compensate you for everything."

"Never!" said Usk, so tragically that Cyril only restrained a smile with difficulty. "I may marry, to please my father and mother, but I can never feel again to any woman as I have done to Félicia."

"Don't be too sure. Why, if you stayed on here for a day or two, you might even find your heart caught at the rebound almost at once."

"If you knew how I have loved and—and believed in Félicia, you wouldn't say that—and I thought she loved me. How could I ever trust a woman again who said she cared for me? I believe these French marriages are better, after all. If you don't love a woman, it can't hurt so much when she plays you false."

"My dear Usk, you will allow me to say that you are talking very great and very youthful nonsense. But I will remember your partiality for arranged marriages, and possibly I may be able to gratify you at some future time. And don't make sweeping statements about women, because that only shows how young you are. You are prejudiced just now."

"Prejudiced? I should think I was!" laughed Usk fiercely. "Why, as I came home just now, I couldn't see a fellow walking with a girl without wanting to call out to him that she was making a fool of him."

"You had better go back to London, certainly, and forswear female society for the present. It would be brutal to inflict you on any unfortunate girl while you are in this state of mind. Your aunt will agree with me, though we shall miss you."

"Oh, but there's another thing!" cried Usk, with sudden recollection. "Don't you think you had better come home too? The Princess of Dardania came and spoke to me this afternoon, and gave me a message for you. She wants the King to marry the girl she's got staying with her, you know, and she says if you don't let him do it, she'll tell Prince Soudaroff all your plans."

"Well, she ought to know by this time that Michael will marry to please himself, and not either her or me."

"Yes; but she thinks you can keep him from marrying Félicia, at any rate."

"I see; you were to warn me and have Félicia back? But you went to her first."

"It didn't seem to strike the Princess that I might prefer her to marry Michael if she wanted him. I didn't need a bribe to warn you. She says that all your arrangements are known to her as soon as they are made, and that she has agents at all your meetings, and that your life is in danger."

"And you remembered what I told you at Llandiarmid, and wisely concluded that the matter was not pressing? Quite right. The Princess knows only of the sham plot, not of the real one. At all the headquarters it is arranged who is to act as her tool, and provide her with carefully edited reports—a sort of bogus information-bureau for her special benefit. She has not the faintest idea that the plot to establish me in Palestine is really one to establish Malasorte in Neustria. To make things safe, in case any genuine spies should be present, he is always spoken of as Mortimer, and Neustria as Palestine, and so on—in fact, there is a regular code. So you see she is quite at fault."

"But you're only thinking of your schemes, and I'm thinking of you. If she and Prince Soudaroff believe in the bogus plot, it's just as dangerous for you as if it was genuine. I don't believe you're safe anywhere but in England or at Sitt Zeynab."

"Why, what should she do—burn the hotel down, or kidnap me? Paschics and Dietrich and I keep a very good look-out, I can assure you. If I believed there was actual danger, do you think I would expose my wife to it?"

"But why not come to England?"

"And leave Michael's affairs to go wrong again? Now that we have eliminated you, as I wished, I hope to set them right before very long. No, don't be afraid; I shall do my work."

"If you had seen her face when she spoke of you——"

"My dear Usk, I don't doubt her will to ruin me body and soul, but merely her power. If she had me anywhere in the wilds of Dardania, now, with a few half-Roumi retainers within call—but she hasn't, and if I can help it, she won't get the chance. That's enough."

Thus dismissed, Usk carried to Queen Ernestine the news of his approaching departure, and noticed that she looked at him with the same anxious, questioning glance as his uncle. She said nothing, however, save to agree that it was better he should go, and he went to tell Nicholson, who was quite prepared to make a personal grievance out of the announcement.

"I'm awfully sorry," said Usk, when a fit of coughing had forced the invalid to desist from his animadversions upon the vile selfishness which was about to deprive him of the only man he knew in this wretched place, "but I really can't stay. You see, I—I—— Well, I didn't know you liked seeing me so much, but I tell you what I'll do. I'll ask my aunt to come and see you sometimes, and that'll be much better."

"Oh, don't alter your plans for me," muttered Nicholson frigidly. "If your aunt cares to come in, I shall be thankful, and if she doesn't, I shan't be surprised. I shan't long be a bother to any one, but I never thought you would go and leave me out here like this."

Usk felt somewhat guilty, but he reflected that, after all, he had not brought Nicholson to Nice, and that his visits had never seemed to give him any particular pleasure. At any rate, he could not bring himself to alter his determination, for the whole aspect of the place was hateful to him now. He thought of London mud and fog with absolute yearning, feeling that this sunlit white and green town with its fringing blue sea could never be anything but a loathed memory in future. Idleness was intolerable, and such sports as the Riviera afforded were not much better. Work was his only hope—to plunge into it, bury himself in it, and thus to forget the dazzling, disquieting, bitterly disappointing experiences of the past few months. Therefore he remained immovable, and, in spite of Nicholson's fretful objections, insisted on bringing the Queen to see him the next day. Nicholson was too ill now to be conscious of the awed satisfaction that the rank of his visitor would have caused him in his days of health, but the gracious kindness which had conquered so many hearts did not fail of its effect with him; and when the Queen had promised to visit him every day, and talk to him a little if he was well enough, he was quite ready to let Usk go. Thus relieved of his chief anxiety, Usk had time to make a farewell call on the Grand-Duke and Duchess, neither of whom he saw, and then applied himself to the preparations for his journey.

Late in the afternoon he was on his way to the station, alone, by his own wish, when he found that his rug had been left behind, and sent his driver back for it, himself walking on to get his ticket. Presently a carriage drew up just beyond him, and a resplendent *chasseur* came to say that the Grand-Duchess of Schwarzwald-Molzau would be glad to speak to him if he could spare her a moment. When he reached the carriage, the Grand-Duchess insisted on giving him a lift to the station, and talked volubly of the loss his absence would prove to his uncle and aunt.

"And, indeed, we shall all be so sorry to lose you—shan't we, Lenchen?" she turned suddenly to her daughter, who had sat silent hitherto, leaning back wearily in her place. It struck Usk that if her face had looked thin the other day, it was now actually pinched and drawn, and he wondered whether it could be merely the afternoon light filtering through the fresh foliage of the plane-trees which made her look so ghastly. Her lips seemed to be moving, but she roused herself with a start at her mother's appeal, and Usk felt that there was strong entreaty in the eyes which met his through her veil as she answered—

"Yes, we shall all be very sorry."

Usk felt vaguely uncomfortable. What could she want him to do? She had blushed violently when his intent gaze showed that he had read her look, and would not meet his eye again; but when the station was reached, and he bade her good-bye, he surprised that piteous glance once more. It haunted him for some time, until at last he thought he had found a clue to it.

"They're worrying her to marry that brute Ivan Petrovitch, and she wanted to have another talk, and relieve her feelings," he said to himself. "It's awfully hard on her, poor little girl! but the Grand-Duchess is a good-natured old lady, and won't let her be badgered into accepting him if she really dislikes him. What a world it is! One can't marry the woman he wants, and another is tormented to marry a man she doesn't want. The pater and mater won't tease me to get married, but I know they'd be awfully pleased if I did—some nice good little girl with nothing baffling or exciting about her, whose mind I could read like a book. There are those two Jones girls, now, the mater would like one of them—be quite her right hand in pauperising the estate. But I don't a bit know which of them is which, and yet they must be quite different, of course. It'll have to depend upon which of them I come across first. No, I really think one might study them a little, even in making a sacrifice of oneself, just to see which was most suitable. But to have the Reverend Goronwy for a father-in-law! Why, he'd be always about the Castle. The mater wouldn't like that. I think we must get him moved to a distance before doing anything serious. That's a respite, anyhow. If the mater is very miserable about me, I can tell her I'm thinking of one of the Jones girls, and she'll be pleased. But I never want to see a girl again. Hope the Trade will move heaven and earth against the Bill, so that we may have a rousing time. Only wish it was the Commons—I do bar the Lords."

"Exit Viscount Usk!" said Maimie, and read aloud from the paper she was scanning: "'Viscount Usk left Nice for England on Wednesday. During the present parliamentary session he will act as private secretary to his father, the Marquis of Caerleon, to whom, as a leading light of the Temperance party, it has fallen to pilot the Anti-Tied-Houses Bill through the House of Lords.' That ends a chapter, Fay."

"Well, I hope you're right happy now. You've destroyed the one chance I had of being a good woman, and don't you forget it."

"I didn't know you had aspirations that way; but I guess Lady Caerleon would receive you with open arms even now if you went back to her properly penitent."

"Not I—but I wish I cared for Usk either more or less. If I didn't care for him, I wouldn't mind his going; and if I was really in love with him, I wouldn't have had him go."

"You don't care for him," said Maimie decisively. "If you did, a crown wouldn't have tempted you. You just felt sort of safe with him, knowing that he would be kind and fair all the time, whatever you might do. And just tell me what would have happened if I hadn't helped you get rid of him? When the Grand-Duke said he understood you were betrothed to the son of the Marquis of Caerleon, and that in view of such an honourable alliance the Emperor might be willing to acknowledge your father as morganatically married, and give you a patent of nobility—didn't that show you where you stood? You were on the very point of losing everything. If we hadn't been able to tell him that there had been some thought of such a thing once, but you had broken it off because Usk objected to your pressing the claim, you'd have been just simply left!"

"That's so," responded Félicia. "It's as well to be through with it, any way. I love that old Grand-Duke—he's a real nice man." The liking was mutual, although Félicia had said things to the Grand-Duke which would have made Helene's hair stand on end with horror if she had heard them. "But I can't just see why he don't have his wife and daughter call on us."

"Why, it isn't advisable yet. They can't treat you as a princess before you are one, and they'd think you wouldn't just choose to be treated as a no-account person. Say, Fay! she's betrothed—that little plain girl." Maimie was still glancing over the paper. "Do you remember the evil-looking Scythian that was riding in the Grand-Duchess's carriage yesterday—the dark man with the beard? That's the happy man. 'A marriage has been arranged, and will take place at Molzau shortly after Easter, between the Grand-Duke Ivan Petrovitch of Scythia and the Princess Helene, youngest and only unmarried daughter of the Grand-Duke and Duchess of Schwarzwald-Molzau.'"

"Shortly after Easter? Then we won't see it!" cried Félicia. "I do think these folks might hustle things a little. To keep me waiting months this way, and not even let me stay here, is just horrid!"

"But the yacht!" Maimie reminded her. "We'll have a lovely time these weeks, and it'll be real elegant to appear among your new relations in your own ship."

"Well, I don't know," said Félicia doubtfully. As delicately as he could, the Grand-Duke had suggested that pending the decision of the Emperor and the Prince of Arragon on her claim, it would be well for her to withdraw herself to a certain extent from the public eye. A sojourn in some quiet mountain village, whither her fame as an American heiress would not precede her, and where her footsteps would not be dogged by reporters, would best suit the views of her father's august relations. Maimie, reading between the lines of his speech, saw that some rumour of the Carnival proceedings and other doings of the kind had reached him, and forestalled Félicia's indignant refusal by suggesting that she should send for the Bluebird, the beautiful steam-yacht which Mr Steinherz had designed and constructed for himself, and sailed in all the Western seas, so as to take a short cruise in the Mediterranean. The idea did not displease Félicia, and to the Grand-Duke it came as such an evident relief that she could not refuse to adopt it, especially when she found the yacht could not reach Nice before Mid-Lent, which would enable her to take part in the Battle of Flowers and other festivities of the occasion. But there were details in connection with the proposed cruise which still rankled in her mind, and again she turned angrily upon Maimie. "And I do think, Maimie Logan, you might have stood by me, so's we wouldn't have an old school-ma'am trail us along everywhere. It makes me real mad to be shepherded around that way."

This referred to a proposal of the Grand-Duke's that the chaperon on board the Bluebird should not be Mrs van Zyl, but a lady of the Pannonian Court, who might give the two girls various useful hints in case of a change in their position. Félicia, who had delightful dreams of fluttering the Imperial dovecotes by appearing among her august relations as a frank and unashamed American, had been horrified to hear Maimie acquiesce in the suggestion. In ordinary society anywhere Maimie felt that she could hold her own and guide Félicia, but on these lofty heights she was at fault, and she had the good sense to see it. Félicia was more difficult to manage than she had expected, but at last she succeeded in making her see that any *faux pas* on her first introduction would produce a bad impression and alienate King Michael, and she yielded with a poor enough grace.

"But you save so much time getting at things on the voyage," Maimie urged now.

"How does that make up, when I wanted to take a real nice party on board, and have a good time? It's nothing but a snub to poor Sadie, I say."

"She won't have you see that she feels it so, any way. She'll conclude to keep track of you, with an eye to the future, I know. And I thought the Grand-Duke fixed it real nicely to have this Baroness Radnika come and stay at the hotel, so's you could just fall in love with her, and invite her to make the cruise with you."

"Oh, it's all awfully smart, of course, and I guess Count Mortimer was somewhere around when it was fixed. But for you and the Grand-Duke both to insist that I must have this old dowd of a Baroness tag after me, just because she knew pappa, and can teach me their tricks—why, it's the meanest thing out! I'm real thankful there's the chance of a frolic or two first. I'll even up my accounts with you, you bet!"

To Maimie this was sufficiently alarming, and yet, although Félicia kept her word, and enjoyed herself thoroughly at the Mid-Lent gaieties, the great and most disagreeable shock which the Battle of Flowers brought with it was not due to her. As a reward for her complaisance in withdrawing from the pleasures of society for the present, she had promised herself the delight of outshining all possible rivals before she disappeared from view.

Her carriage was a bower of irises in all the delicate shades which the flower presents, and the occupants were dressed to correspond. Mrs van Zyl's gown was a soft harmony in yellow and lavender, Maimie wore white and dark purple, and Félicia was in the colour she loved best, a clear pale lilac, emphasised, but not unduly so, by the touches of black velvet demanded by fashion. The scheme of decoration had been kept a profound secret, and the "iris carriage" was greeted with shouts of admiration from end to end of the course. Close at hand rode King Michael, duly masked, but quite recognisable to the spectators, in a rich gold-embroidered Thracian dress of two shades of purple. The understanding which was implied by the correspondence between his costume and those of the ladies suggested a hint of romance which the populace were not slow to take, and he shared in the plaudits which accompanied the carriage in its progress. Maimie felt a little uneasy, wondering whether his action would be considered premature by his relations, but before long she was conscious of quite a different cause for anxiety. Among the mounted men by whom the line of carriages was every now and then broken was one who seemed to be manœuvring to place himself near Félicia, endeavouring also to attract her attention by making his horse prance and curvet. He seemed to be short of stature, but the close-fitting Mephistopheles dress which he wore, carried out not in red but in black, set off a peculiarly graceful figure, and he displayed a complete mastery over his restless steed. His hair was black, and his eyes, when they could be distinguished through the holes in his mask, dark and glittering. His mysterious appearance was well calculated to rouse the curiosity of any one not absolutely engrossed, as was Félicia, by her carriage, her clothes, and her prize, and Maimie saw that King Michael was obviously uneasy. Again and again, when the procession paused for a moment before one of the tribunes, or when the carriage turned at the end of the course, he interposed his horse so that the unknown cavalier should not approach Félicia. His first idea had been that the stranger was his vanquished rival, Usk, but it was obvious that the Englishman's broad shoulders could not possibly be hidden under the black doublet, and he scented a deeper mystery. Presently another stoppage occurred before one of the stands, in which sat the Grand-Duke and Duchess of Schwarzwald-Molzau and the Grand-Duke Ivan Petrovitch. Bouquets were flying fast and furiously, the air was full of roses, jonquils, violets, mimosa; shrieks of laughter arose, now from the carriages and now from the tribune, but King Michael took no part in the fray. In thrusting his horse between Félicia's carriage and the unknown rider, he had forced the latter close to the Scythian Prince, who was staring at him in astonishment, and presently addressed him in his own language. The reply which reached King Michael's ear, "An affair of the heart; you won't give me away?" only deepened his suspicions. Presently he was able to leave Félicia in the safe keeping of his uncle, who asked to be allowed to occupy the fourth seat in the carriage as it moved on again, and he leaned over the railing to the Grand-Duke Ivan.

"Who is the black Mephistopheles?" he asked.

"You won't betray him, I presume? Timoleon Malasorte."

"Then I was mistaken. I thought it was some one I knew, and I wanted to play him a trick." The King spoke with admirable nonchalance, but he was inwardly perturbed. He knew the story of the Pretender's courtship of Félicia, and foresaw a repetition of it, and he blessed the obtuseness of his uncle, who was enjoying himself hugely as the butt of all the hardest bouquets, and claiming Félicia's attention at every turn. She looked round in vain for some one to deliver her, while the Grand-Duke was giving her a long account of his daughter's obstinate refusal to attend the festivities with her betrothed. The Grand-Duchess persisted she was ill; but he had been determined she should go, and would have carried his point if his wife had not called in a rascally, venal doctor to her aid. Félicia did not find Helene's delinquencies at all amusing, but while she sought for help, she did not happen to glance in the direction of her former suitor. King Michael returned to his post in the nick of time, and remained at her side so gallantly for the rest of the afternoon that Malasorte had no chance of accosting her. Apparently accepting his defeat, the Prince dropped behind the carriage, but when King Michael saw him next, he was picking up a spray of white lilac Maimie had dropped, and slipping something with it into her hand. The King nursed his wrath in silence until the return to the Villa, when he stopped Maimie as she was following Félicia upstairs.

"May I trouble you for the note Prince Malasorte gave you for the Princess Félicia, mademoiselle?"

Maimie stared at him in astonishment. She had not at all decided whether to give Félicia the letter which Malasorte, relying on her old friendliness, had entrusted to her, or not, but now she had to come to a decision at once. What was the exact meaning of Malasorte's presence here, where he was at any moment liable to be arrested and conducted to the frontier? Was he on his way to make himself emperor, or was it only that he had learnt Félicia's true descent, and desired the support her family and fortune could give him in his campaign? There were many things it would be well to know before determining the fate of the letter, but here stood King Michael opposite her, holding out his hand for it. "I guess I won't jump at the shadow and lose the substance," she said to herself, and gave it to him. Somewhat to her surprise he opened it immediately.

"I am not like that poor fool Usk, to be deceived and hoodwinked, mademoiselle," he replied to her amazed look. "I protect myself, and it appears it is necessary. Do you not think so?" He read from the note: "'Meet me at eight to-morrow morning in the garden of the Villa Bougainvillea. I must speak to you. I have more to lay at your feet than I had once.—M.' Has he any ground for believing she would be willing to meet him?" he demanded, looking Maimie sternly in the face.

"None. She hasn't a notion that he's around. We lost sight of him years back," she answered, her tone anxious in spite of herself.

"And if he renews his attempt, on which side are you? I wish to know, that I may lay my plans accordingly. I am not to be tricked, mademoiselle."

"On yours," said Maimie firmly. "I don't see throwing away all the trouble and worry we've had these last months."

"You are wise. You will not find me ungrateful, but I beg you to understand that I trust no one absolutely. To show that I am favourably disposed towards you, I may tell you that Count Mortimer has strongly recommended me to see that you are removed from the household of the Princess before she becomes my wife. I mention this that you may arrange with her to retain your services, for I find it desirable to have at hand a trustworthy person with whom I can discuss matters affecting the Princess which might be disagreeable to herself. As long as your influence is exerted in compliance with my wishes, your position in the Court will be secure."

"And when it's exerted against your wishes——?" thought Maimie, as he allowed her to depart. "You scored this time, you consequential little wretch, but I guess you won't do it any more. And as for your dear stepfather, I'll just count the days until I can punish him. Trying to part me from Fay, indeed!"

Nothing more was seen or heard of Prince Malasorte just then, and Maimie guessed that Félicia's non-appearance at the rendezvous had disgusted him beyond remedy. Very shortly after the Battle of Flowers she and Félicia embarked on the Bluebird, accompanied by the Baroness Radnika, for whom, fortunately enough, Félicia had conceived one of her sudden attachments. Maimie, who knew that the Baroness's maiden name had been Aline von Hartenweg, was not surprised by the passionate tenderness with which she responded to Félicia's endearments, and wondered at the practical wisdom which had been shown in selecting Prince Joseph's old love as the instructress of his daughter. Meanwhile, Mr Hicks was summoned from New York, bringing with him the documents committed to his care; and alarming legal personages invaded the parish of St Mary Windicotes, and the peaceful dwelling of the old clergyman and his wife at Whitcliffe, demanding evidence on oath with regard to the marriage of Joseph Bertram and Constance Lily Garland. While the Bluebird cruised in the Western Mediterranean, never spending more than one night away from port, the negotiations dragged their slow length along. About once a-week a hitch appeared, which threatened to bring them to a dead stop, but as King Michael invariably marked these occasions by paying fresh attention to the Grand-Duchess Sonya, matters were smoothed over in some way or other.

The first hitch presented itself just after Mr Hicks's arrival in Europe, when the 'Empire City Diurnal,' a paper which was the unresting rival of the 'Crier,' and even more noted for its skill in exploiting sensations, suddenly published what purported to be an interview with an intimate friend of Félicia's. Her father's history was detailed in a highly-coloured style, embodying just enough of truth to wring severely the withers of the royal and imperial personages concerned, and ending with a claim, put forward apparently in all seriousness, to the crown of Pannonia itself on Félicia's behalf. This claim was further pressed in a fervid editorial, calling upon the manhood of the United States to arise and cross the ocean, and sweep to destruction the effete usurpers who were keeping an American woman out of her rights by force and fraud. A subscription-list towards effecting this noble object followed, headed by the proprietor and ending with the office-boy, and the names of eleven volunteers (others were stated to be arriving in thousands) appeared below. The extracts telegraphed at once to Europe raised a ferment in Pannonian Court circles, and the Grand-Duke of Schwarzwald-Molzau was very nearly driven to wash his hands altogether of Félicia and her claims. Cyril happened to be in England at the time, but Mr Hicks succeeded in saving the situation. An expenditure at which the Grand-Duke stood aghast seemed nothing to him, and he cabled whole columns to his own journal. The next day the 'Crier,' strong in the indubitable fact of possessing one of the trustees of the claimant on its staff, administered a douche of cold water to the excited public of the 'Diurnal.' So far from possessing or advancing a claim to any crown whatsoever, Miss Steinherz was solely concerned to vindicate the good name of her mother; and the 'Diurnal's' polemic was nothing but an attempt to prejudice her in this sacred task by alienating the august relatives who had welcomed the news of her existence with tears of joy, and were only restraining their eagerness to receive her into their midst in order that her claim might be properly substantiated according to law.

"Draw it mild, Hicks!" said Cyril, when they next met, and he read this reply. "Any one can see you had your tongue in your cheek the whole time."

"Is that so, Count? Well now, I'd bet my bottom dollar you're the only man that will see the thing was wrote sarcastic. There were tears in the Grand-Duke's eyes when he read it, any way. And in the States the effect has been colossal, I hear, especially of the paragraph about the 'Diurnal's' stopping the cash-boys' salaries to stick in its subscription-lists. It isn't every day a man can make a big scoop for his paper and pat Europe on the head as well."

In any case, the 'Diurnal's' sensation wilted, as Mr Hicks put it, and no more was heard of it after the paper's unfulfilled promise to publish the name of the "distinguished lady" who had given the information. The next difficulty came from Mr Steinherz's elder brother, Don Ramon, who demanded that before he considered her claim, Félicia should prove her good faith by surrendering her fortune into his hands as head of the house of Arragon. Her father's will provided effectually against this, and led to a deadlock; but as Félicia intimated that her relations' interests would receive careful consideration from her if the relationship were established, the difficulty was shelved. Then a hitch was caused by the discovery that Konstantia von Lilienkranz was not sufficiently high in rank for even the Emperor to raise her retrospectively to a level befitting the bride of a Prince of Arragon. Cyril replied with the terse advice, "Consult the heralds"; and after a little expenditure of time and trouble Félicia's mother was provided with a descent which rivalled that of the Schwarzwald-Molzaus themselves. The difficulty which came next threatened to be more serious; for the Church objected to the recognition of the irregular marriage, on the ground that the Pope's consent to a mixed marriage had not been obtained, and that no provision had been made for the children to be brought up in the Roman Catholic faith. The solution obviously intended was that Félicia should change her creed; but Cyril, on behalf of King Michael, pointed out that this would make her impossible as a Queen for Thracia. The Emperor, to whom the marriage offered a way out of many difficulties, brought a despairing pressure to bear upon the Vatican, and the matter was compromised on the understanding that Félicia should build and endow a magnificent church to her father's memory. She consented at once, as she would have consented to build a mosque had it been required of her; for the nearer she came to her goal, the more intolerable did the thought of failing to reach it appear. It was a joy to feel that Cyril and Mr Hicks were already discussing how her fortune could best be applied to solve the financial problems of Thracia without infringing the provisions of her father's will; a greater joy to learn that King Michael's conditional proposal of marriage had become a definite one; and greatest of all, to receive through Mr Hicks a telegram, half-invitation, half-command, directing her to proceed in her yacht to the Pannonian coast, that she might be presented to her father's family.

CHAPTER XIV.
FOR PITY'S SAKE.

WHEN Usk returned to England, he found his parents in London, established in a corner of the vast mansion which had been built by Lord Caerleon's grandfather, the Peninsular General, and much adorned by his son, the Crimean hero, in the palmy days of landowning. Both these veterans took a keen professional interest in battle-pictures, and had embellished Caerleon House with many square yards of warlike frescoes, which their civilian descendant sometimes wished had been painted on canvas, so that they could be removed and sold. When his father's death, or, strictly speaking, the duties consequent thereon, left Lord Caerleon unable to keep up two establishments, he succeeded in letting the town house on a long lease to a Northern magnate who had made a fortune in sugar-refining, but now sugar, as well as land, had fallen upon evil days. The house was on its owner's hands once more, and it was cheaper to encamp in some of the smaller rooms than to live in lodgings, especially since Lady Caerleon's chief desire was for a drawing-room which she could lend for meetings. Thus, while in the state apartments the blinds remained down, and the furniture looked ghostly in holland wrappings, Usk and his parents lived and worked, interviewed political friends and opponents, and furthered various religious and philanthropic schemes, in the modest suite traditionally allotted to the heir of the house, and called the Viscount's rooms. It did not occur to them to feel ashamed of their obvious poverty, and they found pleasure in entertaining the few, chiefly old friends or fellow-workers, who did not consider that stinted means and lack of "smartness" placed the Caerleons beyond the pale of decent society.

As for Usk, he threw himself so completely into his parents' interests that he had no time to think even of running down to Llandiarmid, and thus the peace of mind of Gwladys and Myfanwy Jones remained undisturbed. Lord Caerleon's Temperance measure had hitherto escaped the different snares and pitfalls in its path, and was rapidly nearing the goal which was the usual fate of the Bills he brought forward—a piteous request from the Government for its withdrawal, since to press it further would jeopardise the success of the complete and carefully drawn scheme of reform which His Majesty's Ministers intended to introduce next session. It is a striking instance of the vanity of human wishes that never in any case did the next session see the introduction of such a Bill.

This was the state of affairs when one afternoon, about the middle of April, Cyril walked into Caerleon House, and found his brother and sister-in-law in the great desolate conservatory, which was sparsely sprinkled with pots of flowers sent up from Llandiarmid. Lady Caerleon thought the conservatory the most country-like place in the house; and her husband preferred it because to smoke in any of the other rooms seemed like sacrilege.

"Why, Cyril!" cried Lady Caerleon, catching sight of him first. "Is the— is Ernestine here?"

"No, I have run over alone. Usk's out, I hope? I wanted to catch you two together. Bill flourishing, Caerleon? The session onward plods its weary way, I suppose? How does Usk work?"

"Splendidly. When we have him in the Commons, we shall begin to move at last, I feel certain."

"Good. No chance that the Southumberland seat will fall vacant just yet, is there, though? Morrell will hang on until death or a general election unseats him, and there's no present likelihood of either, I believe?"

"Not that I know of."

"That's all right, then. I want Usk."

Lady Caerleon turned pale. "Oh, Cyril, has Félicia repented?"

"Never further from it. She is making splendid progress towards her heart's desire. But your maternal instinct was not at fault, Nadia. It is on behalf of a prospective daughter-in-law that I am come to you."

"But Usk has never said anything——"

"About her? I think he has. Has he never mentioned the Princess Helene of Schwarzwald-Molzau?"

"A Schwarzwald-Molzau!" cried Lord Caerleon, but his wife broke in—

"Yes, of course. We saw her engagement to the Grand-Duke Ivan, and Usk was quite unhappy about it. He said the man was a brute."

"Well, it was broken off about a week ago, but I suppose the news has not got into the English papers yet. That is the young lady."

"But, Cyril, I am quite sure Usk has never thought of her in that way."

"It's just possible he might learn to do it."

"But why should he? Oh, you can't mean that she has fallen in love with him, and let other people see it, when he hasn't said a word to her?"

"Why that tone of deep disgust? I seem to remember a young lady once whom I only dissuaded with the greatest difficulty from sending a refusal, in writing, to a man who had never proposed to her."

"Unfair, Cyril!" cried Lord Caerleon. "Nadia couldn't help knowing that I cared for her."

"I can't stand up against the two of you, that's certain. Well, Nadia, let me tell you the circumstances, and I think you will acquit poor little Princess Lenchen of any worse crimes than a romantic disposition, and an ingenuous readiness to take Usk on trust on the strength of a childlike adoration for his uncle."

"Of course I don't wonder at her falling in love with Usk," said Usk's mother.

"Of course you don't. And she never told her love, at any rate, which is an extenuating circumstance. You mustn't think there was ever any affection between her and Ivan Petrovitch. Her parents had been pressing her to accept him, and she yielded suddenly at last, about—yes, it must have been just about the time Usk came home—simply because she had not vitality enough to hold out longer, I should think. She looked like a ghost after the engagement, but she was dragged out to all the gaieties there were, which in itself was nearly enough to kill a delicate girl brought up very quietly in the mountains. She looked worse and worse as the days went on, and Ernestine almost broke her heart over her; but when she spoke to the Grand-Duchess, she only wept, and said her husband was determined the marriage should take place, and she dared not cross him. The climax came at the time of the Mi-Carême Battle of Flowers. The Grand-Duke and the lover insisted upon the poor girl's going, though she had a perfect terror of it, after the fright she got at the Carnival, where Usk met her first. She fainted twice while she was dressing, and the Grand-Duchess was alarmed at last, and sent for a doctor. Very fortunately, the English doctor whom Ernestine had advised her to call in was in the hotel at the moment, visiting Usk's friend Nicholson, who was his patient. He put an absolute veto on the girl's going out that day, and promised to come and examine her thoroughly in the morning. They told him nothing of the circumstances, but after seeing her he said there was some trouble pressing upon her mind, and if it was not removed she would die of sheer terror. The Grand-Duke stormed, but could not shake him, and as no one could pretend not to know what the trouble was, Ivan Petrovitch was sent about his business. I should imagine the Grand-Ducal family went through stormy times for a day or two. The Grand-Duke is not a pleasant man to oppose, but if you have to do it, it's as well to do it with spirit. Félicia and he get on excellently, because if she doesn't like what he tells her to do, she says so, and the matter is at an end. Well, the doctor continued his visits, as the Grand-Duchess asked him, but he told Ernestine privately that it was useless. There was no organic disease, but the child did not seem to have any wish to live. She knew that her parents quarrelled over her, I suppose, and had not the courage to assert herself. She was quiet and fairly happy when once her engagement was broken off, but she didn't get better. And only just seventeen, Nadia!"

"Much too young to be thinking about engagements at all," said Lady Caerleon, decisively but not harshly.

"Ah, well, her parents had put the thought into her mind, you see. Then, three days ago, she had a dreadful shock. Usk's friend Nicholson had another attack of hæmorrhage, and died in the hotel. Ernestine thought him very much softened lately, and he used to like her to read to him. She was with him just before the end, and the Grand-Duchess asked her not to go and see Helene that day, lest she should inquire for him. She took an interest in him as an invalid, you see, and used to send him some of the flowers which were sent her. That afternoon the Grand-Duke came to our rooms in a terrible state of mind. The Grand-Duchess's maid had let out to Helene that Nicholson was dead, and, somehow, it seemed to awaken the child to the fact that she wasn't very far from dying herself. It did not disturb her to realise it, but the Grand-Duke complained that his wife and the other women looked at him as if he was a murderer. He begged Ernestine to go and see them, and even promised that anything she thought might be any good should be done. Of course Ernestine went, and you can imagine the state of things she found—the lady-in-waiting weeping in the *salon*, the maid sobbing in the passage, and the Grand-Duchess herself in Helene's room in floods of tears. I suppose the poor girl thought she had no time to lose, for without giving her mother any opportunity of recovering from the first shock, she had asked for her jewels and other little things, and was saying who she would like to have them. She's such a simple little soul that it didn't occur to her she was doing anything hackneyed—it was just the most natural thing in the world to her. There were bracelets and so on for her sisters and cousins, and some trifle for me, and then she touched a ring which she always wears, which was given her at her confirmation, and said she would like Usk to have it. Her mother was so much astonished that she didn't answer for a moment, and Helene said piteously, 'You won't mind then, will you, mamma? I shall never see him again, you know.' Ernestine thought the Grand-Duchess had gone out of her mind, for she got up suddenly and seized her by the arm and took her out of the room. When the door was shut, she said, 'That's what the child wants! You will help me. We will take her to the mountains at once, and she shall marry your nephew instead of Ivan Petrovitch, and get well. Come, let us tell her about it.' Ernestine begged her to wait and consult the Grand-Duke, but she absolutely refused. She went back into Helene's room, and swept all the jewels into their box again. 'Nonsense, Lenchen!' she said. 'You are not going to die. This place is too hot for you. We will go back to the mountains, to our own Lauterbach, just you and I, and your aunt will come and stay with us.' Ernestine felt obliged to back her up by saying that as I could not leave Nice just at present, she would ask Usk to come and escort her to Lauterbach, and they would stay at the cottage close to the Schloss, so that Helene might be quite quiet. She says she didn't dare to look at the child as she spoke, but she heard her whisper, 'Then I shall see him again, after all!' and for the first time she felt there was some hope."

"But the Grand-Duke!" cried Lord Caerleon. "What did he think about it?"

"Well, Ernestine and the Grand-Duchess very prudently came to our rooms to have it out with him, lest Helene should be disturbed. Of course he vowed he would never hear of such a thing, but for once his wife seemed to have lost her fear of him. She told him plainly that she would separate from him rather than let Helene die when she could be saved; and as the money is nearly all hers, that brought him round. At last he calmed down sufficiently to allow the doctor to be consulted, and he was called in. He approved highly of the mountain plan, and recommended very strongly that the girl's inclination should not be forced in any way. She was so sensitive, he said, that only a man of a most sympathetic type could hope to make her happy. In deference to the Grand-Duke's feelings, his wife consented to leave that part of the programme in abeyance, but they start for the mountains to-morrow, and I should like to pack Usk off to join them, if you have no objection."

"On what footing?" asked Lord Caerleon sharply. "I won't have him bandied about according to the state of the Grand-Duke's temper."

"My dear Caerleon, haven't you learnt yet that the honour—the punctilio, I might say—of the family is safe with me? Usk will be received as a suitor approved by the young lady's parents, though he will not be formally presented to her as such."

"Well," said Lady Caerleon, "if I were in Princess Helene's place, it would not make me better to know that a young man was being brought to marry me, quite irrespective of his own wishes."

"She knows nothing of the kind, and no one has suggested it to her. I don't pretend to say what may be passing in her mind, but I should imagine she flatters herself that she regards him merely as a dear friend. But I seem to be unfortunate in my advocacy, Nadia. Since my words only prejudice you further against the poor little girl, I shall be obliged to show you this, which I didn't mean to bring out if I could help it, for it's not flattering."

He handed Lady Caerleon a photograph, which she took with a stern and unbending aspect, but her look changed suddenly.

"Oh, Cyril, what a sad little face!—and how very————"

"Plain?" suggested Cyril, as she hesitated. "If you saw her, you wouldn't think so. It's the expression that is wanting in the photograph."

"She must have beautiful eyes and hair," said Lady Caerleon slowly. "But, Cyril, Carlino, think of the difference from Félicia! Do you think Usk would ever care for her? And so badly dressed! I should like to take her in hand."

"Come," said Cyril, "this is a ray of hope. Now you realise that she needs comforting and dressing, Nadia, you won't steel your heart against her for long."

"I don't want to steel my heart against her, poor little thing! but you don't seem to see—I daresay it sounds very selfish, but you feel it too, don't you, Carlino?—when Phil is so far away, to have to give up Usk too! I know I ought to be willing to do it, if it's to help some one, but for him to have to go and live in Germany—it would be like losing him altogether."

"No, no, Nadia," said her husband quickly, as she turned to him with streaming eyes, "that's out of the question. Usk has his duties here, and he won't give them up with my consent."

"You both seem to have the worst possible opinion of me," lamented Cyril. "Is it likely that I should deliberately arrange for Usk to become a hanger-on at a petty German Court, where he wouldn't even be welcomed? No; the Grand-Duchess quite sees that her husband and her daughter agree best at a distance. 'The young people will live in England, of course,' she said to me, 'but they must come and see me in the mountains every year, and sometimes I will come and see them.'"

"Is that Usk coming in?" cried Lady Caerleon, starting up.

"Suppose you break the idea to him, Nadia, and see how he takes it," suggested Cyril. "No one wants to force him into anything, of course, but I hardly see how he can do better. And you will manage it much more artistically than I should, for with you I began by giving the poor little girl away, which was the last thing I meant to do."

Lady Caerleon hurried into the house, and the brothers were left together.

"I hope Usk will be able to see his way to it," said Cyril. "Ernestine and I are quite foolish over this child Helene. Imagine my tearing across Europe just to get her what she wants!"

"I can't understand even now how the Grand-Duke came to give in. One has always heard that his views on unequal marriages were so very strict."

"I'm going to give you a tip," said Cyril. "You mustn't allow that it is unequal, on any account. Play the *grand seigneur anglais* for all you're worth when you meet him. Be impassive, bored, contemptuously tolerant of all you see, and let him know that you have much better at home."

"Anything else?"

"It's perfectly true. None of the Grand-Duke's palaces can hold a candle to this house, and there's no need to mention that you can't afford to live in it. And as for Llandiarmid, though Félicia was pleased to turn up her pretty nose at it, it would make him miserably discontented with all his country seats, even if he saw it as it is. To German ears your rent-roll sounds magnificent, and the family jewels are historic. I'm thankful you never parted with them—but they are heirlooms, aren't they? so it was not any virtue on your part. If you have to come to Molzau—for the wedding— make Nadia wear the emeralds, and have the pearls mounted afresh for Helene. That will smooth your path wonderfully."

"If you exalt me much higher, I shall begin to think that it is Usk who is making the *mésalliance*."

"Oh, the rest of the Schwarzwald-Molzau family will soon undeceive you in that case. It's the Grand-Duke's bitterest pill that he has imbued his children so thoroughly with his views that they will all look askance at him now. The youngest son, Prince Franz, who married the daughter of Félicia's uncle, Don Florian, is the only one from whom he can expect any sympathy. Princess Resi is *recht demokratisch*, I understand."

"Nice to be received upon sufferance into a family where only the Radicals will tolerate you!"

"You must make allowance for the susceptibilities of young people who have all married as they were told, and done excellently for themselves. I don't know whether they married for rank, but they have certainly married where rank is. The Grand-Duke has always warned them against the romantic taint which crops out in the family with such curious persistency, and their feelings will naturally be hurt when it turns out that the taint has reappeared and vanquished him in the youngest and most timid of them all."

"And this taint is merely a disposition to marry for love, I suppose?"

"Exactly; the sort of thing which can't be allowed in a semi-royal house. The men in whom it appeared have generally gone to the bad, I believe, and the women become *dévotes*, after experiences which proved how wise their family were in refusing to listen to their wishes. It doesn't seem to have struck the family that it would have been cheaper, and saved a good deal of scandal, to allow the delinquents to resign their rank, and settle down in private life with the objects of their affections. Their domestic squabbles would have served as awful warnings to the next generation. Perhaps that is the secret of the Grand-Duke's yielding now."

"Cyril!" Lord Caerleon turned and looked fixedly at his brother. "I hope there's no morganatic foolery about this business? That I won't stand."

"Certainly not. Our Plantagenet blood, which your Radical friends think so lightly of except when they want you to push their Bills in Parliament, has stood us in good stead here, as I have often found before. But I own I never expected to be grateful for poor old O'Malachy's descent from Irish kings. It was a happy thought of his to have that elaborate pedigree drawn out, though I believe it was the only thing he had to leave Nadia at his death, wasn't it? I must have it copied to take back with me, though I remembered enough of it to quiet the Grand-Duke's apprehensions as to Usk's mother's possessing the regulation number of quarterings. But it is a curious thing that you, the most typical Englishman I know, should apparently be doomed to associate with foreigners. You have a foreign wife, so have I, and now everything is conspiring to provide you with a foreign daughter-in-law."

Lord Caerleon growled impatiently. "It doesn't seem to have struck any one to ask how Usk and his wife are to live," he said. "Has the Princess any money?"

"In Germany she is regarded as something of an heiress, and her fortune undoubtedly looks rather imposing reckoned in marks. I should say she would have about eight hundred a-year—pounds, I mean."

"Even with what I can give Usk, it'll be precious little to support such a lot of grandeur upon. They won't have much margin."

"She is sure to be a good housekeeper. All German girls are. By the bye, what about that new railway which was to pass Llandiarmid and open up the hill district? Is it still on the *tapis*?"

"Rather. But Nadia and I both felt that we ought not to run up the price of the land, as the line is so much needed."

"You didn't tell the Company that, I hope? Don't, pray, feel that you must love your neighbour better than yourself. Let them make the first offer. You may be sure they won't propose to give more than the land is worth, but you certainly ought to get enough out of them to increase Usk's allowance to something a little more in accordance with his position."

In the meantime, Lady Caerleon had intercepted her son in the hall, and drawn him aside into the library.

"Your uncle is here, Usk, and he and your father are having a little talk. Come in here. I—I want to speak to you."

"Anything wrong?" he asked in surprise. "Why, you've been crying, mater! What is it?"

"No, dear, there is nothing wrong. It was foolish of me to cry. I ought to feel very glad and proud, after what I have just heard about you."

"There's little enough about me to make you either glad or proud, I'm afraid," he said bitterly. "But I'm glad you're pleased, mater, whatever it is."

"But I am not pleased!" cried Lady Caerleon. "At least, as I say, I ought to be. But if it is to make you happy, I *will* be pleased."

Usk changed colour. "Mother," he said, almost breathlessly, "if it's any message about—anything from Félicia, it's no good. I don't want to hear from her. I could never trust her again."

"No, no! It's about the Princess Helene of Schwarzwald-Molzau. Her engagement to the Scythian Prince is broken off."

"Is that all?" cried Usk. "What a start you gave me! And what in the world has it to do with me?—though of course I'm glad for the poor little girl's own sake."

"Usk," said his mother quickly, "had you any idea she cared for you?"

"For me? Princess Helene? What an idea! Of course not."

"She has been very ill, and when she thought she was dying, she begged that the ring she always wore might be given to you. And now—they hope she will not die."

"I—I don't think you ought to have told me this," said Usk awkwardly. He looked with a kind of reproach at his mother, who could not meet his eyes. "You see," he went on more firmly, "she's such a nice little girl that it's a shame to say that sort of thing about her. She's as innocent as a baby,

- 161 -

and it would get her into dreadful trouble with her people if they thought it was true."

"It is true," said Lady Caerleon desperately, "and your uncle would like you to marry her. Could you care for her at all, Usk?"

"No one could help caring for her, she's such a gentle, friendly little thing. But not in that way! Mater, say you're joking."

"I wish I could, but everything is arranged in a way. They think she is pining after you—no, I know it doesn't sound kind to say it, Usk, but what am I to say? You were kind to her, weren't you? and she misses you, and they say it would cheer her if you went and stayed with your aunt near her, and saw her every day. It doesn't sound much to ask, but then it involves a good deal more."

"But why?" asked Usk quickly. "I shouldn't a bit mind seeing her as much as she liked, and—anything of that sort. Why shouldn't it stop there?"

"I suppose people would talk—I don't know. Besides, if she really——"

Usk stopped her. "Please don't. It would make her so awfully miserable if she knew things of that kind were being said about her. Feeling as I do, I have no business to listen to it. If I cared for her, it might be different."

"But couldn't you? Do you never mean——"

"To marry? I don't know. Perhaps some day it will seem more possible than it does now. Mother, think! If you knew how I loved and trusted Félicia, you would know that I could never feel the same to any woman again, never! If she had even broken it off at one wrench, it would not be so bad; but she played me like a salmon, pretending to let me go, and then drawing me back again, until every feeling of that sort seems quite dried up."

"But you are young, Usk. You will get over it some day."

"Possibly. I don't feel like it just yet."

"And a good girl—not one like Félicia——"

"Do you realise what Félicia is—how beautiful?—'witchlike' Princess Helene called it once, I remember. If she was looking at me, I should know it, though I was at the other end of the room and there was a crowd of people between,—I should feel it all over me, somehow. I couldn't feel like that for the little Princess. I should like to make her happy, to take her away from her father and be kind to her, and see her begin to assert herself, and hear the funny things she says, but I couldn't marry her on that, could I?"

"But pity is akin to love."

"Mater, you're weakening! You don't mean to say you would wish it?"

"I don't wish it, but—I'm beginning to be afraid it may be your duty."

"And then it's all up, isn't it? What a thing it is to have a mother with a conscience!"

"Don't talk so hardly, Usk. I can't help thinking how we should feel if the poor girl died. You say you would not make it up with Félicia if you could; don't you think you may be called to make this sacrifice?"

"It's not a sacrifice altogether," admitted Usk. "I really do like her, you know, but not in that way. The question is, is it fair to Princess Helene herself? No; certainly it would not be such a sacrifice as marrying one of the Jones girls," he added with a laugh.

"What, Gwladys or Myfanwy? My dear Usk!"

"Why, mater, I had made up my mind to propose to one of them in due time, simply because I thought you were so fond of them."

"As helpers in the parish, perhaps. But not to marry you."

"It's just as well that we have had this explanation, then, for I should certainly have done it."

"I am most thankful you haven't. And Mr Jones—oh, Usk!"

"Mater, I'm afraid you're a very worldly woman."

"Am I? I hope not. But perhaps I am, though I don't think there's anything wrong in preferring a Princess of Schwarzwald-Molzau to Miss Jones. No, I'm afraid you're right. I have always been so anxious people should not think your father had done himself harm in marrying me. It was pride, of course, because I used to hope you would both make brilliant marriages. But I couldn't wish Phil to have chosen differently—though I wish she lived in England. But I should like you to marry well, Usk."

"Then, on your own rule of conduct, I ought to go and propose to Miss Jones at once, so as to mortify your pride, oughtn't I?"

"No, it would not be fair to Princess Helene. We have her to think of too, you know." Usk raised his eyebrows at this sophistry. "I—I should like you to go back with your uncle, Usk."

"And propose immediately to the poor little girl?"

"Oh no, that's not necessary. Only go and be kind to her. You may find that she doesn't care for you, after all, or you may come to care for her, in time."

"And in any case I shall be safe from your friends?"

"Don't, Usk. I only want to see you happy, you know that. Any woman that can make you happy again will be welcome to me."

"Then the Princess Helene shall have the honour of trying the experiment," said Usk.

CHAPTER XV.
NOT LONG A-DOING.

IT was night when Usk arrived at Lauterbach. At the little station, far down in the valley below, Queen Ernestine's solemn Syrian major-domo and several of the Schwarzwald-Molzau servants had met him with horses and pack-mules, and they had ridden up and up all through the hours of the spring evening. When they reached the tiny table-land on which the Bergschloss stood, it was too dark to distinguish anything but towering peaks on every hand shutting out the stars, with a gleam of whiteness at one side, cast by the waterfall which filled the air with such a tumult of sound that Usk wondered how the dwellers on the plateau ever heard each other speak. He was to learn later that those who were accustomed to the noise did not even hear it, and that they could distinguish other sounds as though it had not been. Even now Helene, lying awake in one of the turret-rooms of the Schloss, the twinkling lights of which showed its position against the dark mountains, heard the sound of the horses' feet as they passed, and said to herself, "He is come, then, at last!" But although Usk, as he rode under the walls of the castle, wondered for a moment which was Helene's room, he thought no more of her that night after reaching the smaller house, called Luisenruh, after its builder, the mother of the present Grand-Duke, where his aunt was staying. Queen Ernestine had much to ask him about his parents and his work in London, and he had to tell her the various incidents of his journey, and as if by a tacit understanding they held aloof from the delicate matter which had brought him to Lauterbach.

In the morning, however, he found that they were to join the Grand-Duchess and her daughter at the Schloss for the late breakfast; and he walked with the Queen through the gardens, which adjoined each other so nearly that few people could have told where the grounds of the cottage ended and those of the Schloss began, and learned from a servant who was sent to meet them that the meal was served in the Chinese pavilion. There were several of these summer-houses dotted about in the gardens—a Greek temple, a hermitage, a Persian mosque, an Arcadian shepherd's hut, all absurdly incongruous in their architecture as in their names, but affording pleasant retreats in hot or wet weather, and fine views of the mountains and the waterfall at all times. In the Chinese pavilion, which had a range of pointed roofs one above another, with little bells hung at every possible extremity, the visitors found the Grand-Duchess, whose nervousness was concealed under a restless activity which would have been called bustling in a lady of lower rank. Helene, very thin and bright-eyed, with a red spot in either cheek, was propped up with pillows on a couch which commanded the finest of the views.

"What do you think of my mountains?" she demanded eagerly of Usk, as soon as she had greeted him, and she smiled with pleasure over his answer that they looked jolly. "You can't know them properly by only seeing them from this distance," she went on. "I shall show you all my own special views and paths, and all the things I used to discover."

"No mountain-climbing just yet, Lenchen!" said the Grand-Duchess. "You are to walk a little every day as soon as you are rested from the journey, you know, but it must be only about the gardens, where the paths are level."

"Walking where the paths are level! Why, mamma, in a fortnight I shall be bicycling again. We will keep the level paths for that. I want to take Lord Usk up the mountains, and see all my friends."

But in spite of Helene's eagerness for exertion, it was long before she could attempt the mountains. Naturally enough, when the excitement of returning to her favourite scenes, and of welcoming Usk, had passed, she seemed to lose strength, and to the anxious eye of her mother appeared actually worse than she had been at Nice. Almost in desperation, the Grand-Duchess threw herself upon Usk for help, and adopted him as the natural sharer of her anxieties with a calmness that surprised him.

"You must help me to save her," she said. "Here are the doctor's directions, and I look to you to carry them out."

Somewhat amused though he was at being turned into a sick-nurse, Usk accepted the position, which he found to be no sinecure, and which made him feel by turns horribly cruel and a good deal of a fool. Helene was to live almost entirely in the open air, it seemed, and to take exercise at stated hours and for a fixed period of time. If she grew tired too soon, it was his duty to pretend not to notice it, and to talk to her as she walked until she forgot it too. Or if, as sometimes happened, she was ready to wander on when the stated time was over, he was obliged to induce her to rest, which could occasionally only be done by pretending that he himself was tired. It struck him once, when he was hurrying after his patient with a rug, because she would not sit down anywhere but on the grass, that his position was a good deal less romantic than might have been expected from his conversation with his mother. Helene talked to him as naturally as if he had been her brother, and he could not flatter himself that her frank pleasure in his society, and her readiness to turn to him for everything she wanted done, sprang from any stronger feeling than pure friendliness. His uncle and the Grand-Duchess must have been mistaken, he decided, and the fact produced in him curiously mixed sensations. On the one hand, when Helene was better, nothing more would be expected of him, and he could go his way in peace; but, on the other, he felt that he had to some extent been fooled when he was induced to screw himself up to the performance of a tremendous exploit which now appeared quite unnecessary. But he grew genuinely fond of Helene in a brotherly way, and was as proud as her mother when she began to show unmistakable signs of returning health. When she refused breakfast one day, and the Grand-Duchess only waited until she was out of sight to weep, Usk showed no disappointment. His prescience was rewarded in the course of the morning, when Helene confessed suddenly that she was "so hungry," and asked him to fetch her something to eat. Then there was the day when for the first time an expedition was undertaken beyond the grounds, and Helene proudly introduced him to one of her friends, the wife of a goatherd who lived on the mountain-side. The good woman set before her visitors a meal of black bread and goats' milk; and this simple fare, which Usk privately thought very nasty, Helene ate and enjoyed, and the Grand-Duchess wept again, but this time her tears were of joy.

Now that Helene was sufficiently recovered to take longer walks, her mother thought it advisable to consider the conventions once more. At first she succeeded in putting a veto on any distant expeditions by the plea that Helene would overtask her strength, but when Usk had suggested taking a pony with them, on which she could ride when she was tired, it was necessary to provide suitable companions. Neither the Grand-Duchess nor the Queen were equal to the exertion involved, but the former invited her youngest son and his wife to pay a visit to Lauterbach. Prince Franz Immanuel had been educated in England, and Usk and he had been contemporaries at Eton for some years, so that they had many interests in common, while Princess Theresia, the daughter of Félicia's uncle, Don Florian of Arragon, was so fond of things English that she was known at the Pannonian Court as the Anglomaniac. To her the Grand-Duchess had divulged her scheme concerning Usk and Helene as soon as it was formed, hoping to gain one firm ally, and the event proved that her object had been attained. The elder children of the Grand-Duchess, to whom the secret had not been revealed, were already writing from their married homes to inquire suspiciously why "that man Mortimer's nephew" was being thrown so much with Lenchen, and prophesying that complications would occur; but Princess Resi was an ardent supporter of the match, and insisted that her husband should share her views. He had been inclined at first to adopt the natural Schwarzwald-Molzau attitude, and scout the idea of a *mésalliance*; but he and his wife were a most devoted couple, and she fairly talked him over. Plied all day and every day with arguments in favour of love-matches, unequal marriages, unions in which the parties were of different nationalities, and harassed by the unreasonable conduct of Princess Resi, who insisted on taking any opposition as a reflection on herself or her mother, whose admission into the house of Albret-Arragon had only been secured by her immense dowry, he yielded at last, and when they arrived at Lauterbach his wife had him well in hand. He was further cheered by finding that Usk showed no signs of undue elation, and that the intercourse between him and Helene was of so free and brotherly a nature as to suggest that the Grand-Duchess's plan had miscarried.

Prince Franz and his wife were ideal companions on the expeditions Helene loved. Princess Resi's Anglomania was of so pronounced a character as to degenerate occasionally into caricature, especially in the matter of the costumes she adopted for climbing; but she made it a point of honour to do as much as her husband, and they followed Helene uncomplainingly into all the nooks and corners of the mountains. So tireless was Helene herself that Prince Franz unhesitatingly expressed his opinion that she had never been ill at all, and that her ailments had simply been assumed as an excuse for leaving Nice and returning to her beloved Lauterbach, but his wife reproved him for this in private. She understood from the Grand-Duchess, she said, that Helene's recovery was almost entirely due to Usk's care of her, and the firmness with which he had carried out the doctor's orders, and if things of that kind were said, he would think her friends grudged him his fitting reward. Even now, said Princess Resi, she thought his feelings must have been wounded in some way, for she took care that he had an opportunity nearly every day of speaking to Helene, but it was clear he had not done it yet.

As for Usk, about this time he wrote to his mother alluding gloomily to Miss Jones, without specifying which Miss Jones he meant, and advised her to make up her mind to welcome that young lady into the family after all. It is possible that he was influenced by an incident from which he drew, perhaps, larger deductions than he should have done.

He was mounting the stairs which led to the morning-room at the Schloss one day when he heard a sound as of paper being torn violently, and then Prince Franz's voice raised in protest.

"What in the world are you doing, Lenchen? That paper is mine."

"Then you had no business to bring it here. It's a shame!" The stove-door clanged, and there was a sound of fire-irons. "As if I would let it lie about for him to see! She must be wickeder than I could ever have imagined it possible for a woman to be, to go and break his heart——"

Usk stood hesitating on the threshold as Helene, with a flushed face, rose from her knees before the stove. It had not struck him at first that he was one of the persons alluded to, but now the truth was clear. It was something about Félicia that she had been unwilling for him to see, and of late he had thought less and less about Félicia, and might almost be said to have forgotten her. Helene read in his face that he had heard and understood, but she misread the blankness of his expression when he realised the change which had come over his mind.

"The new guide-book has come. Wouldn't you like to look at it?" she asked, beckoning him into the library. No sooner were they out of earshot of Prince Franz than she turned to him with tears in her eyes.

"I am so sorry," she said. "I only wished to save you pain."

"You are very good," said Usk, "but I don't quite understand——"

"Oh, it was a portrait of the Princess Félicia, and an interview with her, in an American paper, and I knew it would bring it all back to you—all the pain. If——if——" she hesitated—"if it would comfort you at all to talk to me about her, please do. I am so very sorry for you."

"I'm afraid it wouldn't," said Usk, feeling rather guilty.

"I thought if you felt that it wasn't her fault—that she was coerced by her family—it might comfort you to say so."

"It was something much more vulgar than that—simply the desire for a crown." Usk spoke with momentary fierceness, born of recollection.

"Ah, you are bitter. I do not wonder. You have borne it all in such silence. I have felt for you, but I did not like to say anything, lest you might be beginning to forget. I hoped you might still be able to believe the best of her, for that is always a comfort, isn't it?"

"But you don't," objected Usk.

"How could I, when she has made my friend suffer?" demanded Helene passionately. "But I would if it would comfort you," she added.

"You are too kind," said Usk, with sufficient moodiness to satisfy her; and when he was alone he told himself again that he had been brought here on a fool's errand. When Helene sent him the ring, she only meant to assure him of her sympathy under the treatment he had met with from Félicia.

Hence it was somewhat disconcerting to Usk when his uncle appeared suddenly on the scene, for whereas he was quite satisfied to go on from day to day enjoying the present and not troubling about the future, it was only too probable that Cyril would look to hear something definite. He met the party as they came down from the mountains one evening, sunburnt and hungry after a long day's wandering. The two girls had decorated themselves and the pony with wreaths of flowers, and even Prince Franz's Tyrolese hat was ornamented with a garland which he was forbidden to remove on pain of his wife's severe displeasure. Usk, in consideration of his nationality, was allowed to escape with a buttonhole, which Helene had made up for him with great care; and Princess Resi's obedient husband hinted that he would not mind being an Englishman too for once.

"But this is treason, disloyalty!" cried Theresia. "How shall we punish him, Lenchen? Oh, I know! If you say another word, Franz, we will put a wreath round your neck as well. We have plenty of flowers left."

"You have, indeed," said a new voice, as Cyril came face to face with them at a turn of the path. "Princess Helene might be posing as Flora."

Helene smiled shyly from her high seat on the pony, where she was holding the luncheon-basket heaped up with flowers, and offered him a mountain-rose for his coat.

"After this mark of favour, I think I ought to be allowed to lead the pony," said Cyril. "Usk, the Princess will dispense with your services for the present."

Usk looked round in apprehension, fearing that his uncle had misunderstood the state of affairs, but Helene spoke hastily, lest his feelings might be hurt.

"Oh, please, if you would not mind Lord Usk's walking on the other side," she said anxiously to Cyril. "The pony knows him so well."

Cyril smiled, and allowed Usk to retain his position. "Surely there can be no fear of the pony's running away?" he said. "Even music seems to have no effect upon him. I found my way to you by hearing your singing far above me. I hope I did not put a stop to it?"

"We were pretending to be peasants," said Theresia, "but we had left off singing before we met you, Count. We are getting so near the castle, you see."

"Arcadian peasants, surely?" said Cyril, with an involuntary glance at Prince Franz's hat. "And is the Princess Helene sorry to leave the upland meadows and the flowers, and come back to reality?"

"Oh no; we are bringing the flowers with us, you see," answered Princess Resi for her.

"Which things are an allegory," said Cyril; but what he meant he did not explain just then. He spent the evening at the Schloss with Queen Ernestine and Usk, watching all that went on without seeming to do so, and gaining a much clearer idea of the state of affairs than his nephew gave him credit for possessing. When they returned to Luisenruh, and the Queen had gone indoors, he suggested to Usk that they should smoke in the garden, and Usk could not think of any sufficient reason for declining.

"Well?" said Cyril at last, when Usk had exhausted himself in the endeavour to confine the conversation to general subjects. "Any news, Usk? Have you settled anything?"

Usk's first impulse was to feign ignorance, but he knew it would be no use. "With Princess Helene, do you mean?" he asked. "No; I haven't settled anything, because there's nothing to settle. You were all mistaken. She only cares for me just as she does for her brother."

"This is really very strange," said Cyril gravely. "I should have thought the girl's own mother ought to know the state of her feelings, but of course the girl herself must know it better. Do you say she told you this plainly? In that case, surely you would have found it better to leave at once? You have your father's dignity to think of as well as your own, you know."

"I'm afraid she might make herself ill again if I wasn't here to look after her," explained Usk anxiously; and Cyril was seized with a violent fit of coughing, due, he remarked, to something wrong with his cigar. "But she didn't tell me all this," Usk added, with some reluctance. "I saw it for myself."

"You mean you have never proposed to her yet? But you must, you know. It will be merely a formality, of course, since you are aware what the answer will be, and you can go away immediately afterwards."

"But," objected Usk, "she might be afraid—of giving me pain——"

"I'm afraid I don't quite follow you. Oh, you mean she might accept you for fear of hurting your feelings by refusing? That would put you in a very awkward position, certainly. Your feelings have not changed, I suppose?"

"How could they?" was the tragic reply. "Félicia is still—nothing can——"

"Nothing can undo the fact of her intervention in your life, you mean? Quite so. When you start with an absolute impossibility of that kind, it simplifies matters, if only in the direction of cutting off one way of escape. Otherwise I should have thought—— I may be at fault in such a delicate matter, but if you were each prepared to marry out of pure tenderness for the other's feelings, it seems to put it on rather a fair footing, doesn't it?"

"No doubt it all strikes you as awfully funny, but——"

"My dear Usk, far from it! I fully appreciate the seriousness of a situation in which it is equally difficult for you to propose or not to propose, to be accepted or refused. I never remember coming across anything quite like it before. If you see any way in which I can help you, pray tell me. How you and Princess Helene are ever to learn each other's real sentiments while sparing each other's feelings, I don't know. Unless, perhaps, you were to intimate that you intended to serenade her one night, and I took your place, *à la* Cyrano. But I am getting rather old to play Romeo, and, besides, your aunt might object."

Usk growled angrily but incoherently, then turned to his uncle.

"Why you should think it funny I don't know," he said, with some inconsistency. "I don't. But what I want to know is, why should I propose to her at all? Why not simply go away?"

"But I thought her health would suffer? You don't think so now? Because you have been received here as a suitor accepted by her parents, and it would be a blackguardly thing to do. It would be a cruel slur on the lady herself, and a most undeserved insult to the Grand-Duke and Duchess. Surely your father's son is bound to be a gentleman, Usk?"

Even in the darkness Cyril was conscious of the start with which his nephew flung up his head. "You don't understand," said Usk coldly. "I am only anxious to do what is best for her. But think of it, Uncle Cyril," his tone changed suddenly; "she is such a child, so young. I don't believe she has ever thought of this kind of thing at all."

"Girls have a habit of growing into women very much more suddenly than you would expect. At least you might try if she understands."

"I don't like to disturb her. She has been so perfectly happy lately."

"My dear Usk, this idyllic life in meads of asphodel is very nice, but it can't last always. Little Helene must learn to come down into reality like that pleasant sister-in-law of hers, and she will do it with a much better grace than you think. She will bring the flowers with her, as Princess Franz said, if only you will let her."

"But why not let things go on as they are? We might drift into an understanding at last, without making such a fuss about it."

"Because the rest of the world is not standing still while you are drifting. In plain English, we must begin to make arrangements for Michael and Félicia's wedding. Things are so far advanced that it's safe to go to work quietly. It is not expedient that they should be married in Thracia, as they are both Protestants. They can't be married at Vindobona, for the same reason, and therefore Molzau, as the seat of his family, is the natural place.

Unless you have any objection, I should prefer to get you out of the way first. You have no particular wish to hang about at the ceremony, have you?"

"I? No, indeed!" Usk shuddered. "Well, I'll speak to her somehow, and get something settled, but I shall always feel myself the biggest blackguard on the face of the earth."

All the next day Usk went about with a remorsefully resolute expression, which was correctly interpreted not only by his uncle but by Princess Theresia, who was sympathetically prepared to give him every possible assistance. The wanderings of the four young people led them that day into one of the most difficult parts of the mountains, and about noon they left the pony at the hut of one of the Grand-Duke's gamekeepers, since it would only be an encumbrance in their climb. The girls were very tired when they approached the hut again in the evening, and, to her husband's alarm, Princess Resi seemed even more exhausted than her sister-in-law. She hung heavily on his arm, and walked so slowly that Usk and Helene were soon out of sight in front.

"You are much more tired than Lenchen," said Prince Franz. "You must ride instead of her, or at least you must take turns."

"I won't! Why, it would spoil everything. No, you are not to shout to them, Franz. I won't have you interrupt them." Then, as he looked at her in astonishment, "He has been making up his mind to do it all day, and he shall have his chance."

"To speak to Helene, do you mean? Well, I hope you see now that even an Englishman feels a little diffidence in the presence of a daughter of Schwarzwald-Molzau?"

"Because he has taken so long about it, you mean? Franz, it does surprise me to see how foolish even a rather nice man, such as yourself, can be!"

"At least I'm not too dull to see that your fatigue has suddenly disappeared in the heat of argument."

"Ah, you only *see*. I *know*, and I know just what his feelings are."

Prince Franz received this assurance with a shout of laughter, but he consented to lag behind with his wife. Usk and Helene had not noticed their considerate conduct, however. Helene was keeping up bravely, in spite of her fatigue, laying plans for fresh expeditions, and wondering why her companion received them in such a half-hearted way. He did not seem to be listening, she thought, and at last he broke into one of her sentences.

"Take my hand here, won't you? It's a stiff bit." Then a few moments of silence, and he spoke again suddenly. "I'm afraid I shan't be here much longer. My uncle was saying last night that I ought to be off."

This was the plan Usk had devised, after much cogitation, for breaking the ice, and preparing Helene for the proposal which was bound to be so startling to her, but its immediate effect alarmed him. He felt her stumble, and a shiver ran through the arm which was passed through his. Presently she said wearily—

"I am so tired—so terribly tired. Do you think you could leave me here, and fetch the pony from the hut? I feel as if I could not walk any farther."

Much perplexed, and wondering guiltily whether his announcement was to blame for this sudden exhaustion, Usk sought out a large stone by the wayside.

"Of course. Sit here, and I will bring the pony to you in a minute. What an idiot I was not to see that we were going too far for you! But you will catch cold."

He felt in the inner pocket of his jacket for the warm scarf his mother had placed there, adjuring him always to wear it in the mountains, and wrapped it round Helene's neck, tucking the ends into her coat and buttoning it. She pushed his hands away.

"Oh, don't! I can't bear it!" she cried, then added hastily, "I shall be too hot, I mean."

"I am a brute!" thought Usk, lingering near her, but she bade him go with a gesture which aroused in him something of indignation. Helene to treat him in this way! Then he realised the truth of his uncle's words. She was a woman, after all.

Usk made short work of the climb to the gamekeeper's hut, and himself helped to saddle the pony. Helene had not been alone five minutes when the clatter of hoofs on the stones announced his return. She began to apologise for her rudeness in a gentle, tired voice from which all ring of happiness had departed, but he seemed to have no time to listen to her. He had her mounted and well on the homeward way before he would speak, in his new-born terror lest Prince and Princess Franz should come up and interrupt them.

"I want to ask your advice, Princess," he began. "I am in trouble—in a difficulty."

"Oh, if I could help you," she said, with a quick return of pleasure.

"It's about a man who—whom I know. He can't make up his mind what to do. May I tell you about him?" She gave him a breathless permission, and he went on. "This man was in love with a girl, awfully lovely and all that, and she—jilted him for some one else. Then he met another girl, and got very fond of her, but he felt that he never could love any one again as he had loved the first girl. And it seemed to him that it wasn't fair to ask the second girl to love him when he couldn't care for her as he ought. I can't tell you exactly how he felt about it——"

"Perhaps I can," she said. "The first girl was so beautiful that she had only to command, and it was a joy to him to obey. She seemed to know the right thing to be done, as if she had been a prophetess, and the second girl was only a poor little thing to whom he had been kind. She could not advise him, and he would never think of asking her for advice. But because he had been kind to her, he pitied her, and cared for her in a sort of way——" her voice thrilled with pain.

"No, no!" cried Usk. "It's not that. He really is awfully fond of her, but he can't feel that it would be fair to ask her to marry him when he doesn't love her as he did the first girl."

"He adored the first, and the other he is only—fond of?" said Helene. "I think the second girl should be asked whether that is enough for her."

"Is it, Lenchen?" He looked up at her as he walked beside the pony.

"One thing I must know first," she said hastily. "See, she comes to you again, the Princess Félicia, and holds out her hands. She says, 'I am free. I hardened my heart against you for the sake of a crown, but I find that I cannot live without you. I have always loved you best, and I have broken loose and come back to you. Take me.' And you would, would you not?"

"Rather not!" cried Usk. "She has broken me of that kind of thing. I should only want to know what she expected to gain by it."

"You."

"But that's not enough for her. She despises me, you see. And I come and offer you what she despises. Do you wonder I'm ashamed?"

"And I accept it," said Helene. "Does it seem to you very poor-spirited to be content with what you offer me? Perhaps it is, but—I can't do without you. All my strength seems to forsake me when you are away. The day you left Nice, when we met you on your way to the station, I was praying—oh, so earnestly!—that the good God would change your mind, and make you decide to stay. It would have been a miracle, you say? But why not? I knew I could not hold out against my parents and Ivan Petrovitch if you were gone. But you went away, and I seemed to have no power to resist. I allowed papa to tell Ivan Petrovitch that I would marry him, and I prayed that I might die soon, before the day could come. Do you wonder, then, that I am content now? But listen to me, please." She laid her hand on his shoulder as he walked beside her. "I am glad you have told me all your feelings, because it relieves me from one of my fears, at least. I am content, but I am not satisfied. I shall not be satisfied until you can tell me from your heart that you love me best."

"But really, you know," protested Usk, "it's simply that I can't help knowing that if I had to live the time over again since last August I should do exactly the same—as regards Félicia, I mean."

"I know—and I want you to be able to say, 'If I had known Helene then, I should have loved her best.' It sounds impossible, does it not? and you are honest; you will not say it does not. But let me try. Do not steel your heart against me, that is all I ask. You promise, then?" as Usk took her hand and pressed his lips to it. "And you will say nothing of this to any one? It is our secret, yours and mine."

"I feel as if every one ought to know how wretchedly, miserably ashamed I feel beside you," he muttered.

"So? I would have liked you to feel proud—and just a little pleased," and Helene smiled at him with trembling lips. Usk looked at her as if he hardly realised the meaning of her words, then his strained expression relaxed, and he smiled too.

"This part of the path is rather steep. I think I ought to hold you on the pony," he said, and did so.

"There's one thing I want to ask you," said Helene presently.

"To the half of my kingdom, such as it is! Only let me hear it."

"You have a Christian name, haven't you? I want to have a name for you that other people don't use—not to have to call you after a place, like a king in Shakespeare. Do you think Cordelia called her husband 'France'?"

"My Christian name is Edmund," said Usk gravely.

"Oh, and Edmund in 'King Lear' is so horrible! I couldn't call you that."

"I'm sorry. It's a family name, you see. But as you're such a Shakespearean scholar, have you ever read 'Henry V.'?"

"I don't think so. No; I'm sure I haven't. But I will, as soon as I get home."

"Oh no; you needn't," hastily. "There's a fellow in that called Nym—a delightful person—and Nym was short for Edmund, you know. That's a name you can have quite to yourself, if you like it."

"Yes; I like it. But I shall only use it when we are alone, lest other people should find it out. Nym!—I believe it is the name of a horrid person after all," as Usk smiled involuntarily. "Then I shall call you by it all the same, just to punish you. Well, Nym, do you still think you must go away soon?"

"Not without you. I shall want you to help me with my election when I get back to England. I'm sure I could never get through it alone."

"Oh, do you mean that I may help you—really help you—in your parliamentary work? What may I do? I know so little."

"Oh, you can help me with my speeches—look up references, and that sort of thing," said Usk vaguely. "And you could canvass, of course."

"Canvass? But that is to ask people to vote for you, is it not? And the English great ladies allow the voters to kiss them, don't they?"

"*You* had better not, unless you want me to fight the voters all round. No; the way of going to work nowadays is to get at the electors' wives, and make them promise to influence their husbands."

"I see. I am to say to them, 'You must tell your husband to vote for mine, because I am the person who knows best, and I can assure you how good he is.'"

"You are nothing but a child after all," laughed Usk. "And a few minutes ago I thought you had turned into a woman who was quite a stranger to me."

"A child for you to love, and a woman to love you," said Helene, very low.

CHAPTER XVI.
BEYOND RECALL.

"OH, Nym, I am so frightened!"

"Why? About what your father will say, do you mean?"

"No; it's something I have done."

"What wickedness have you been up to now? An infant like you!—aren't you ashamed of yourself?"

"Not exactly ashamed," said Helene seriously, "but terrified."

"Hadn't you better confess? My mind is duly prepared for horrors."

"If you'll call me Little Nell, I will."

"Little schemer, I think. Well, Little Nell?"

Helene put her hand through his arm, and clasped his wrist tightly. "It seemed such a splendid idea when it came to me first. It was the very evening that we were—engaged, you know, and I was so happy I could not sleep, and rather frightened, too, because mamma had been sitting by me and crying, and saying all the relations would be so angry. Then I remembered that the Emperor Sigismund was hunting near Neuburg this week, and I thought I would write to him, and get him on our side. And I did."

"How frightfully enterprising! And what does he say?"

"There hasn't been time for an answer yet. But last night it seemed to me that it would have been so much better not to write to him until—until everything was over, you know. And the answer might come to-day, if he wrote at once. And I am so frightened. I don't know what to do."

"It strikes me you're much too independent for an engaged young woman. You deserve a good scolding. Why didn't you say anything to me?"

"I thought it would be such a nice surprise. I never imagined he might be angry, somehow. Please scold me, Nym. Then perhaps I shall not be so frightened."

"I don't think there's much need for me to scold you," said Usk gravely, rising to look down the path which led to the Lauterbach plateau from the lower world. He and Helene were sitting on the roof of the Moorish kiosk which was one of the less bizarre erections scattered about the gardens, and commanded one of the widest views. "There are people coming up, Lenchen, and one of them looks like——"

"Not cousin Sigismund himself? Oh, Nym!" She was white and trembling, and her hands gripped his arm convulsively. "Can't we escape?"

"Where to? Why, Nell, what is there to be afraid of? He can't eat you."

"But if he should want to send you away? He shan't, he shan't! If he does, I will go too. You won't give me up, Nym?"

"You silly child! I shan't be asked. They'll want you to give me up."

"Then we are quite safe, for I won't."

"He's looking this way; he's seen you, Nell. Wave your hand and don't be frightened. We've done nothing to be ashamed of."

"Of course not. I'm not ashamed. Oh, Nym, he is telling the rest to ride on. He is dismounting and coming up here. What shall we do? Let us go down—quick!"

"Remember that you'll have to ask if you may present me," said Usk hurriedly as he followed her down the outside stair. At the foot he waited, expecting Helene to go forward alone to greet the soldierly man in hunting costume and Tyrolese hat who had just mounted the knoll on which the summer-house stood, but she caught his arm and dragged him forward with her.

"Oh, cousin Sigismund, please—this is Usk!"

A more informal presentation there could not have been, and the Emperor, finding his hand forced, looked almost embarrassed and decidedly annoyed. He acknowledged Usk's presence coldly, greeted Helene with paternal kindness, and sat down on the piazza of the summer-house, motioning her to a seat beside him; but she preferred to stand, still gripping Usk's arm as though to hold him fast.

"I don't think your friend will run away, Lenchen," said the Emperor, with an involuntary smile, as he glanced at the two culprits before him; and Helene laughed nervously as she released Usk's arm, still retaining her hold of his hand, however. Her eyes sought her cousin's face anxiously.

"I suppose you know you are a very fortunate young man?" said the Emperor abruptly to Usk; and both hearers felt that it was not at all what he had intended to say.

"Most fortunate, sir." Usk squeezed Helene's hand reassuringly.

"Have you any explanation to offer of your pres——" Usk felt that Helene darted a look of angry reproach at the questioner—"of the ambition which has led you to seek an alliance with the house of Schwarzwald-Molzau?"

"I can't say it was exactly ambition, sir. I—I love the Princess——"

"I love him," interrupted Helene calmly.

The Emperor frowned. "My dear cousin, as a favour to me, allow Lord Usk to answer for himself. Do you intend to seek a career in Germany, Lord Usk? You hold a commission in the British army, I believe?"

"Only in the Yeomanry, sir. If I might speak freely to your Majesty——"

"By all means. That is what I desire."

"I have no wish to live anywhere but in England, sir. I am my father's only son, and have many ties at home. I hope to enter Parliament before long, and devote myself to a political career."

"And we shall live in a tall, narrow black house in a square, and I shall drive him to the House of Commons every evening, and sit up and look out quotations for his speeches until he comes back," said Helene ecstatically.

"At least you have not idealised the prospect!" said the Emperor drily to Usk, then turned to Helene. "My dear little cousin, might I ask you to be so very kind as to go and tell your mother of my arrival? You will do me this favour, won't you?"

"If you command me as Emperor, I suppose I must," said Helene undauntedly, though Usk could feel that she was shaking; "but for anything short of that I can't—I mean, I won't go."

"Really we could talk business much better," said Usk, aghast, and at his wits' end to know how to act and speak without either offending the Emperor or wounding Helene's feelings. She looked at him with high disdain.

"The Emperor wishes to get rid of me that he may say things to you which will make you give me up, but he shall say them before me, or not at all."

"As you will, little cousin," said the Emperor carelessly. Then he turned suddenly a penetrating gaze on Usk. "What part does this intended marriage of yours play in the plans of your uncle Count Mortimer? If there is any question of a revival of your father's preposterous claim to the throne of Thracia, understand that it will not be permitted. The unbridled ambition of you Mortimers has already endangered the peace of Europe too often."

This time it was Usk who could not help smiling. "If your Majesty knew my father, you would see how strange it sounds to hear you speak of unbridled ambition in connection with him. He went to Thracia against his will, led on by circumstances, and left it with the most intense pleasure. He would do anything rather than go back there or allow me to go."

"You will find it more generally accepted that your father's ambition failed him at a critical moment. He aspired to enter the ranks of reigning sovereigns without submitting to their limitations, and preferred a marriage of affection to one arranged for state reasons. I am only doing honour to the foresight of that most accomplished statesman, Count Mortimer, when I say that if the marriage he projected for his brother with the lady who is now the Dowager Princess of Dardania had taken place, we should probably have had a Mortimer dynasty firmly established in Thracia to-day, and the Balkans would be less of a menace to European peace. But your father withdrew from Thracia, and neither he nor his son will be allowed to return there."

"May I remind your Majesty that my uncle has devoted his life to the work of strengthening the throne of the present King of Thracia?"

"I do not presume to fathom your uncle's plans. But I see that he has reappeared on the political stage after the check he received in the Scythian occupation of Jerusalem, and I augur badly from that."

"Indeed, sir, he is visiting Europe purely on King Michael's account."

"And yet I know him to be at this moment the centre of a widely extended conspiracy, the object of which is to establish him as ruler of Palestine. You would have me believe that he contrives to ally himself with half the reigning houses of Europe in a fit of absence of mind, as you English like it to be thought that you built up a world-empire? No; if Count Mortimer really wished only to set the affairs of Thracia in order, and return as a private person to his retreat in the desert, his judgment is at fault. He should have married his stepson to the Princess Helene, and you to the American heiress, leaving her in her original obscurity until the wedding was over."

"But I would never have married Michael!" cried Helene, in dismay.

"You would if Count Mortimer had wished you to do so, much as you are now marrying his nephew, my dear Lenchen," was the reply. Helene was about to make an angry answer, but Usk stopped her.

"It is not for me to defend my uncle," he said hesitatingly, "but if your Majesty would grant him even a short interview, I think he would be able to convince you of the honesty of his intentions."

"Count Mortimer is as yet scarcely in a position that would entitle him to ask for an interview," was the reply, "and in view of the propaganda he is carrying on, I must decline to receive him in audience. My Chancellor would no doubt be interested in his plans if he cared to impart them to him. I can quite believe that you have the fullest belief in your uncle," this as Usk was digesting the snub as best he might, "but it is merely another proof of his astuteness. If you have any regard for his safety, you might warn him that to persist in his present course will be dangerous in the extreme. He is too much of a firebrand to be left at large in Europe, and if I feel this, what must be the sensations of those whose policy he is deliberately opposing? He will do well to bury himself in the desert again as soon as possible. This morning I should have advised him also to give up all hope of the ambitious alliance he has devised for you, but provided that you and your father refuse to allow yourselves to be drawn into his schemes——" the Emperor paused.

"Oh, you are going to be kind? You will take our part?" gasped Helene.

"Certainly not. I cannot bestow my approval on such marriages as this, but in the circumstance, and especially if Count Mortimer leaves Europe immediately, I will not oppose it."

"The Princess Helene and I are most grateful to you, sir," said Usk, wondering that Helene did not speak. But as the Emperor rose to meet her mother, who had heard of his arrival and come to look for him, she pressed her lover's arm.

"You do believe that I love you, Nym? Even if we have to part, you will never let anything keep you from believing that?" and her face was pale and anxious again.

"Why, of course not!" said Usk. "But what should part us now?"

It happened that Queen Ernestine was spending the morning at the Schloss, and when the Grand-Duchess brought in the Emperor she was unable to escape, much to her disgust. The Emperor was very glad to meet her, and anxious to talk to her about King Michael's marriage, but he was careful only to allude to Cyril as if he were still a trusted minister of state. The Queen had far too much *savoir faire* to expose herself to such a rebuff as Usk had incurred, but it was gall and wormwood to her that her husband's existence should be thus pointedly ignored. Her cousin had played a prominent part in bringing about her unhappy first marriage, and this still rankled in her mind, so that the time seemed interminable to her which she spent in answering his questions and receiving his suggestions. The Emperor departed after lunch, and she returned quickly to Luisenruh, where Cyril came out to greet her with a smile.

"Well, Ernestine, so you have had a visitor? The excursions and alarms penetrated even to my quiet retreat here. Was he in a good temper?"

"I think so—for him. He won't object to Usk's marrying Helene, though he doesn't approve of it, and I am thankful for that. And he approves of all that has been arranged about Michael—thinks that Molzau is quite the best place for the wedding, and that your idea of getting my aunt Amalie to escort Félicia to meet her father's people is excellent. But, Cyril——"

"I thought there was something behind. What is it?"

"I don't think he wants you to be at the wedding."

"Is that all? I never thought of being there. The apple of discord would be nothing to me. The party would scarcely separate without bloodshed."

"Then I shall certainly not go either."

"My dear Ernestine, you must. How could you, Michael's own mother, and on excellent terms with him, be absent? Without me you will have no difficulties about precedence. Do you think I could stand your reducing yourself to a Countess, as I know you would do when you saw me relegated to my proper place? You must think of Michael's feelings a little."

"I shall speak to Michael. He can't be so ungrateful as to let you be slighted after all you have done for him."

"What can Michael do when he comes in conflict with the unbending laws of etiquette? No, Ernestine, listen; I have it all nicely mapped out. We shall both be at Helene's wedding, at any rate; we won't let them do me out of that. Then we will pick up your aunt Amalie and run down to Nice again, and see Félicia safely into the hands of her father's family. You will return to Molzau for the wedding, and I shall go on to Thracia. Michael and Mirkovics have give me *carte blanche* as to reorganising the government offices, so as to prevent corruption in future, and you will join me at Bellaviste. Then we shall be ready to welcome Michael and Félicia, and as soon as they have settled down we will take our leave and be off to Sitt Zeynab, and spend a quiet old age dispensing justice to the Arabs under our own palm-trees."

"But I would rather not wait for that until after the wedding. I should like to go back at once, Cyril—at once, this very day."

"I'm afraid we can't annihilate time and space quite to that extent. But I suppose this means that the Emperor has been saying unpleasant things? I have had Helene here, drowned in tears, and offering to give up Usk if his marrying her would really bring me into danger. What does the man mean by trying to frighten two women? Why not say what he has to say to me?"

"He told me distinctly that you were in danger as long as you remained in Europe and persisted in your schemes. Poor little Lenchen must have heard the same."

"Probably. If we were punished as severely for our evil deeds as for our good ones, we should come off pretty badly, shouldn't we, Ernestine? I'm sure the best thing I ever did in my life was when I threw myself on your mercy and induced you to marry me, and I'm tolerably certain the next best was bringing Usk and Helene together, and yet it's just those two things these people can't forgive me."

"But must you stay, Cyril? Do let us go."

"Before we have seen the young people made happy? No, no; we'll see the thing through after having so much to do with it."

"Well, then, as soon as Michael's wedding is over, you can meet me at Trieste, and we will leave for Beyrout at once. Why should you run into danger for the sake of Prince Malasorte?"

"It's not that. I failed my friends when they trusted me, and now that they have thrown in their lot with Malasorte, I won't spoil their plans a second time, as I should do if I left Europe before he brings off his *coup d'état*. They trust him, and I don't, but if I can help them a bit by getting public suspicion concentrated on me instead of him, I will. And that's my last word, Ernestine."

With a couple of weddings approaching, there was no time to lose, and the Schwarzwald-Molzau family were most anxious to get the less important of the two over, and be able to devote themselves to the preparations for the gorgeous state ceremonial which would mark the marriage of King Michael. Hence Usk made a hasty business journey to England very shortly after the Emperor's visit, and when he returned it was in company with his parents, who were duly installed by the Grand-Duke, not with the best possible grace, in a wing of the great Schloss at Molzau. The transaction with the Aberkerran and Western Hills Railway Company, to which Cyril had alluded, proved, when carried out on the lines he suggested, highly beneficial to Lord Caerleon's exchequer; and he was able to leave on the minds of the Molzau people an impression of sober magnificence which checked any misgivings as to the match their little Princess was making. Quite unintentionally, Lord Caerleon also produced a distinct impression on the Grand-Duke, who revenged himself afterwards by alluding to him as "the stone image," but at the time actually asked Cyril whether his brother would like to be received with the honours due to an ex-sovereign, purely as a compliment, of course, and without prejudice to King Michael's rights. Cyril declined the offer on Caerleon's behalf, but he derived a good deal of amusement as well as relief from the fact that his brother could overawe the irascible Grand-Duke to such an extent that the occasion was not marked by a single burst of temper. The wedding was very quiet. Princess Theresia induced her mother to be present, and that amiable lady, who was always at her daughter's beck and call, shed the lustre of her historic jewels on the ceremony, but Europe as a whole turned its head away and refused to be aware of what was taking place. When the wedding was over, the bride and bridegroom, with what Usk regarded as a preposterous retinue of servants, and Helene as the lowest number with which it would be respectable to travel, betook themselves to the Lebanon, where they were to meet Philippa and her husband, who had been prevented from coming to the wedding by the authoritative claims of a son and heir only a month old. The Grand-Duchess, who had maintained for the past three months a defiant attitude towards circumstances irresistibly suggestive of a ruffled hen defending its brood, bewailed the loss of Helene with floods of tears to Lady Caerleon, Queen Ernestine, Princess Florian, and Princess Resi by turns, and then settled down to her usual duty of acting as a buffer between her husband and his surroundings. Lord and Lady Caerleon returned to England, and Cyril and his wife journeyed back to Nice, in company with Princess Amalie of Weldart, the Queen's aunt, who disapproved highly of Helene's marriage, but had not been able to bring herself to stay away from the wedding.

Félicia was now very near the realisation of her hopes. Princess Amalie, who was her great-aunt, was to take charge of her at Nice and deliver her over to Don Ramon of Arragon, who was to await her with his family at the Pannonian seaport close to which her father's youth had been passed. Her position was now recognised in the Court circle, and after the reception by her uncle it would be made evident to the world. With considerate regard for the endurance both of Félicia and her new-found relatives, it had been arranged that her marriage with King Michael was to follow as soon as the long journey from the coast to Molzau would allow, and this visit to Nice was for her a delightful whirl of congenial toils. Dresses, jewellery, furs, decorations and furniture for the palace at Bellaviste, servants' liveries, the exact constitution of her court, all these things had to be thought of, discussed, decided upon. King Michael was determined to spare no pains nor expense in gratifying the wishes of his bride; and it was well that Félicia had the good taste and loving advice of the Baroness Radnika at hand, and also the wide experience of Mr Hicks, whose sarcastic humour restrained her from not a few follies. Revelling in the interest she excited, for her story had long since leaked out, she was absolutely busy and perfectly happy, save for one shadow of a cloud in her sky.

"Maimie," she exclaimed incredulously, as they were looking through the letters and papers that awaited them on their arrival at Nice. "Come and look here—right now. Usk is married!"

"Well, I guess he hasn't wasted much time lamenting you," said Maimie.

"It's to the Grand-Duke's daughter, the little pale girl—and they haven't ever told us!"

"Why, you know every one said she must be in love with some other man when she was engaged to the Scythian Prince and looked so miserable. Of course it was Usk, and now Count Mortimer has had him marry her."

"He'll be real good to her," said Félicia slowly.

"What's that to you, any way?" was the sharp response.

"Oh, I don't know. Say, Maimie, is the 'chapel attached to the Grand-Ducal Palace at Molzau' the same as the Schlosskirche where I'm to be married? No bridesmaids, of course—I do hate that. I always meant to design the cunningest costumes for my bridesmaids. 'The Marchioness of Caerleon was gowned in panne of an exquisite shade of heliotrope, with the famous family emeralds'—guess she looked just elegant, don't you? 'Her Royal Highness Princess Florian of Arragon in *gris argent* brocade, the corsage almost covered with the magnificent Mohacsy diamonds,' 'the Princess Franz Immanuel of Schwarzwald-Molzau'—that's my cousin Resi, of course—'in pink satin and pearls.' What did the Grand-Duchess wear, I'd like to know? Crimson velvet, I guess. 'The bride's travelling-dress was trimmed with exquisite Eastern embroidery, sent from Palestine by the bridegroom's sister, Lady Philippa Mansfield.' Did Phil mean that for me when she bought it, do you think, Maimie? But there don't seem to be much to say about her wedding-gown—just that she wore the Caerleon pearls. I guess I shall go one better in gowns, any way."

"I just know you will," responded Maimie. "Why, you'll be a queen, Fay."

"That is so." Félicia's tone sounded a little wistful. "I can't seem to feel real happy, Maimie. It'll be you and me one side, and Michael the other, all the time. Being queen will be just elegant, but—— Michael's awfully in love with me, but I don't trust him, and he don't trust me."

"And Usk you did trust," cried Maimie, much alarmed by the turn the conversation was taking, "and he marries another girl right away, before you're married yourself, even. Don't you see the way it is, Fay? It's just that he won't look as if he had been jilted—just pride, and not anything more. He don't care a red cent for this other girl, but he's set on making you mad. I wouldn't have him do it."

"No, I don't feel mad, only a little sorry. And not real sorry, either, for I wouldn't go way back now. It's just that it's the end, Maimie."

"That's so, and I'm real glad of it, for you won't ever be able to reproach yourself about Usk again. And as to Michael, don't be afraid. We'll fix him up some way. You and I will have some place just all to ourselves, so's we can forget all of the stuff the Baroness has been teaching us, and have a good time together, chewing gum and talking the way we choose, and no other person shall come in there."

"And you don't hate turning into a hired girl?" asked Félicia, rather doubtfully.

"Not a cent, so long as you are queen. I'd as lief be hired girl as not, so's I can fix it that I wait on you. They won't turn you into a statue while I'm around."

It was only when she was alone with Félicia that Maimie ventured to speak thus freely nowadays. She had fallen quite naturally into the position of her friend's confidential lady-in-waiting, and had profited by the teachings of Baroness Radnika a good deal more readily than Félicia herself. Her influence was invaluable, said the Baroness, and no one dreamed of the absolute equality to which the two girls returned when they were unobserved. When Princess Amalie arrived, she took a great fancy to Maimie. Félicia was just a little difficult to manage sometimes, she admitted, "but that good creature Logan" could nearly always persuade her to see reason. Princess Amalie was a cheerful old lady, whose temper did not seem to have been soured by the fact that her lack of beauty had driven her family to provide for her by making her a canoness. The semi-conventual title ensured her a position of independence, a sufficient income, and a home at the Stift, or Institution, whenever she was not visiting her relations, which was very seldom, for she made up for not possessing a family of her own by taking the keenest interest in the affairs of her large circle of nephews and nieces. In nearly all the Courts of Europe she was "everybody's aunt," and every one confided in her, although she had a perfect genius for betraying secrets to the very people to whom they ought not to be told. Very soon after her arrival at Nice Félicia knew of all the discourteous and uncomplimentary remarks her uncle Don Ramon had made when he found himself forced to acknowledge an American niece, and Maimie had heard a second time that Cyril had advised King Michael to get rid of her before he married Félicia. Both of them had drunk in with keen delight Princess Amalie's account of the disgust felt by all the younger branches of the Schwarzwald-Molzau family and their relations over Helene's marriage, and the almost total lack of wedding-presents and royal guests. It was this which pleased Félicia most, but Maimie took an even greater pleasure in the further resolution which seemed to have been generally formed by King Michael's family, that they would not attend his wedding if Count Mortimer was to be present. Any slight inflicted upon the man who had tried to separate her from Félicia she accepted as a boon to herself, and it happened that there was another person who felt with her.

About three days after Princess Amalie's arrival, it struck her suddenly that she ought to call upon the Princess of Dardania, who was also her niece, but whom she had not seen for some time, owing to the unfortunate series of events which had long ago alienated the Princess from her relations. Félicia was driving with Queen Ernestine, with whom she agreed as well as could be expected when they had not a single taste or thought in common, and as Princess Amalie's own *dame d'honneur* was ill, she borrowed Maimie for the afternoon. Maimie had by this time become accustomed to being regarded as a mere chattel, an appendage to Félicia, and was by no means loath to accompany the old lady, from whose chatter she expected to pick up a good deal of useful information. She knew that the Princess of Dardania had an old grudge against Count Mortimer, and as she sat silent and apart during the visit, holding Princess Amalie's lap-dog, she heard, as she had anticipated, the canoness beginning her tale afresh. Every disparaging remark, every calculated rebuff, was detailed over again, the Princess of Dardania listening with lazy satisfaction, commenting on what she heard rather with her great black eyes and arched eyebrows than by word of mouth.

"Then what is the poor Count to do, while Ernestine queens it at Molzau, and he is shut out?" she asked at last. "Will he go to England, to his brother?"

"I don't quite know," said Princess Amalie, unwilling to confess herself at a loss. "Ah, but Miss Logan will know. They were explaining their plans to Félicia last night, and she was there."

"And did Miss Logan happen to hear how Count Mortimer proposed to enjoy his week of liberty?" asked the Princess.

"He is going to Thracia, madame, and her Majesty is to join him there."

"To Thracia—from the south of Pannonia? It will be a long journey."

Maimie was conscious of something in the Princess's tone which seemed like repressed excitement. She answered promptly, "He intends to go through Illyria, madame. There is only a few miles of country between the Pannonian and Mœsian railways, and he will save time by driving from one to the other instead of taking the long round."

"To drive across Illyria—— Ah!" said the Princess slowly. Again there was that hint of eagerness in her manner, and Maimie caught it. The Princess looked up, and saw the responsive sparkle in her eye. Instantly her own face changed. "Illyria is a country of very beautiful scenery. I have travelled there a good deal," she said, with a dead calmness in her tone, and Maimie was left to wonder what memory, or what project, had provoked that sudden excitement. For some reason she suspected that it did not bode well for Count Mortimer, and she was glad of it, though it was not evident to her what the Princess could do to annoy him.

A few days later, the Bluebird left the Western Mediterranean for the port at which Don Ramon of Arragon was to welcome his niece. The Queen and Cyril were on board, so was Princess Amalie, and so also was Mr Hicks, who was understood to occupy the position of the late Prince Joseph's man of business. A high honour was awaiting Félicia, for the Emperor of Pannonia happened to be visiting the port; and when Don Ramon's arrival was delayed, through some accident or mistake which was hinted not to be altogether accidental, he took upon himself the duty of welcoming her and Princess Amalie. Queen Ernestine went northwards to Molzau, Cyril started on his journey to Thracia, and Félicia, with her train of followers, was delivered into the hands of her uncle. He proved to be a stern-faced elderly man, early soured by the loss of all his prospects, and interested in humanity only from the point of view of a student of brain disease. His wife was so completely his shadow that she was known as "la Ramona" at the Pannonian Court; but she had individuality enough to disapprove very heartily of heretics, Americans, and people who were not *hoffähig* generally, and to regard Félicia as an example of all three. The daughters were uninteresting girls, keenly on the look-out for something shocking in everything their new cousin said or did, and Félicia expressed privately to Maimie her opinion that even if her whole fortune had been divided among them they would not have married. But these unpleasing family characteristics were merely spots in the sun. Félicia's ambition was on the eve of attainment. She was recognised as a daughter of Arragon, and as the Princess Doña Feliciana Josefa was on her way to Molzau to receive a crown—and incidentally, to marry a king.

CHAPTER XVII.
MISSING.

"WELL, Phil, what do you think of your sister-in-law? Isn't she an amusing child?"

"She is amusing, but she's not a child—or at any rate, she's a woman as well."

"No, Phil, I swear to you I feel like a showman, or old Barlow in 'Sandford and Merton,' or a benevolent uncle taking a small kid to the Zoo—like anything but a husband. Now, do we look like a married couple?"

"Not a bit. How funny! It was only this morning that it struck me you looked like a kind elder brother taking his little sister out on a half-holiday. Helene was hanging on your arm and looking up into your face, and chattering hard the whole time."

"Of course. She's nothing but a child. She has been nowhere, seen nothing, heard nothing, and her mother has done all she could to keep her a baby. Everything is new and interesting to her, and life is a nice new game. I keep thinking of that absurd story of the wife of some literary man who chose a house because 'the garden would be so lovely for her and Percy to play in.' I'm certain Helene would be attracted by a good lot of bushes. She'd think they would be so convenient for hide-and-seek."

"I'm glad the more obvious literary parallel hasn't occurred to you," said Philippa severely.

"More obvious even than that? Oh, I know! David Cop——"

"If you say it, I shall throw this book at you. She is a dear little thing, Usk, and you don't appreciate her a bit."

"I know she's a dear little thing, and I'm awfully fond of her. And no doubt it's most excellent for her to be firmly convinced that I know everything. Plenty of men would give their ears for their wives to think so. But it's horribly embarrassing for me when she looks up at me just like a child and asks some perfectly impossible question."

"No, not like a child. A child is never satisfied if you can't answer it. 'Don't you know? Why don't you know? Does anybody know? Then *why* don't you know?' You used to go on like that yourself; I can remember it quite well. But when Helene finds she has asked a question you can't answer, she's dreadfully afflicted, and looks round to make sure that Fred and I haven't noticed."

"Poor little girl! But really, Phil, we get on perfectly well, and she's continually assuring me that she was never so happy in her life."

"Yes; but I am in constant terror that her eyes will be opened. I always try to draw her in when you and I are talking. Don't you see how it is? You consult me about what you are going to do, but you tell her about it when it's all settled. And she has a right to be consulted."

"Oh, nonsense! I don't want her to worry herself. She's a dear little comrade as it is, and I believe I'd rather she remained a child, after all. She—she's so awfully contented and satisfied now, you know."

Philippa nodded her head sagely. "That's just it. You think that as a woman she would demand more from you. But she is a woman in the way she loves you, Usk. I can see that."

"My dear Phil, you are most penetrating and far-sighted, I don't doubt, but after all, I'm Helene's husband, and I may be allowed to know her better than you do. Look at her now, tormenting old Fred with a catechism on vine-growing. She's only a child, vividly interested in everything, and devoted to me just because I've been kind to her—as if I could help it. I suppose she'll grow up some day, but I'm not going to turn her into a little old woman before the time."

Philippa rose and looked over the carved wooden railing that safeguarded the balcony, for the house stood on a precipitous hillside. Up the winding path her husband and Helene were slowly climbing, with a pleasant murmur of voices, after visiting the vineyard which occupied a more gradual slope below. Far in the distance could be seen the blue of the Mediterranean, with a wilderness of hills between, some bare and rugged, others cultivated almost to the summit. The native house in which the Mansfields had taken refuge from the heat and possible fever of the Palestinian lowlands where their work lay was situated on the western slope of Mount Lebanon.

"They won't be here for a minute," said Philippa hastily. "Usk, tell me quickly—I'm most frightfully anxious—is it because you are still in love with Félicia that you can't care properly for Helene?"

Usk laughed. "You've quite determined that I'm a brute to Helene. No, Phil, I can't say that I feel the very slightest envy of King Michael. If Félicia was cruel, she was kind too. As I was not to love her, she left me nothing to do but hate her. No, I don't mean that exactly. You know, don't you?"

"And now she has probably had her wish, and been a queen, for two days. It doesn't seem at all fair or moral. Even Becky Sharp never quite succeeded in getting what she wanted. But she's out of your way, and I'm glad of it. Poor little Helene must 'dree her ain weird,' I suppose, as you won't listen to what I say about her."

"A telegram!" cried Helene, running up the steps at the end of the balcony. "We met the servant coming from Beyrout with the letters, and he had this for you, Usk. What can it be?"

"What can it be?" echoed Usk, as he tore open the envelope. "I say!" his tone changed. "Just listen: 'Your uncle has disappeared. Meet me immediately at Novigrad, *viâ* Trieste.—ERNESTINE.' What does it mean?"

"Uncle Cyril disappeared!" gasped Philippa.

"They've murdered him at last!" cried Mansfield. "Don't stand staring, Usk; they shall pay for it! We'll track them to the world's end."

"It doesn't say he's dead," suggested Helene, very pale. "Perhaps it's brigands, and they are holding him to ransom."

"Well, at any rate, we must find him," said Mansfield. "If we go down to Beyrout to-night, we can catch the steamer to-morrow morning, Usk."

"No, no," said Usk, recovering himself. "You must stay here. We can't leave the girls alone. Besides, there's your work."

"Hang the work!" cried Mansfield. "The girls will look after one another."

"No," said Helene, very quietly, but with white determination, "I am going with Usk."

"Nonsense, Lenchen! I can't take you. You'll stay with Phil and the baby."

"I am going with you," repeated Helene. "Or if you refuse to let me come with you, I shall follow you by the next steamer, and Phil will help me, because she knows I am right in going."

"She is, indeed, Usk," said Philippa. "With you to take care of her, what reason is there why she shouldn't go?"

"Why, dozens! It's simply preposterous. I shall be rushing about into all sorts of places, where I couldn't take a lady. You don't know how rough things are in Illyria."

"I can live upon black bread and goats' milk," said Helene calmly, "and you couldn't."

"But I can't trail about a whole procession of servants. Everything may depend upon following up a clue quickly."

"Then we will leave some of them behind. I promised mamma I would never travel without Hannele and Jakob—she was afraid of my becoming English and independent, so she made me promise not to go about unattended," explained Helene rather piteously to Philippa—"so we must take them; but with your William besides, we can manage quite well."

"Now you know you only want William because his name is the same as the groom's in 'Mademoiselle Mathilde,'" said Usk unkindly.

"No," said Helene, with dignity. "It is because it is not suitable for my husband to have no attendant while I have two."

"And look here, Usk," said Mansfield; "you can establish your wife and the servants comfortably at some safe centre while you go off and follow up clues. It'll be much better for her to have some one with her."

"That is not what I want," objected Helene—"to be left safe and comfortable while Usk goes into danger. I want to go with him and help."

"Oh, but you don't want to be in the way, Lenchen," said Philippa, speaking with the authority of a whole year of matrimonial experience. "You will do as Usk thinks best, I know, and he'll take you with him wherever he can, won't you, Usk?"

"Rather!" said Usk forgivingly, and Helene brushed away a threatening tear or two, and smiled up at him.

"Because, you see," Philippa went on, "this is such an awful thing that we must none of us think about ourselves at all, only about Uncle Cyril and how to find him. We had better settle that you are to telegraph for Fred the moment you want him, Usk. I don't think he ought to leave Palestine until you see what there is to be done, for I know the Chevalier Goldberg considers his presence here very important."

"I hate being made a part of a plot and not seeing how it works," said Mansfield gloomily. "If you wire I'll come like a shot, Usk. Which is the quickest way?"

"To land in Dardania and cross the mountains, if the steamers fit. Why does Aunt Ernestine tell me to come round by Trieste, I wonder?"

"Because she has reason to distrust Dardania, probably. It's quite possible that our friend the Dowager Princess has allies there still."

"You are puzzling Helene," said Usk. "She doesn't know all the ins and outs of the family differences."

"Oh, I know that Cousin Ottilie was very angry about Aunt Ernestine's marriage, and said horrid things about the dear Count," said Helene; and then the subject dropped, as Philippa suggested that it was time to pack.

Five days later Usk and Helene, with their diminished retinue, were landing at Trieste, after eagerly seizing upon the papers brought out by the boats which boarded the steamer outside the harbour. When they left Beyrout, no news had arrived concerning the disappearance of Count Mortimer beyond the Queen's telegram, but in these European papers it was the sensation of the hour. The circumstances appeared equally simple and perplexing. The Count, with his secretary and valet, had left the Pannonian railway at its termination on the eastern border of the Illyrian Provinces, and, like other travellers, hired a carriage to convey him across the debatable land which was owned by Roum, partially occupied by Pannonia, and unceasingly coveted both by Dardania and Mœsia. The Roumi Government had refused persistently, and from its own point of view wisely, to allow any railway to be built across this strip of territory, but there was a carriage road, kept in good order by Pannonian military engineers, which connected the Pannonian railway system on the western border with that of Mœsia on the east. Quitting Novigrad in Illyria, the party had arrived safely at a posting-station bearing the uneuphonious name of Klotsch, situated near the point at which the main road into Dardania crossed, almost at right angles, that which joined the two railways. Here, while the horses were changed, the travellers alighted for dinner, only to find when the meal was over that their driver had got drunk. The landlord volunteered to provide another, but he had to be sought for in the village, and Count Mortimer, who was obviously impatient at the delay, decided to walk on with his secretary, and allow the carriage, with the valet and the luggage, to overtake him. It was a long light summer evening, and he was anxious to reach the Mœsian frontier that night. The carriage started about a quarter of an hour later, but the driver and the valet were astonished to find that they did not come up with the walkers, although the horses were fresh and the road good. In ever-increasing astonishment they drove the whole way to the customs-station on the Mœsian border without meeting any one, and learned there that Count Mortimer and his companion had not arrived. The valet became immediately very much excited, and demanded a force of gendarmes from the Pannonian frontier-post, in order to go back and make a thorough search on both sides of the road for his master, who, he declared, must have been waylaid and murdered. The officer in charge of the post received the demand with contempt and some resentment, for the road was regarded as particularly safe, but the valet's earnestness, and his declaration that he believed his master had enemies who would stick at nothing to get him out of the way, induced him to send a patrol with torches to search the roadsides as far as Klotsch. Messengers were also sent along the road which led into the Dardanian highlands, to inquire whether the two men had taken the wrong turning and gone that way by mistake; but neither at the one country-seat which stood in the neighbourhood, nor in any of the poor hamlets along the road, had anything been seen of them. The country-house belonged to Prince Valerian Pelenko, a cousin of the Prince of Dardania, and he himself, travelling to "Europe," had passed through Klotsch with his attendants shortly after the carriage had started. He had not met it, for it would have passed the cross-road before his carriage turned into the main highway, and most certainly he had not met the missing men, for his attendants would have been sure to report at the posting-station the astonishing sight of two "European" gentlemen walking unattended along the road. Extraordinary as it seemed, there was no doubt that Count Mortimer and his secretary had disappeared as completely as though they had not been, and that the disappearance had taken place on the high road and almost in broad daylight. There were no signs of a struggle, and tentative suggestions of a landslip, or a fall over a steep place on the edge of the road, were scouted at once, for there was absolutely not the slightest indication of either. The English papers, taking up Count Mortimer's cause with a vigour they had seldom displayed during his career, were drawing parallels between his disappearance and that of the unfortunate Mr Benjamin Bathurst in the early years of the nineteenth century, and hinting that as similar influences were in all probability at work, the fate of the one was likely to remain, like that of the other, an unsolved mystery. The Neustrian, Scythian, and Roumi papers, relying on the known antipathy of their respective Governments to the Pannonian occupation of the Illyrian Provinces, were urgent and eloquent in their representations that Pannonia had now conclusively proved herself unfitted to discharge her duties, since she could not even protect travellers on the high road. The Pannonian papers, unable to deny the facts, took refuge in the assertion that Count Mortimer's disappearance was purely voluntary. For reasons of his own he had made up his mind to vanish, and he had done so, and who could be held responsible for the doings of a man whose pride it had always been to baffle and astonish the rest of Europe? This was the state of things at present. Queen Ernestine, in the deepest grief and anxiety, was at Novigrad, where Lord Caerleon had joined her as fast as steam could bring him from England, and they were making a comprehensive search throughout the whole district, aided by the best detectives that money could procure.

"It looks hopeless!" said Usk despondently to Helene, as they walked up the quay at Trieste. "One almost wonders—— Now then, where are you going to?" The words were addressed to a loutish youth, apparently a dockyard loafer of the usual type, who had lurched up against him; but as the man withdrew with a surly apology, Usk found a piece of paper in his hand. Guessing that it contained some secret information, he unfolded one of the newspapers he had bought, as if to look at the page again, and laid the paper against it. "Look here, Helene!" he said.

Helene glanced quickly at the scrap of writing.

"When you leave Trieste this afternoon, watch out for me. I shall be fooling around at the depot with a camera, and I don't want to have you seem to know me. Get into talk with me the way you would with a stranger, for I must speak to you.—HICKS."

"This gentleman is some English peer of your acquaintance?" said Helene, looking respectfully at the signature.

Usk smothered a laugh. "Not exactly," he said. "He's the American newspaper man you've heard so much about, and a real good fellow. If you'll excuse me, Nell, I'll light a cigar."

"A long way round!" said Helene, as he twisted the paper into a roll, and striking a match, set light to it, instead of lighting the cigar with the match.

"If you mean a roundabout way, my child, why not say so? Don't you see that Hicks evidently expects us to be watched? I daren't leave that paper lying about, or even tear it up. Now will you keep your eyes open this afternoon, and express innocent wonder if you see a long scraggy fellow, with a thin grey beard, taking snap-shots? That'll give us an opportunity to get into conversation."

Helene promised to be on the watch, and very soon after they reached the station she pulled Usk's sleeve. "Do look at that gentleman taking photographs," she said, with admirable innocence. "It must be so interesting to be able to do it! All these quaint costumes——"

"They're nothing to what you'll see in the Balkans," said Usk. "What a pity we didn't think of bringing a kodak. But we might send for one, of course. Would you mind allowing my wife to see how your camera works?" he asked of the photographer, who had been listening with a twinkle in his eye while pretending to focus an Albanian group on the opposite platform.

"Why, certainly," was the hearty response. "You hold it this way, and you put your eye here—— But if we move away a step or so, we won't be so crowded. I have a whole-souled admiration for your manner of meeting me, sir," added Mr Hicks, in a lower tone, as he exhibited the camera and appeared to be describing its mechanism. "And this is the little Princess?"

"No," said Helene. "It is Lady Usk."

"Is that so?" asked Mr Hicks slowly, manipulating a screw. "Well, I incline to think Lord Usk has struck ile."

"I don't know English quite well yet," said Helene apologetically.

"I guess your husband has found the pay-streak, then."

"I'm afraid there must be a great many words I don't know. I must look them out."

"Mr Hicks wants me to understand that I've married a treasure, Lenchen. Does that satisfy you? Well, Hicks, what's the plan of campaign?"

"Why, just this, sir. There are the Queen and your father turning the Illyrian Provinces upside down, and a whole army of detectives figuring around. But those that took on this big risk mean to see it through, and they will pour out the dollars like water to keep truth at the bottom of her well. They know just who's on their trail, and they have covered their tracks. I have concluded to work back of them, instead of in front, which is high-toned, but renders a man more liable to sudden death than appeals to me. I am working up the Illyrian Provinces with typewriter and camera, *sabe?* on behalf of a monster tourist agency in the States that's set on exploiting them, and you may bet your last red cent my eyes will be open for any suspicious circumstances. I'd like to fix up a code for communicating with you——"

"Oh, please," said Helene, "pardon my interrupting you, but I have just seen my cousin, the Princess of Dardania, getting out of the train at the end of the platform, and I thought from what Usk said——"

With great dexterity Mr Hicks withdrew himself behind a pile of luggage. "You're real smart, Lady Usk. If her Royal Highness had seen us together, it would have been just about the meanest trick fate could have played us. Coming off the cars from Illyria, was she? Now what's she been doing way down there? She was at Nice yet when we quit it before the wedding. You don't think she saw us, do you?"

"No, I'm sure she didn't, but she is coming this way."

"Helene, you'll have to face her," said Usk. "I must arrange things with Hicks. If I establish you on this seat, with a bodyguard of servants in the background, while I go and see about the luggage, you won't move away till I come back, will you? and you'll try to keep her in talk?"

"But there is no need to see about the luggage," Helene called after him, as he hurried away; "the railway officials look after that, or you can send one of the servants." But he was already out of earshot, and Helene rose to meet the Princess, who swept towards her with outstretched hands, making her feel incredibly young and small.

"Why, my little Lenchen!" cried Princess Ottilie; "do I find you alone? What has happened to the Fairy Prince—fairy peer I should say, should I not?"

"Usk is gone to look after the luggage," said Helene.

"The ruling passion of the Englishman on his travels! And are you tired of one another yet, my romantic Lenchen?"

"I am certainly not tired of him, Cousin Ottilie."

"What freezing coldness, little one! But I forgot that you had married into a romantic family. The Mortimers and their wives are always absurdly attached to one another. It is quite *bürgerlich*—middle-class, I suppose your new relations would call it."

"If it is middle-class to be fond of one's husband, then I am middle-class," said Helene.

"You—the descendant of Charlemagne! And you are allowing your husband to drag you into exile already? Where are you going with this wonderful luggage which needs so much looking after?"

"Can you ask, Cousin Ottilie? Of course we are going to Novigrad, to help look for the dear Count."

"To help look for——? Oh, Count Mortimer!" the Princess broke into a soft peal of laughter. "My darling Lenchen, you must forgive me. It really did not occur to me whom you meant. Has it never struck any of you that Count Mortimer might prefer not to be looked for?"

"How could it? What can you mean?"

The Princess drew a letter from her pocket. "Of course Lord Usk won't believe me," she said, "but I should really like to save you two from taking a journey into the wilds for no reason at all."

"Cousin Ottilie! why shouldn't Usk believe you?" cried Helene, aghast.

"My dear child, he is prejudiced, of course," but the Princess seemed a little confused, and unfolded the letter quickly, as though to forestall further questioning. "This is from my husband's cousin, Valerian Pelenko. I have just been paying a flying visit to Dardania—to see the new baby, not to stay; Emilia and I agree better apart—and I wrote to ask whether I might spend a night at his house near Klotsch on the journey. Here is what he says: 'Pray consider my house as your own, as often and as long as you like. I am sorry to be away. By the bye, I had a curious *rencontre* just as I was leaving home. Do you remember the man Mortimer, who made rather a laughing-stock of himself at Ludwigsbad two or three years ago by aspiring to your particular favour? Naturally you will remember him; he found your cousin Ernestine of Thracia less hard-hearted than yourself, I recollect. Well, as I was driving towards Klotsch, before we turned into the Novigrad road, we met another carriage, and in it I saw Count Mortimer and a lady, with whom he seemed to be on excellent terms——'"

"Oh, it must be a mistake!" cried Helene. "Why, Aunt Ernestine was at Molzau, at Michael's wedding."

"My dear Lenchen, let me entreat you not to make that remark to your husband when you tell him this, or he will set you down for ever as a fool. Valerian goes on: 'There were servants and luggage, and all the necessaries for a long journey, apparently. Doubtless your friend was bound, by way of Dardania, for the Ionian Isles, or some similar region of delight, where a spot or two may yet be found destitute of the moral code, as I once heard an Englishman say of the East generally. Happy he! What are your plans for the autumn? I am too late for Ludwigsbad this year, alas!' That is all that concerns the Count," said the Princess, folding the letter, as Helene sat dumb. "And here is your husband, come to sweep you into the train with the rest of the luggage, I suppose. How do you do, Lord Usk? So delightful to get this short glimpse of little Lenchen! She really looks younger than ever since you married her."

Helene was still speechless as the Princess bade her an affectionate farewell, and gave her hand to Usk that he might lead her to her carriage. When he returned to warn Helene that their train was coming in, she turned an ashy face to him.

"Oh, Nym, I must tell you. She says such things——"

"Wait until we're in the train," said Usk; and it was only when they were moving out of the station that he turned to her with, "Well, what is it, Nell?"

"She says that the dear Count went away of his own accord, with—with a lady, and that he doesn't want to be found."

"Not content with kidnapping him, they try to take away his character, do they?" said Usk savagely. "She wants to hurt Aunt Ernestine, do you see, Nell? We won't tell her if we can help it. Of course you don't believe the story?"

"Of course not. But it is so dreadful that people should say such things about him, when we know how good he is, how——" Helene's voice failed.

"Well, we know that no one will believe it who knows anything of him. She must have thought you very young, and ready to believe anything, mustn't she? Poor little Nell!" He put his arm round her, and drew her close to him, regardless of the fact that the guard might appear at any moment.

"But how terrible that she should say such things, when she knows they are not true! Our own cousin, Nym!"

"Oh, well, you see, she has a grudge against him."

"But why? What has he done?"

"Well, she wishes it to be understood that he proposed to her at Ludwigsbad a year or two back, and she refused him. That sort of thing generally makes a woman pursue a man with implacable hatred, doesn't it? What do you say?"

"Why, I should have thought just the opposite—that she would be as kind to him as possible, and fearfully sorry that he should love her in vain."

"So should I. And we think, all of us—mind, he has never said a word on the subject—that she—well, that it was the other way about."

"That she proposed to him, and he refused her? Oh, Nym!"

"And he married Aunt Ernestine. That's where the sting comes in, you see. Why, what's the matter, Nell?" for Helene was crying.

"I never thought people could be so wicked," she murmured at last.

"Ah, you'll find worse things done than that," said Usk sagely. "Now do you see why Hicks thinks the Princess is mixed up in whatever has happened?"

"But what could she have done?"

"He's quite certain there has been foul play, and he thinks the most likely thing is that they have hired a band of brigands to carry him off into the hills. You see, the district is a sort of No Man's Land, and the brigands may have come from any part of the Balkans. They may even have taken him down into the Roumi territory to the south, where an army couldn't find him. But Hicks doesn't believe it's as bad as that," quickly. "He thinks it's much more likely they have got him somewhere in the Dardanian mountains."

"And does he hope to find him?"

"He's going to try. By the bye, he is to get a camera for us, and send us hints on photography from time to time, and we have arranged a code with the technical words. So cheer up, Nell. We'll outwit them yet."

CHAPTER XVIII.
WANDERING FIRES.

IT was on a day of appalling dust and heat that Usk and his wife arrived at the Illyrian town of Novigrad. The place stood among hills which had been left stony and treeless by several centuries of Roumi domination, but up which patches of woodland were beginning to creep under the fostering care of the Pannonian officials in charge of the province. There was a sparkling river which flowed in a rocky channel through the town, and many of the houses on the outskirts were embowered in greenery, but the general impression was of glaring white walls, dazzling roofs and blinding dust, and an atmosphere of heat from which no refuge could be found. Helene was nearly fainting when Usk helped her out of the carriage at the door of the solitary hotel, and her plight moved an elderly man of Jewish appearance, who was sitting in a dejected attitude on the terrace in front, to catch up a glass of sherbet, and hasten to her assistance with a murmur of sympathy.

"Place de younk lady in dis chair off mine, sir," he said. "Heat such as dis iss killink for dose not accustomed to it. Your business must be fery pressink, iss it not? But why! it iss my frient Lord Usk and his most gracious lady! Ah, den I need not ask your reasson for comink here. What a loss iss dis we hef all sustained!"

"I never thought of finding you here, Chevalier," said Usk, administering a few drops of the sherbet at a time to Helene, "and yet of course it's the natural thing. Helene, this is the Chevalier Goldberg, my uncle's great friend——"

"Alas, no!" cried the Chevalier, raising his hands deprecatingly—"not his frient, his enemy. It is my embition, my esspirations, det hef led to all dis! De Queen says it; she will not receife me. I may not help efen to search for him, but I remain here, in case I may yet be permitted to do somethink."

"But you didn't help to lead him into danger?" asked Helene anxiously.

"I kennot tell. De Queen says it. It seems he hed receifed warninks; I wass not told. Rader would I hef postponed efen de triumph off my nation den risk his life, his freedom."

"Then where is the Queen?" asked Usk.

"She is spendink de day at Klotsch, and your fader also. So it iss efery day. Dey go dere to exemine all de neighbourhood demselfs, and come beck at night to receife de reports off deir achents. But her Machesty will not see me, nor allow me to take any part in de search."

"We will speak to her, and ask her to let you help," said Helene. "It must be so sad for you not to be allowed to do anything."

The Chevalier pursued her with his fervent thanks as Usk supported her into the hotel, but the task she had undertaken proved more difficult than she expected. When Queen Ernestine returned, she refused to have anything to do with the Chevalier Goldberg. He had sacrificed her husband to his plots, she declared, with a violence of unreason which reminded Lord Caerleon of those early days when she had done her best to make Cyril's life a burden to him. The stately gentleness which had characterised her of late years seemed to have disappeared, and she was simply a woman fighting wildly for her husband's life. The fearful anxiety of the last few days had driven her almost mad, as she joined feverishly in the searches made in the district round Klotsch, or sat waiting for messages, not knowing whether to look forward to their arrival with fear or with hope. But so far no news whatever had been received.

"It's quite natural she should feel prejudiced against the Chevalier," said Lord Caerleon to his son, as they walked up and down the terrace, while Helene sat with the Queen, and tried in vain to cheer her, "but it's very unfortunate. These Jews have a natural instinct for ferreting out mysteries, and Goldberg can set in motion a whole army of helpers all over Europe. But I can't urge her against her will. I wish your mother was here."

"What is the mater doing, by the way?" asked Usk. "We quite thought we should find her here."

"Pauline Vassilievna is dying. We were just starting for Geneva to be with her, when your aunt's telegram came, so your mother went alone to Switzerland, and I came on here."

"And King Michael—what about him? What an ungrateful beast he must be!"

"Oh, he is away on his honeymoon, in the Bluebird, and your aunt wouldn't allow him to be told. He was only to be troubled with absolutely necessary State business, and she doesn't particularly want him here. He could do no good."

"Usk," said Queen Ernestine from the window, and Usk noticed the new tone of sharpness in her voice, "you and Helene are not to stay here more than one night. Helene looks ill already, and Mirkovics tells me she was nearly dead when she arrived. You must take her up into the hills, to Drinitza, in the morning."

"Oh, please not," Helene's voice interposed, from the sofa. "Dear Aunt Ernestine, we have come here to help. You will break our hearts if you send us away, and won't let us do anything."

"Hush, Lenchen!" said the Queen harshly. "I will not have more trouble brought upon the innocent by their connection with me. How could I ever forgive myself if you fell ill?"

"Besides," said Lord Caerleon, in his calm tones, "you can be very useful at Drinitza. It is not so far off, just above the underground cavern out of which this river here flows, and you will be able to explore that part of the country as we have been doing the other side. It seems quite certain that your uncle has not been taken across the Dardanian frontier, and therefore he must still be on this side of it. That will be your work, to search the Drinitza district."

"But Helene is not to be sacrificed. I will not have her sacrificed," repeated the Queen feverishly. "If there is a curse, it shall rest on me alone."

"No, no; who is talking of sacrificing Helene?" asked Lord Caerleon. "She is going to spend these hot weeks at a pleasant little place in the hills, and take plenty of walks and drives with Usk. That will suit you, little girl, won't it?"

"Oh yes; if we can really help in that way," said Helene eagerly.

"I am having the buggy sent out which I had built for you," Lord Caerleon went on. "It is intended for rough roads, and I have my eye on a pair of fair enough horses which one of the officers in the town, who is ordered back to Vindobona, wants to sell. Usk will give you driving-lessons, and take you with him on all his expeditions wherever the buggy can go. When he can't be with you he'll leave you in charge of his man William, who is the nephew of our coachman at Llandiarmid, and knows all there is to know about horses."

"Oh, thank you. You have arranged everything so nicely," said Helene.

"We will take a carriage and go over to Drinitza in the morning to see about rooms," said Usk. "Will that suit you, Aunt Ernestine? You evidently share Phil's opinion that I don't take proper care of my wife."

"It is not that. I have brought trouble on so many——" began the Queen.

"By the way, Ernestine," said Lord Caerleon, with some impatience, "are you still thinking of a personal appeal to the Emperor of Scythia? If so, we shall want to leave some one in charge of things here. Are Usk and Helene to come back from Drinitza?"

"Ah, you are trying to persuade me to accept the help of the Chevalier Goldberg!" said the Queen. "Well, I cannot say yet. I must wait until all the detectives have reported to me. Then, if there is still no news," she shuddered, "we must think what is to be done."

Early the next morning, while the air was still comparatively cool, Usk and Helene hired a carriage and drove out to Drinitza. Their road zigzagged up and down the hill-sides, and crossed several bridges, all over the same river. The hamlet for which they were bound stood near the crest of a hill, looking as if it might at any moment slip from its little terrace of rock over the stupendous cliff below. Behind the hotel the wooded summit rose sheer; in front there was the pretence of a garden, with arbours (a little the worse for dust), and a fountain or two, and a piazza which commanded a pleasant view. At the foot of the cliff, in a cool glen cheerful with singing-birds, and bright with crimson-flowered bushes and masses of white-blossomed creeper, was the mysterious cavern from which the river burst forth full-grown. The landlord of the little inn, an old Pannonian soldier, was eloquent in his description of the wonders of the cavern, the blueness of the water inside it, and the strange shapes of the rocks, but it seemed that he had only explored it to a point from which the entrance could still be seen. He was too wise, however, to dash the hopes of prospective guests, and promised to provide a boat and plenty of torches, and do his best to find two boatmen, if the "gracious English nobilities" wished to make a more thorough search at any time. The place was beginning to become known, but the old man's principal customers were still the officers and townspeople who drove out from Novigrad on Sundays and holidays, and he was delighted to let his best rooms to such distinguished persons as Lord and Lady Usk. In his abounding satisfaction he escorted them up the wood-paths to the top of the hill, and pointed out in the valley far below on the other side a white thread, which he told them was the road into Dardania.

"Then where does Prince Pelenko live?" asked Usk, while Helene gave a gasp. They might even now be looking at the scene of the final act of the tragedy which was baffling them all.

"Yonder is his Highness's house," answered the old man, pointing to a large white building dimly seen among the trees, "but his property extends for miles, as far as the Dardanian frontier."

"Then we shan't be able to walk through those lovely forests, as he is away from home, and can't give us leave," said Helene.

"Ah, the gracious lady need not grieve herself," said the old man, with a knowing look. "The Prince started, certainly, but he is back at home now, sure enough, though it is not every one that knows it, and it will be easy to obtain his leave for the noble lady and gentleman to go where they like on his land."

"At home? Oh, Usk, we must go and see him, and find out whether he really——" but Usk pressed her arm.

"Is it true that the river flows underground before it reaches the cave, and that there is a place where it disappears into the earth?" he asked the landlord. Volubly the old man assured him that it was perfectly true,—that close to the Mœsian frontier, on the north-east, there was a spot called Bagnanera, where the river disappeared suddenly into a cave of awful blackness, and that objects thrown into the water there had in due time been found in the river below the hotel.

"How dreadful!" said Helene, shuddering. "Why," her tone changed, "there is a European coming up the hill—not an officer. Have you any other visitors?"

"It is the great Scythian nobleman who has been visiting the Pelenko mansion. Will the nobilities excuse me?" asked the old man hurriedly. "I must see that his horses are ready."

"How awfully unfortunate!" said Usk quickly, as the landlord hastened back to his house. "It's Prince Soudaroff, of all people! and there's no hope that he hasn't seen us. Well, we had better face it out, Nell, and just admire the view till he gets up here."

The recognition seemed to be mutual, for the gentleman who was mounting the steep path stopped and hesitated perceptibly when he saw the two figures on the hill-top, but coming, apparently, to the same decision as Usk, he resumed his climb, and advanced towards them with beaming countenance and uplifted hat.

"I assist at an idyll!" he said in French as he met them. "Youth, beauty, and nature—I enjoy them all at one glance. Let me congratulate you, Lord Usk, on the spot you have chosen for your sojourn. It is evident that you are of the few who have discovered the charms of this corner of Europe, you and—may I say Madame la Vicomtesse?"

"Oh yes, please," said Helene, flushing with pleasure. Here at last was some one who understood her wish without being told.

"It isn't the scenery that has brought us here," said Usk bluntly.

"Ah no, I understand. A family bereavement, is it not? and one of a particularly distressing character. You have no good news yet, I fear?"

"Fear? you mean hope!" was Usk's unuttered comment. Aloud he said, "None."

"But we hope to learn something soon," said Helene eagerly. "We were so glad to hear that Prince Pelenko has returned home, because he seems to have seen Count Mortimer later than any one else on the evening that he disappeared, and we want to ask him so many things."

Again a look of uncertainty flitted across the Scythian statesman's face. "Ah, I see!" he exclaimed. "I fear you will be disappointed, madame. It is not Prince Valerian, the head of the family, who is at the Pelenko mansion, but his younger brother, Prince Shishman Pelenko, who holds a commission in my imperial master's bodyguard, and it is on his account I am here. Ten days ago this young man was engaged in a duel, and had the misfortune to kill his opponent. The sad event preyed so much upon his mind that he wrote a hasty resignation of his commission, and retired to the family estate, to bury himself among these hills. My august master received his decision with much regret, and graciously entrusted me with a mission to the unfortunate young man, and it is from the discharge of this mission I am returning—unsuccessful, alas! Ah, madame, how can I hope to explain to one so youthful and innocent as yourself the depth of grief, of remorse, in which this unhappy Prince Shishman is plunged? He confines himself to the enclosed grounds immediately surrounding the paternal abode, and in these narrow limits he paces up and down like a caged tiger. Until the unfortunate dispute which separated them, he and his rival had been the closest of friends, and now no assurances that his conduct throughout was that of a man of the nicest honour will comfort him. He cannot forgive himself," and Prince Soudaroff, deeply affected either by his own eloquence or by the moving picture he had conjured up, brushed away a tear.

"I am so glad you have told us this," said Helene, in conscience-stricken tones. "We were going to ask leave to walk through the woods on the estate."

"But why not, madame? In this I can serve you, I am happy to say. At the inn I will write a note to Prince Pelenko's steward, and he will send you the necessary permission without troubling the unhappy Prince Shishman. Of course I will assure him that you will confine your walks to the unenclosed woods, and not threaten the privacy of the mourner."

"Surely that assurance is scarcely necessary, Prince?" said Usk haughtily.

"You must pardon me, my dear Lord Usk. I was only considering how, as a friend of the family, I could best ensure the goodwill of an old family servant. You intend to spend some time here? I myself am leaving at once, summoned to the sick-bed of my sister-in-law, Pauline Vassilievna, or I should have been delighted to do anything in my power to show you the neighbourhood."

"We stay here," returned Usk, with unconscious grimness, "until we have cleared up the mystery of my uncle's fate."

"Indeed?" Prince Soudaroff raised his eyebrows. "It is a delicate suggestion to make, but are you sure you are quite wise? Is it kind to condemn madame to a possibly lifelong sojourn among these hills? When one wishes to disappear, one is generally able to baffle pursuit."

"Count Mortimer didn't wish to disappear!" cried Helene indignantly. "It is his enemies who have got him imprisoned somewhere."

"Ah? 'The Prince of the Captivity,' indeed!" said Prince Soudaroff pleasantly. "I would not for the world destroy your faith, madame. But I must reluctantly depart. I trust we may often meet again. Farewell, madame! farewell, Lord Usk—surely all the world must be jealous of your happiness?" and kissing Helene's hand gallantly, the diplomatist departed.

"Usk," breathed Helene, clutching her husband's arm, "that man knows!"

"Knows what?"

"Where the dear Count is. I saw it in his eye."

"Oh, nonsense, Nell! He's much too wily for that."

"I don't care. I don't know how it is, but I know that he knows."

"If it was certain, it would be maddening," cried Usk; "for you might as well tell me that the General of the Jesuits knows. We are just as likely to get it out of him. But we'll tell Aunt Ernestine what you think when we get back to Novigrad. It may help to decide her plans."

"Prince Pelenko is not at home, after all," said Helene to the old landlord when they returned to the hotel. "It is his brother, Prince Shishman."

"So the noble Scythian gentleman told me, gracious one. I did not see the Prince come home; I only saw smoke coming from the chimneys, and the Dardanian servants hanging about, and I knew that one of the family must be at the house. I guessed that there were creditors waiting to make themselves troublesome as soon as his Highness arrived in Europe, as has happened before, and that he had therefore returned."

As Usk had anticipated, the chance meeting with Prince Soudaroff decided Queen Ernestine to make an immediate appeal to the Emperor of Scythia, who was far more likely to listen to her, now that the influence of his terrible Chancellor was temporarily removed. At the moment he was paying his annual visit to his relations at Kaufenhafen, the capital of Cimbria, and the Queen made up her mind to follow him thither, trusting to the kind offices of their common cousins to secure her an interview. It was a relief to Lord Caerleon that his sister-in-law should be willing to take this long journey, for the whole of the district round Klotsch had now been scoured, without revealing the faintest trace of the missing men, or anything that could throw light upon their fate, and he feared that her brain would give way under the continued anxiety. In view of this personal appeal she became almost hopeful, for she and her helpers were now beginning to feel convinced that Count Mortimer and his secretary had been kidnapped either by Scythia or by persons in Scythian employ, and conveyed in some mysterious way into Scythian territory, to be there imprisoned.

"I will go on my knees to the Emperor to release him!" she said. "I will promise anything in his name—anything, even that we return at once to Sitt Zeynab and never leave it again. Cyril will keep the promises I make for him—he may hate me for making them, but I can bear that, if only he is restored to me safely."

The Chevalier Goldberg, whom she had at last consented to receive, and even, on Lord Caerleon's advice, to leave in charge of affairs at Novigrad, was equally ready to make sacrifices on Cyril's behalf. If it was the plot to place Cyril on the throne of Palestine that had led to his disappearance, the plot should come to an end and the plotters be disbanded the moment he was released, and the heads of the great Jewish syndicate called the United Nation would pledge themselves that he should never again be brought forward as a candidate, and would enforce the same pledge on their poorer brethren the Children of Zion. Besides these concessions, the importance of which was, to the initiated, rather apparent than real, the Chevalier was prepared to give other aid, but the nature of this he did not mention to the Queen, although Lord Caerleon understood that the journey would be as easy as the financier's influence could make it. At every stopping-place an agent of the Chevalier's was at hand, to see whether anything was needed, and at Kaufenhafen his representative had *carte blanche* to take any measures advisable for furthering the interview. These included the discreet distribution of presents among various high functionaries of the Scythian Court, and the expense was likely to be considerable.

Usk and Helene drove into Novigrad to see the Queen and Lord Caerleon start on their journey, and returned rather dolefully to Drinitza. They had never anticipated anything like this resultless and hopeless waiting, this wall of silence which seemed to close them round. Even a rumour, though it might be proved baseless, would have been some comfort; but no one came forward with false clues, as generally happens in more thickly populated countries. The disappearance was complete.

"Look here," said Usk, rousing himself, as they sat silent on the terrace over their after-dinner coffee, "we're getting into the blues, Nell, and I won't have it. I shall wake you up jolly early to-morrow morning, as soon as ever I come back from the river, and you shall have a good stiff driving-lesson before breakfast. Give you something else to think about."

Helene smiled faintly, but she was destined to be waked even earlier than her husband intended, and the driving-lesson was not to take place that day. Usk went down to the river for a swim every morning, and he was still absent when Helene was aroused by hearing a horseman dash up the steep road, and ride clattering into the stone-paved courtyard beside the hotel. She heard him inquire eagerly for the English nobleman, and peeping out of her window, she saw the tokens of dismay, horror, and astonishment exhibited on the faces of the audience which gathered round him. She saw him ride down the road again to find Usk, escorted by several volunteer guides, and she rang wildly for her maid, and sent her to find out what had happened. To her dismay, the landlord returned a polite message that the rider had brought news for the noble Viscount, and for him alone, and that it was of too horrible and appalling a nature for any one else to take the responsibility of communicating it to the gracious lady. From this decision he could not be moved, and Helene, in terrible anxiety, flung on her clothes in wild haste, regardless of the protests of the discreet Hannele, who owed her position to her supposed power of keeping her young mistress within bounds. Dressed at last after a fashion, Helene rushed out, hatless and in slippers, and ran down the sunny, rocky road towards the glen. Before she had gone half the distance, she met Usk hurrying up, some way in advance of the messenger and his friends, and ran to him. She could not speak, but he read her question in her eyes.

"No, he's not dead—at least we don't know that he is, but they have found Paschics's body in the river between here and Novigrad."

"Dead—murdered?"

"I don't know. I am going into the town to see. No, you had better not come. I'll send out to tell you anything we may discover."

"Oh, I must—I must come," cried Helene, clutching feebly at his arm, and forthwith stultified herself by spinning round and falling in a dead faint at his feet. To Usk's intense relief, there appeared at this point a sufficiently comical procession, consisting of Hannele with her Highness's hat, Jakob with her Highness's shoes, and William, pressed into the service, with her ladyship's sunshade. With their assistance, Helene was carried back to the hotel and up to her room. When she recovered consciousness, her first thought was to send Usk off to Novigrad at once, and she went so far as to promise to stay in bed until he came back, although the scandalised Hannele was not a very agreeable sick-nurse, even when her company was the only alternative to Helene's own anxious forebodings. It was a long, weary day, but Usk returned at last, though without any comfort to offer her.

"It is poor Paschics, sure enough," he said.

"And he has been murdered?"

"That's what we can't be sure about. The body is terribly bruised, but there seems to be no injury sufficient to cause death."

"But perhaps he was drowned?"

"No; the police-surgeon seemed quite certain it was not that. He rather thinks that death was due to heart-failure following on a violent shock of some kind."

"Oh, Usk, how terrible! If he could only speak! But the bruises?"

"I have a theory which may account for them. Do you remember what the landlord said about this river flowing underground from Bagnanera, fifteen or sixteen miles away? Well, suppose the poor fellow was thrown into the water there, whether dead or alive, in the hope that he would sink and never be heard of again, but that the river carried him all the way to this place? The bruises would be easily accounted for then, you know."

"Isn't it horrible? Oh, Nym, do you mean—you can't mean that they did that to the dear Count too, and that he has not been found, and we shall never know? What are you going to do?"

"I think of going over to Bagnanera. We never dreamed of extending the search in that direction, it seemed so entirely out of the way. I only wish I could get hold of Hicks to come too."

"The camera he was to send us came to-day."

"That won't tell us where he is, though. We must only hope that the thought of the underground river will strike him when he hears about this. There are not many things that don't occur to him."

Very shortly it was evident that Mr Hicks had a correspondent in Novigrad who kept him in touch with the course of affairs, and that the idea which occurred to Usk had struck him also, for the next day a telegram was brought out from the town which read—

"Hope camera arrived safe. Bagnanera good place for views. Am going there to-morrow; will coach Lady Usk if you come. Bring films."

"We must make a day of it," said Usk.

"And you'll have to take me," said Helene.

"I've a good mind to take Hannele too, to look after you," returned Usk; but Helene smiled contentedly, in the certainty that Hannele could not possibly be accommodated in the buggy. In accordance with the cryptic direction at the end of the telegram, William and Jakob accompanied the carriage as a mounted escort, and Mr Hicks smiled when he met the procession, in spite of the seriousness of the occasion.

"Your outfit is real elegant, Lady Usk," he said, as he helped Helene out. "Guess the natives will be 'most too frightened to stop and look at you."

"Do they make any opposition to our exploring the place?" asked Usk.

"Not a cent, sir. I've been figuring around as cross-examiner all of the morning, and I can't dig anything suspicious out of them. The whole township isn't anything but rocks and a few goats, and there's not a sign of plunder or bribery in any of the houses. Of course, they may all be in it together, and have hidden everything dangerous, but I can't quite fix it so. And now, if her ladyship will be so good, after a few hints from me, as to work that camera all it's worth, and make love to the women and the population generally, you and I will strike for the disappearing river."

"Oh, mayn't I come?" asked Helene anxiously.

Mr Hicks appeared to consider deeply. "Well, Lady Usk," he said, "I'd as lief have you come as not, but you could assist us far more by exercising your fascinations upon the villagers. A few nickels laid out in bribing the children to have their pictures taken might raise us up friends that would justify their existence."

"Then of course I will go to the village," said Helene.

"Between you and me, sir," said Mr Hicks, when he had explained the working of the camera, and Helene, attended by Jakob, had begun to climb the steep street of the hamlet, "I have no use for her ladyship the next hour or two. It's a real ugly place, this cave, with a current that runs like Niagara, and a sweet reputation among the people. They won't go near it for their lives, and would consider it profane to build a boat. I propose that you and I and your groom should take it in turns to explore, one man swimming, and the other two holding the rope and lighting him."

Usk agreed, and the first sight of the cave proved to him that Mr Hicks's precautions were not unnecessary. The river, running swift and dark, lost itself under an overhanging brow of rock, and it required a good deal of nerve to plunge into the blackness within, even when secured by a rope. Various ways of obtaining light were tried, such as burning candles at the entrance, fixing a lantern just inside it, or fastening a candle in the cap, miner's fashion, and the cave was explored for some distance. Usk, indeed, ventured too far, being caught by the swift current, and only saved by clutching at a rock past which he was swept, until he had regained sufficient strength to add his own efforts to those of Mr Hicks and William as they hauled desperately at the rope. He returned silent and grave, for, as he confided to Mr Hicks, he felt he had been very near death. In the narrow passage he had reached, the torrent took a downward course, and above the rush of the current he believed he could distinguish the roar of water falling from a great height. What fate could be more awful than a plunge over a subterranean cataract, to be dashed and beaten and choked to death in the bowels of the earth? No attempt was made to penetrate farther, but there were some gruesome experiments to be conducted with the carcases of goats, in order to ascertain whether a body thrown into the river here could possibly reappear below Drinitza. The result, it may be mentioned, was of a negative character. Two of the carcases were actually found the next day in the river above Novigrad, but the rest were never seen again, so that the experiment proved little, either as to the body of the unfortunate Paschics or the still unknown fate of Count Mortimer.

CHAPTER XIX.
A CHANCE WORD.

THE result of Queen Ernestine's journey to Kaufenhafen was in one respect satisfactory, although it threw no light upon the mystery of her husband's fate. The Emperor of Scythia received her kindly, and pledged his imperial word that neither he nor his ministers had had any hand in Count Mortimer's disappearance, nor had they the slightest idea where he was at present. No reference was made to the Zionist plot, and the Emperor did not express any disapprobation of Cyril's late political activity, which, said Prince Soudaroff when he heard of the interview, was a clear waste of a heaven-sent opportunity. Even if the Emperor did know nothing about Cyril, he might surely have dissembled his ignorance, and obtained some useful pledges from the Queen by means of vague promises and hinted hopes. But the whole subject of the interview amused Prince Soudaroff extremely, and he confided his *bon mot* respecting the "Prince of the Captivity" so freely to the two or three kindred souls he contrived to gather round him even at Geneva, that it was repeated all over Europe before the end of the week. It was generally added, and the addition may also have been due to the kindred souls, that the Emperor had been wise in asserting his Chancellor's non-participation in the *affaire Mortimer* before, and not after, questioning the Chancellor himself on the subject.

Heart-sick from her failure, the Queen was driven almost mad by the accounts which reached her from Illyria of the discovery of Paschics's body and the abortive search at Bagnanera. Fresh confusion had been imported into the matter by a surgeon of high reputation for whom Usk had telegraphed to the capital of the province, for he certified that the bruises on the body had been caused before death, and could not, therefore, be the result of a buffeting in the subterranean river. Anxious to examine into the mystery herself, and also pay the last tribute of gratitude to her husband's faithful servant by attending his funeral, Queen Ernestine hurried away from Kaufenhafen, only to fall ill on her journey to Illyria. A nervous fever, brought on by grief and overstrain, kept her a prisoner at Vindobona, tended by her aunt Princess Amalie, who was almost as much at home in the sick-room as at a wedding, and watched over by Lord Caerleon, who had not the heart to leave her and go on to Novigrad.

Then, before Prince Soudaroff's witticism had time to grow stale by repetition, and when the papers, having made the most of the sensation afforded by the medical evidence as to the cause of the secretary's death, were beginning to hunt for a fresh topic of interest, there came a rush of events which swept the "Balkan mystery" clean out of men's minds. Just at first it was remembered sufficiently for Prince Soudaroff's friends to say among themselves, with exquisite glee, that if he had his secrets from the Emperor, the Emperor clearly kept one or two things secret from him. But as Prince Soudaroff only looked wise and said nothing in public, the world in general thought he had known of the matter all along, little guessing the gnashing of teeth and tearing of hair which had taken place in certain chancelleries, that of Scythia not excepted, when the news came. There was a revolution—the fifth, if minor outbreaks are left out of the calculation—in Neustria.

This new revolution was the crowning glory of its kind. Other revolutions had been bungled at their inception, or had dragged on for several years before they could fairly be considered successful, but this one seemed to have been born full-grown. One night Prince Timoleon Malasorte was a casual sojourner in a Lutetian hotel, so little thought of as a political personage that the police either were not aware of his arrival in the forbidden capital, or winked at it. The next night he was master of the army, and by its means of every fortress in the country, master of the ecclesiastical system, and through it of the women of Neustria, master also of the national purse-strings. The whole thing came about with almost the suddenness of a transformation scene. It was never known publicly when and how the idea of the revolution had taken shape, or how long the astutest minds in Europe had toiled by devious and underground paths to prepare its way; all that was certain was that one morning the city was white and purple with unauthorised proclamations, posted in all sorts of forbidden places. The police tore them down, only to find that whatever way they turned, fresh bills were posted behind their backs, and while they did their confused best to keep pace with the bill-stickers, a drastic "Pride's Purge" was being administered at the centre of parliamentary life. The Senate and the Chamber of Deputies were found to be surrounded by troops, and the alarmed legislators saw their sacred precincts invaded by armed men, headed by—as it seemed to their startled eyes—the counterfeit presentment of Timoleon I. Without giving them time to recover from their surprise, the new Timoleon informed them that he had assumed the office of Dictator in order to save the country from the evils menacing it, and announced a dissolution. Before even the most violent deputy could raise his voice in protest, soldiers were filing down the alleys between the rows of seats, and arresting one man here and another there. Those arrested were taken at once into safe keeping, where they met many of their friends in other walks of life, who had been apprehended at their homes or places of business. The city Municipality, indeed, found its numbers almost complete in this new place of meeting. The whole scheme could not, naturally, be carried out with the same celerity and certainty as these preliminary steps, and in the streets of Lutetia there were a number of spasmodic attempts to erect barricades. But Prince Timoleon and his supporters were not men to be trifled with; troops had been posted at strategic points throughout the whole city, and there were cannon ready wherever they were likely to be needed. In these circumstances the barricade-builders found it well to carry back into the houses the bedding and furniture they had requisitioned, to restore the overturned cabs to their normal position, and even to lay down again the torn-up paving-stones. In the more respectable portions of the city no opposition was offered to the new rule. The better class of people were so sick of their late government, so weary of a long succession of mediocrities diversified by knaves, that they were ready to welcome any change that promised stability and some measure of relief from corruption, and above all, they hailed the advent of a man—a commanding personality who would not only command but be obeyed. The priests headed processions of their flocks to take the oath of allegiance to the new government, and—surest sign of the strength that lay behind the movement—the credit of the country rose higher than before, and the Dictator had no difficulty in obtaining money. In all the larger provincial towns a similar change of affairs had taken place, and each town saw that the district round it followed its example. The rural inhabitants submitted to the altered conditions quite philosophically. They had always been of the opinion that they lived in the worst possible world for honest people, so that it was clear they could not become worse off. There was some fear lest the sacred names which had been handed down from the days of the first revolution should be lost to sight, and an absolutist empire, supported, as it was now currently believed this new enterprise had been throughout, on one side by the Jews and on the other by the Jesuits, be set up. But the Dictator was too wise for this. The proclamation which he issued on the night of his triumph, dated from the Presidential palace (which the former occupant had quitted in haste and without much reluctance), was a model in its way. After a short sketch of Roman history, appropriate to the occasion, Prince Timoleon called the nation to witness that he had been welcomed as the saviour of society by the whole people, and established at the head of the government with scarcely the shedding of a drop of blood. There was the inevitable reference to the deeds, sacrifices, and triumphs of his ancestors; but with touching modesty and fairness Timoleon Lucanor, Prince-Dictator, concluded by saying that he proposed immediately to take a *plébiscite* of the whole nation on the question of reviving the imperial form of government in Neustria. This clinched matters. Timoleon Lucanor trusted the people.

When the great news was flashed over the wires from Neustria to Illyria, and the flock of newspaper correspondents which had settled upon the country round Novigrad, like rooks upon a ploughed field, pocketed their notebooks and their fountain-pens, and took the quickest way back to Europe, they were followed also by all the detectives who had been engaged in the search for Cyril. Curiously enough, as it seemed to Usk and Helene, these men all saw in the Neustrian revolution a chance of exercise for their peculiar talents, and no bribe would induce them to remain. Consequently, to continue the investigation of the mystery there were only Mr Hicks, still pursuing his inquiries in the Bagnanera district, the Chevalier Goldberg, who was called away every few days to Vindobona on business of European importance, but returned doggedly to Novigrad when it was settled, and the two young people at Drinitza, who were now absolutely at a loss, and could not even think of anything more that might be done. They made long driving excursions, during which Helene was duly tutored in the use of the reins, and which were always made the occasion of questioning any country-people who might be met on the road, and they wandered through the beech-forests on the Pelenko estate, and invented wonderful series of events which might happen, to crown all their work and anxiety with success, if only some clue would opportunely show itself. But in the minds of both there was surely growing up the conviction, hateful and long resisted, that the black pool in the cave at Bagnanera held the clue to the secret.

Riding back to the inn one day from Novigrad, tired and dusty, and perhaps a little cross, Usk caught sight of Helene talking to a lady on the terrace. The lady's face was not familiar to him, and there was something about her look and dress which made him think she was not likely to be an acquaintance of the Schwarzwald-Molzau family, but Helene was so deeply engrossed in listening to her that she had not even heard him ride up.

"Who is the lady talking to Lady Usk?" he asked of the landlord, who came out to take his horse.

The old man looked embarrassed. "It is a Scythian lady, honourable sir, who has driven out to see the glen. Her name is—at least she calls herself—Mlle. Garanine."

"Tania Garanine—the actress?" cried Usk.

"I know, honourable sir. She is not suitable company for the gracious lady, but what could I do? It was not for me to——"

Usk had left him, and was hastening round the corner of the house. As he reached the terrace, however, he saw the stranger already descending the steps to her carriage. She glanced over her shoulder at him—he noticed that her eyelids were artificially darkened—and laughed gaily when she saw his angry face. In a moment she was driving away, kissing her finger-tips lightly to Helene. The action raised Usk's wrath to white heat.

"How dare you take up that woman?" he demanded fiercely of Helene. "Surely your own self-respect ought to have kept you from speaking to her."

"I thought she wasn't very nice," murmured Helene, gazing at him with dilated eyes. "Her hair was such a strange colour—I think it must be false—and her skin looked—oh, so *dead* when she came close. But she sat down here by me, and talked."

"She's one of the most notorious women in Europe," fumed Usk, "and now she'll spread it abroad that you have noticed her and received her, and what will your people think of me for letting you do it?"

"But you couldn't help it, nor could I," pleaded Helene.

"Why didn't you get rid of her, when you saw the kind of woman she was? I thought exalted persons like you always knew how to dispose of people who tried to force themselves upon your notice?"

"I don't know how to be rude," said Helene, with heightened colour. "No one who was unfit to speak to me has ever been allowed to come near me before."

"That's a nasty one for me!" said Usk, whose wrath was beginning to evaporate.

"Oh, Nym, I am so sorry; I didn't mean it. And see, I will tell you how it was that I felt obliged to listen to her. I didn't dare even to try to cut her short, lest I should lose something important. She talked about the dear Count."

"I might have known it! More lies, I suppose?"

"I don't know; I suppose so, I hope so. She said, just as Cousin Ottilie did, that he had gone away of his own accord, but—I couldn't quite understand—I think she wanted to make me believe that she was the lady Prince Pelenko said he saw in the carriage with him. At least, she talked as if she knew him quite well, and could tell us where he was now, and she said such horrible things. I don't know whether she only suggested them, or really said they had happened, but I know she hinted that the Count had—had got rid of poor M. Paschics because he knew too much, and he had no more money with which to keep his mouth shut. And she talked about a gay life among the islands somewhere, and then she spoke just as if the dear Count was mad, and told me a dreadful story about some one she knew once who had spent all his money, and was found by his relations, quite by chance, in a refuge for lunatics somewhere near Trieste. She said they had advertised for him everywhere, but he had forgotten his own name, and it was only because his nephew happened to catch sight of him that he was recognised. Do you think—she could mean—that the dear Count is in one of those terrible places?"

Usk pondered a moment. "No; I don't!" he cried suddenly. "They want to get us out of the neighbourhood, Nell, that's it! Now that Malasorte has made his *coup d'état*, they see through the bogus plot, and they want to undo their work, if they can. I'm certain they have him hidden somewhere near— in a cave or something of that kind—and find they can't get him out of the country without our knowing. We'll stick on here and tire them out. To-morrow I'll go over and bring Hicks back with me, if I have to drag him by main force. If the whole crew know he's on our side I don't care. He's the man to smell them out."

"How clever you are, Nym! I never thought that it might be a trick. I do wish I was older, and—and———"

"Wiser?" suggested Usk.

"Yes, wiser, and able to give you good advice."

"Thanks; I'd just as soon not. I probably shouldn't take it, you know."

"Oh, Nym, I wish you wouldn't laugh. I want to be a better wife to you."

"You're tons too good as it is, so don't get any better. Was I awfully down on you just now about that Garanine woman, Nell? I didn't mean it, but you must learn to protect yourself, you know. Just say, 'I was a silly little idiot, and I'll never do it again.'"

Helene repeated the words with admirable docility. "But I do wish I could think of clever and useful things like you," she added with a sigh.

When Usk betook himself to Bagnanera the next day, he left Helene listless and unhappy. The actress's words had affected her more than she knew, and the vision of Cyril, nameless and robbed of everything, in a pauper lunatic asylum, was constantly before her eyes. The prospect of spending the whole day alone, since ten hours at least must elapse before Usk could return, if he was to bring Mr Hicks with him, was terrible, for she could think of nothing but that vision. At last she took herself resolutely in hand, determining to set to work at something that would occupy her thoughts. She would spend the day in the beech-woods, and make a sketch for her mother, setting herself the task of finishing it at a sitting. Telling Jakob that she would need his attendance, she went to her room to get out her colour-box. Hannele, who was mending a torn gown, was pleased to approve of her intention. Sketching was a lady-like and elegant accomplishment (provided the sketcher took care not to sit on the grass), and far more suited to the daughter of a princely house than tearing about over the country with a husband as thoughtless as herself. Helene felt that the rebuke was not undeserved, for she had torn the gown disgracefully in scrambling through a thicket with Usk, and she did not venture to suggest that it might be discarded, although Hannele, in her huge spectacles, had the half-resentful, half-triumphant aspect of an unwilling martyr. Hannele was grumbling monotonously on, therefore, when Helene silenced her suddenly by an imperative gesture. Standing near the window, she had been half-unconsciously aware that two Englishmen who had spent the night at the inn were discussing the views as they breakfasted on the terrace, but now her full attention was aroused by hearing the name of Shishman Pelenko mentioned.

"Queer thing that we should have come straight from Shishman Pelenko to his ancestral halls," one man had said.

"Would it be well to call? The place looks inhabited."

"I think not. We know that Shishman isn't there, and though he's a good sort, his elder brother is a queer lot, I believe."

Helene dropped her paint-box, and running down the stairs, presented herself suddenly before the astonished tourists.

"I must ask you to excuse me for disturbing you," she said, with the little air of dignity which sat so oddly and yet so well on her, "but I think I heard you mention the name of Prince Shishman Pelenko? He is a kind of relation of ours—at least, he is the cousin of a cousin—and his movements have—have puzzled us a little of late." Was this untrue? she wondered uncomfortably.

"He is an erratic fellow," said the elder of the two Englishmen—they had both risen politely when she addressed them, "but I am glad to be able to assure you that he was all right ten days ago, Fräulein. We have been mountaineering with him in the Caucasus for more than two months, and though he has had several hairbreadth escapes, he's as fit as he can be."

"We heard a rumour—about a duel," hazarded Helene.

"He has had no opportunity of fighting a duel for three months at least, madame"—the speaker had caught sight of the wedding-ring on Helene's finger. "Indeed, I know, for he told me himself, that his last duel happened quite three years ago."

"Thank you. You have relieved my mind very much," said Helene simply, but she returned into the house with slow, dragging steps. Was her mind relieved, or was it oppressed with a new and vague anxiety? Prince

Shishman Pelenko had never been in the neighbourhood at all; his duel, his remorse, his flight from society, were all alike inventions of the Scythian Chancellor's fertile brain. But if he had not been occupying the Pelenko mansion, then who was the recluse there, who never walked beyond the garden, whom no one in Drinitza had seen? Conviction forced itself upon Helene. The Princess of Dardania's apparently purposeless display of Prince Valerian's letter, the visit and the glib falsehoods of Prince Soudaroff, the strange hints of Tania Garanine—all pointed to one fact and one alone. Cyril was imprisoned down there in the Pelenko mansion, and Helene could take no steps to rescue him for a whole day. The idea was intolerable. She must at any rate try to find out whether she was right—and in a moment she saw how this might be done. Only once had she and Usk approached the great house closely in their walks, and then they had noticed a corner of the garden wall where a tree, growing against the masonry, had forced the lower courses out of position, and dislodged the upper stones. Usk had remarked that it was a standing invitation to burglars, and now she would play burglar.

Her face was flushed with excitement when she entered her room again, and she gathered her paint-brushes together with shaking hands. She could think of nothing but her scheme, and did not at first perceive that Hannele was grumbling still.

"Going out alone on the public terrace and speaking to two strangers—Englishmen, too, who have no reverence or good manners! That was not the way your august parents taught you to behave, Highness. And asking after a young rip of a Scythian captain as if life and death hung upon it! What's Prince Shishman Pelenko to your Highness, I should like to know? I wonder what your noble husband will think when he hears?"

This it was which reached Helene's ears at last. She turned angrily upon the woman. "Silence, Hannele!" she said, with a decision Hannele had never seen in her before. "I justify myself to my husband, not to you."

Leaving the maid crushed but indignant, she quitted the room with her painting materials. Jakob was in waiting, with her camp-stool and umbrella, and they climbed to the top of the hill, and plunged into the beech-woods on the other side. When Helene was as near the Pelenko mansion as seemed prudent, she chose a spot in a long grassy glade, bordered on either side by huge trees which were beginning to show the first touch of autumn, and set to work with uncertain fingers, wondering how long it would be before Jakob went to sleep. She had decided not to make him a partner in her enterprise. For one thing, there might be danger for him where a girl would pass unscathed; and again, he would be very likely to presume upon his long service with her family to prevent her doing anything. It seemed to her that her henchman was provokingly wakeful to-day. Generally it needed but a few minutes to set him propped against the trunk of a tree, slumbering peacefully, with his mouth as wide open as if he wished the squirrels to drop beech-nuts into it. But on this occasion it almost seemed that he must have been making resolutions against his drowsiness, so unwinkingly watchful did he remain. Helene thought hours must be passing before his rigid frame relaxed, and his grey head dropped gently back against the tree. When at last he was undoubtedly asleep, she tore out a leaf of her sketch-book, wrote on it in pencil, "I am going to seek another view. I will return here," and laid it near him with a stone upon it to keep it from blowing away. Then she stole noiselessly past him, and made sure that the tree was between him and herself before she ventured to turn in the direction of the house. She was not long in reaching the corner of the wall, and although it was harder to climb than she had expected, she succeeded in getting over. Inside the wall was a thick belt of shrubbery, so wild and unkempt that it might almost be called a wood, and with beating heart she forced her way through this. There was a clear space in front, she saw, and presently she reached its edge. Crouching down and peering through the bushes, she found that she was close to the house, which looked much less imposing near at hand than from a distance. Originally a pretentious building of the sham classical style dear to the heart of the Europeanised Illyrian, with a good deal of ornamental work in plaster about it, it was now little better than a ruin. Great masses of the balustrading had fallen from the edge of the roof, the walls were cracked in many places, and there were only a few remnants of glass left in the windows. The garden was utterly neglected. Grass was springing up between the stones of the paved pathways, and the water in the large square tank was foul and choked with weed, above which the melancholy fragments of a broken fountain reared themselves. It was evident that whatever debts Prince Valerian Pelenko had contracted in Europe, he had not spent the money on his family seat.

As Helene peeped through the bushes, a slight movement attracted her attention to two persons whom she had not at first noticed—an old man, sitting on a stone seat beside the tank, in the shade of a clump of overgrown myrtles, and a servant, like his master in European dress, lounging against the wall of the house a little behind him. The picture was so pathetic that Helene felt the tears rise to her eyes—the old man sitting there among the ruined glories of his house, his gaze fixed on the dull stagnant waters of the tank. But there was a rustling in the bushes behind her; and turning her head, she saw that a huge fellow in the gorgeous Dardanian dress, his sash bristling with knives and pistols, had tracked her through the wood, and was now within a few feet of her, his cruel eyes gleaming in his fierce face. With a shrill scream she threw herself wildly forward, hoping to find safety in the company of the musing old man, but her foot caught in a briar, and she felt her pursuer's great hand upon her throat. Her scream had aroused the two occupants of the garden, however, and she saw the old man look round.

"What is it that Danilo has found in the shrubbery—a child?" he asked the servant in French, and bewildered and shaken as Helene was, it seemed to her that the voice was familiar. The servant's reply was inaudible, but she heard the old man say sharply, "Bring her to me, and I will reprove her. I will not have children mauled by these rough fellows."

Helene's captor released her reluctantly as the servant approached, but it appeared to her that the new-comer helped her up with equal reluctance, and cursed her under his breath. He gave the Dardanian some direction in his own language as he led Helene to his master, but she had no time to think what the words might mean, for it was Cyril who sat on the stone bench—Cyril whose clear blue eyes met hers without a trace of recognition. For a moment she was staggered—it could not be Cyril—but even before he spoke again she had no doubt. Old and white-haired and broken, this was the man to whom her childish devotion had been given.

"Do you know, young lady, that you are a trespasser?" he asked her in French. "Doubtless you found your way in by the little door in the wall?" Helene opened her lips to deny this, but he went on without giving her time to speak. "I know one of the servants was going into the town, and they are careless about the door. But you would hardly have gratified your curiosity by entering if you had known that my seclusion here is a matter of life and death."

Helene gazed at him, unable to speak, and he went on.

"Probably you are unaware that my life is perpetually in danger? You know my name—Shishman Pelenko? But you will not have heard that my steps are continually dogged by hired ruffians. I can't quite remember why it is—it happened a long time ago—but I am not safe except within these walls and under the protection of my faithful servants. This is Dr Gregorescu, my medical attendant"—he indicated a lithe dark-bearded man who had come up with a cat-like swiftness and softness of tread—"who is good enough to live here with me and watch over my health. My life may not be of much value to the world, but it has still some little charm for myself, and some value for my few friends, I think?" He looked round waggishly at Dr Gregorescu, and laughed—a foolish crackling laugh.

"Your life is most valuable to your friends, Highness," replied the doctor, not smiling in return, but piercing Helene with his black eyes, "and I fear this young lady's entrance here may endanger it."

"Oh, nonsense! she is only a child, and what can she tell the ruffians outside but that I am well guarded? Desire the ruffians on our side to show themselves, if you please."

"The young lady will be frightened," objected the doctor.

"All the better for her—teach her a lesson," was the testy answer. "What, am I to command twice?" he rattled his stick on the stones. "I wish my guard to be visible for an instant."

For the moment Helene felt like Fitz-James at the instant of his introduction to Roderick Dhu, for at the word of command, reluctantly uttered by Dr Gregorescu, the belt of shrubbery seemed to be suddenly alive with stalwart Dardanians. They sprang up from their lairs in the underwood or started out from behind trees, and stood in full view for a moment, then, at a wave of the doctor's hand, disappeared again, while the self-styled Prince Shishman improved the occasion.

"You have seen how thoroughly I am protected, young lady," he said impressively. "Now I do not think, from your face, that you are in the pay of my cruel enemies outside, but if you should be questioned, you may say that these faithful fellows, all trained fighters from their cradles, keep guard over me day and night, and would rejoice at the chance of a fight. You may say also that Dr Gregorescu and the indoor servants are well armed, and that there are underground——"

"Is not your Highness afraid of giving publicity to the exact details of our defences?" asked the doctor smoothly, and Cyril nodded.

"You do well to remind me of prudence, Gregorescu. But I think the young lady, at any rate, will not penetrate within our walls again, for she will remember that to do so would cause great anxiety and pain of mind to a cruelly persecuted man. If you will be good enough to send for the key of the small gate, we will let her out, and see that the door is properly fastened."

"Pray don't trouble yourself, Highness," said Dr Gregorescu hastily. "I will conduct the young lady to the gate."

"No, Gregorescu. It is not that I distrust your vigilance, but I must satisfy myself that the gate is properly locked. It is a perfect nightmare to me. I am thinking of having it bricked up."

The doctor offered no further objection, and Helene was conducted to the gate in solemn procession. Cyril bade her a lofty farewell, the bolts grated home, and, dazed and bewildered, she found herself outside.

CHAPTER XX.
FOILED.

FOR a moment Helene stood irresolute, unable to realise her position. Then the nearness of the fierce Dardanians and the still more terrible doctor occurred to her, and she walked away with tottering steps. Fear drove her on, for even when she had plunged into the wood, she thought she heard the bushes crackling behind her, and she could not feel safe until she came upon Jakob once more. The quiet glade, with the old man still snoring peacefully under his tree, seemed a haven of refuge, and she staggered towards him, her knees knocking together, and collapsed helplessly on the ground. The gasping sobs which she could not repress awoke Jakob, who was much concerned to find her in such a state. She would not tell him what had alarmed her, and as Jakob was firmly under the impression that he had only dozed off for a second or two, he attributed her fright to a snake, and expended much energy in beating about among the tree-roots and last year's dead leaves with a stick. He found nothing, naturally, and seeing that Helene was quite incapable of going on with her sketch, suggested that they should return to the inn, lest Hannele should scold him for allowing her Highness to sit on the ground. There were unmistakable marks of mould on Helene's linen skirt, which meant a cross-examination from Hannele, and in desperation she stood up, supporting herself against a tree, while Jakob removed the stains as well as he could with his handkerchief and the water he had carried for her painting.

"There, Highness!" he said at last, looking up with honest pride. "It will dry before we reach home, and Hannele will be none the wiser."

"Thanks, Jakob," his mistress answered absently. "Do you know whether the two English gentlemen who were on the terrace this morning are staying another night?"

"Their horses were being saddled when we started, Highness," replied Jakob, with placid indifference. "There is nothing to see at Drinitza except the river-cave, so why should they stay?"

Helene's heart sank. For a moment the wild idea of rescuing Cyril immediately had occurred to her. Usk was away, and William with him, but surely those two Englishmen might be depended upon to help another Englishman? Now that hope was gone; and with deeper sinking of heart she remembered that the Chevalier had started on one of his periodical journeys to Vindobona, so that it would be no use to send in to Novigrad. There was the landlord, at any rate, an old soldier, and there were two or three men employed about the inn, and several strong fellows in the village, and there was Jakob, who might be trusted to follow her leading—but was it right, was it even prudent, to oppose these men, practically unarmed, to the Dardanians, each of whom was a kind of walking arsenal? She turned the matter over in her mind as they walked back to the inn, and at last decided to lay it before the landlord, and see what he thought. But disappointment was awaiting her when she arrived, for the landlord had gone into Novigrad for the day.

This last blow was too much for Helene, and she resigned herself meekly into the hands of Hannele, who had brooded over her mistress's sharp words all the time of her absence, and now had the additional grievance of her evident exhaustion to gratify her. She took peremptory possession of Helene, removed her gown and shoes, fed her with soup, and made her lie down, scolding all the time, and having adjured her to go to sleep, went away to scold Jakob.

Helene had yielded to her ministrations and reproaches because she had no spirit to resist; but the moment the door had closed behind the maid her head started up from the pillow. She could not think properly lying down, and that great guarded house in the forest seemed to be crying out to her to do something. What should she do? what could she do? The memory of that helpless prisoner, who did not even realise that he was in prison, drew her back to the Pelenko mansion as though with cords. If only she had made herself known to him, spoken to him in English, addressed him by his own name, surely recollection would have returned to the dulled brain? And she had remained speechless, not uttering a word, terror and astonishment holding her so fast in their grip that she had made no use whatever of this tremendous opportunity! How could she meet Usk and Mr Hicks, who had dared so much for Cyril's rescue without result, if she had to confess to them that she had been face to face with him and had not even spoken?

The thought was intolerable, and in a moment she was out of bed and throwing on the pink cotton gown which Hannele had finished mending, and had left prominently on the back of a chair as if to reproach her. Too much engrossed in her quest to think of her own dignity, she crept down the stairs with her shoes in her hand, and once safely past the room in which she could hear Hannele's voice rating Jakob, put them on, and turned into the path which led up the hill. At the summit she paused, breathless, and put on her gloves. There was absolutely no reason why she should feel so frightened, as if she were doing something dreadful. Why should she not go out for a walk alone if she chose? She was an Englishwoman now, and Usk had often laughed at her because she disliked to go down the street without Hannele or Jakob in attendance. She was simply taking an afternoon walk, and what possible objection could there be to her going round by the Pelenko mansion? She did not even know that she should try to obtain entrance to the grounds—certainly not by that dreadful corner, which the Dardanian who had watched her must know well, if Cyril did not—but it might save time later if she walked round the place and looked carefully to see if there was any other way of getting in. As if to emphasise to herself the perfect propriety and openness of her intentions, she did not take the usual way through the forest, but went straight down to the high road, and walked along it in a westerly direction until she could see the battered chimneys of the house rising above the encircling trees. She shivered as she turned into the rugged lane, miscalled a road, which led up to the gates, and her eyes sought narrowly among the undergrowth on either hand for the brightness and glitter of the Dardanian dress. There seemed to be no one lying in wait just here, however, and she went on to the gates, which had always been fast shut when Usk and she had caught a glimpse of them hitherto. A gasp of astonishment broke from her when she reached them. On this day, of all days, they were open, as if to invite her to enter.

"It is a miracle!" thought Helene reverently; "a sign, perhaps, that the good God will allow me to do something to help the dear Count," and with a prayer on her lips she passed fearlessly in. The drive which led through the thick shrubbery was as rough and full of ruts as the lane outside—nay, the shrubbery was encroaching upon it, for bushes were springing up among the weeds which concealed the gravel. As she neared the house, however, she heard the pawing of impatient horses, and thought it prudent to creep into the wood. Reaching the end of the drive, and peeping through the branches, she saw to her amazement a carriage, laden with luggage, standing before the door. Several of the Dardanians were at work adjusting the various packages, and others were lounging about in front of the house. Presently Cyril appeared on the steps, and for one moment she thought he had seen her, for his eyes seemed to meet hers, but he turned to send his servant back for something, and, without looking at her, began to wave and twist his hands about in a way that appeared to her woefully aimless and imbecile. Apparently impatient of the delay, he entered the carriage after a moment or two, and drawing up the window nearest her, proceeded to trace figures of some sort listlessly upon the glass with his finger. To Helene, as she watched, it looked as if he had written the word "Not," but she could not be sure, since she naturally saw it backwards, as if reflected in a mirror. Before he could get any further, Dr Gregorescu came quickly down the steps, and apologising for being late, stepped into the carriage. Helene watched breathlessly to see what would happen next; but just as one of the Dardanians mounted the box, something was flung over her from behind, and she felt herself pulled down among the bushes.

It was no use to struggle, and she could not cry out. She was held down firmly, and the cloak, or whatever the covering might be, was pressed tightly over her face. She had almost lost consciousness when the pressure was relaxed, and she lay helpless and motionless until she felt some one shaking her by the shoulder, and heard a voice speaking in an unknown tongue. She looked up into the sunken eyes of an old woman, who was holding in one hand the rough woollen cloak which had served as a gag. The stranger was blaming her for venturing into such a place, Helene gathered, and warning her that if she had been discovered, her life would have been the forfeit. Realising the old woman's meaning, she remembered suddenly all that had passed, and springing up, she peered through the bushes again. The carriage and its attendants were gone, and the crushed weeds in the drive showed where it had passed. She turned to run after it, but the old woman caught her by the arm, and intimated by signs that it was travelling so fast she would never catch it. Resorting to signs in her turn, Helene did her best to inquire whether the old woman could take her by a short cut through the forest to the road, that she might see what direction the carriage was taking, but the old woman expressed the most lively fear at the prospect, moderating her gestures, however, when she saw Helene put her hand into her pocket. It was not often that the girl carried a purse, for there was nothing to buy at Drinitza, and she rather liked making Usk pay everything for her when they went into Novigrad, but it was well to have a little loose change at hand ready for going into the village, on account of the beggars. If the beggars were not duly noticed and relieved, they were apt to curse the passer-by, and Helene had a nervous dislike of being cursed. Her purse happened fortunately to be in the pocket of the pink gown, and she emptied the store of small coins it contained into the old woman's hand, with the result that the owner grinned widely, and made signs indicative of her willingness to start at once.

They crept down the drive again, and once outside the gate, plunged into the forest to the right, avoiding the lane, and very soon found themselves mounting a steep slope. This part of the woods Helene had not explored with Usk, and she was therefore obliged to rely entirely on the old woman, who hobbled along, helping herself up the steepest places by clutching at the bushes, with wonderful agility. On they went, now up and now down, through such mazes of forest that Helene decided she must come back by the road, or she would never be able to find her way home by herself. Moreover, as the first excitement of the chase died down, she became conscious that she had gone through a good deal since first starting out that morning, and that her limbs, shaking with fatigue and agitation, would scarcely carry her. But she struggled on bravely, and at last the old woman stopped on the very brink of what seemed to be a wooded cliff, and pointing straight downwards, said something which Helene took to mean that the road was there.

The declivity was not quite so steep as it looked, but Helene soon found that it was impossible to walk down it. The only plan was to run whenever a clear space appeared, bringing up against a friendly tree when she was out of breath, and then picking her way slowly from one trunk to another. It was natural that she should run faster than the old woman, and therefore it did not surprise her to find herself in front; but when she reached the foot of the cliff, and discovered that her companion had not followed her, and she was all alone, it struck her that she had been rather shabbily treated. She sat down, thankfully enough, upon a fallen tree, keeping in the shade so that her light dress might not attract attention, and with her eyes fixed upon the stretch of road to the left, waited patiently. This was a part of the road that she and Usk had never reached, even in their drives, and she felt sure that she must be a good deal in advance of the carriage, which had to follow the many windings necessary for the maintenance of a comparatively slight gradient. For a time she was so glad to rest that she thought of nothing but the relief to her tired feet, but after a while it occurred to her that the afternoon was wearing away, and that she had a very long distance to walk home. Moreover, the road was lonely. Not a creature had passed while she sat on the log, and there was no sign of a human habitation anywhere. The best plan would certainly be to walk back towards Drinitza, and so meet the mysterious carriage. On that quiet road she would hear it coming a long way off, and be able to hide in the wood until it had passed. Or perhaps it might not pass at all—which was a contingency that had not occurred to her before—but in that case she would know that it had taken the only other direction possible, the road leading to Klotsch, so that her walk would not have been in vain.

Rising from the log, she turned to the left, in the direction, as she had never doubted, of Drinitza, and set out boldly along the road. Before she had gone far, however, it struck her that the sun, now approaching its setting, should have been behind her, instead of which it was in front.

"How stupid I am!" she said wearily, beginning to retrace her steps. "My head is so confused that I was actually going the wrong way. And yet I don't see how—but it's no good trying to work it out now. I must simply go on."

On and on she went, still without recognising any familiar landmark, until she was too tired to look at anything but the long white ribbon of road which seemed to unfold itself endlessly before her. At last the growing dusk made her lift her eyes to the sky again, and there was the sun, now sinking behind the hills, in front of her once more! The truth flashed upon her. The unfamiliar scenery was accounted for. She had been right at first, but at that point the road doubled back upon itself, in order to skirt the base of the cliff she had descended, so that for a little while its direction was actually west instead of east. But at the end of the turn she would have found herself looking eastwards again, whereas now she had been walking away from home with every step she took.

For the moment Helene was overwhelmed. She could never walk back to Drinitza now, she knew, and she was utterly alone, in a district which did not seem to possess a single inhabitant. Tired and cold, and faint with hunger, she sat down by the roadside and cried weakly. Unless another miracle occurred to help her, she must spend the night where she was, and even in the morning Usk would have no means of knowing where to look for her. But again she saw a miracle in what followed close upon the despairing little prayer she sent up. From the forest behind her came the lively sound of ungreased waggon-wheels, faint at first in the distance, but gradually increasing in nearness and excruciating distinctness. A vehicle of some kind was jolting over a rough forest-track, and presently she could hear the ejaculations addressed by the driver to his oxen. So comforting was the knowledge that a fellow-creature was at hand, that she ran forward impulsively as the heads of the oxen appeared, but the driver was far too busy to notice her until he had safely manœuvred his team and the long rough waggon, laden with wood, from the side-track into the main road. Then he seemed suddenly to become aware that he had heard a human voice, and he looked down from his stately height—he was a huge Dardanian—to see a little pale girl, in dusty and draggled European dress, weeping bitterly, and sobbing forth entreaties in two or three languages. It was well for Helene that her giant was better-tempered than giants are generally supposed to be, and kind-hearted as well, for although he could not understand either French, German, or English, and shook his head vigorously when she tried to explain that she wanted to get back to Drinitza, he offered her a seat on the wood in his waggon, and actually lifted her up there when she hesitated. She made no further opposition after that. Where he might be taking her, she had no idea, but presumably it was to his home, and possibly to some place where she might find the means of communicating with Usk.

The oxen tramped on patiently, and the waggon began to jolt again as the road became worse, but Helene dozed spasmodically on her rough couch. It was not until the waggon came to a standstill that she really awoke, to find herself in the one street of a little Dardanian frontier village, the white walls and dark roofs of which were glorious in the after-glow of sunset, and made a kind of theatrical background for the gigantic men and strapping women in red and blue and gold-embroidered white garments who were crowding round to hear of the strange adventure which had happened to Petros. Before Helene was fairly awake, the smallest man in the crowd asked her in broken German for her papers, and it was evident that a bad impression was produced by her confession that she had none. The small man had something to do with the customs, apparently, for she gathered from the cross-examination which followed that he suspected her of smuggling, though it was not clear what she had to smuggle, with the exception of her worn and weary self. Moreover, he fastened upon her statement that her husband was English as his own excuse for not understanding her German, and they argued at cross-purposes for some time, while the listening villagers made remarks that were evidently uncomplimentary in their nature. To Helene's horror, he succeeded at last in making it plain that she would be detained for the night as a suspicious character in the hut in which the customs business was carried on; and already she saw herself led to prison before the eyes of the crowd of curious villagers, and locked up hungry and tired, and, above all, alone. In despair, she turned to the tallest man in the crowd, who also seemed to hold some position of authority, and fortunately remembering the word used by the Dardanians to designate their ruler, did her best to explain that the Prince was her cousin, and would hold the villagers responsible for their treatment of her. She could not be sure that she was really understood, but the people seemed to be impressed, and the tall man and the small man consulted together. Presently she distinguished a sound sufficiently like the Illyrian word for "telegraph" to assure her that they were talking of telegraphing somewhere for directions, and she seized upon the proposal with almost hysterical joy.

"Oh, let me telegraph to my husband!" she cried to the little man, "and just let me rest somewhere till he comes, and he will pay anything you like."

Whether the mention of payment stimulated the official wits, or whether the man was afraid of getting into trouble through over-zeal, he appeared to understand and approve of the suggestion. The big man lifted Helene down from the waggon as if she had been a baby, and after she had thanked the driver for his kindness, the scene changed to the post-office, of which the big man was in charge. Here a fresh difficulty occurred, for Helene had no money, and the simplicity of modern dress precluded her from resorting to the time-honoured expedient of offering jewellery in pledge. She had not even a watch with her, and the postmaster became stern and implacable once more. The little man came to the rescue by pointing out that she had a gold ring on her finger, but she pleaded so piteously that she could not give up her wedding-ring, that matters were at a deadlock again. Then the postmaster, apparently prompted by his handsome, slipshod wife, proposed a compromise. He would send the telegram, and wait for the payment until the morning; but Helene and the ring must remain in pawn, so to speak, since she would not be separated from it. She should spend the night in the post-office, which was a lean-to attached to his own house, and could only be entered through the room in which he and his family slept; and if there was no answer to the telegram in the morning, the ring must be given up. There were few things to which Helene would not have agreed at that moment, and she wrote out the telegram, surrounded by the eager and curious circle of villagers, all bristling with weapons. She wrote it in German, as the customs-officer's help would enable the postmaster to make it less unintelligible in that language than in French or English; and when the whole assembly had looked at it wisely, heard it translated and explained, and discussed the meaning, it was allowed to be sent. When, after a good deal of squabbling between the postmaster and the customs-officer over the spelling of the words, the message had at last been despatched, Helene, who had been upheld by her anxiety so far, staggered forward, and clutching feebly at the office-desk, slipped to the floor. Instantly the postmaster's wife, who seemed to have been severely repressed hitherto by her husband, took possession of her, and ordered the other villagers out of the room. It was clear she was saying that whoever the girl might be, she was faint and exhausted, and should not be tormented any more by stupid unsympathetic men. Even this good Samaritan could not provide a softer couch than the bench which ran along one end of the room, but she brought a sheepskin as a coverlid and a rolled-up apron for a pillow, and a frugal meal of black bread and milkless tea. She was so obviously sympathetic and compassionate that Helene kissed her impulsively as she covered her up, and the Dardanian woman smiled broadly as she kissed her in return, and patted her shoulder with a friendly hand as she bade her sleep well and not be frightened.

The inhabitants of this primitive village appeared all to retire to rest as soon as darkness came on, so that Helene had enjoyed a long, dreamless sleep when a furious knocking at the outer door aroused the household, although dawn was only just breaking. The postmaster was disinclined to rise, thinking that some impatient neighbour had come early to inquire for a letter, and that the labours of the department would be appreciably increased if such proceedings were to be allowed. But the knocking continued, and a voice shouted something threatening in an unknown tongue, which was emphasised by vigorous kicks at the door, and the postmaster's wife suddenly shrieked a malediction at him.

"Fool! pig!" she screamed. "Can't you hear? It is the little white lady's husband. Let him in this minute."

The postmaster obeyed, not forgetting to don his beltful of weapons before he opened the door; and it was with a huge revolver in his hand that he confronted the young man who entered with a hasty step, but recoiled abruptly when he met the intent gaze of the rest of the family, peering at him over their sheepskin coverlids.

"Where is my wife?" he demanded, holding out a telegram to the postmaster, then began a hasty apology; but the postmaster saw no need for shyness. Striding to the door of the office, he threw it open, and bowing to Usk, invited him to enter, while the wife and children sat up in bed, their eyes bright with interest. A moment later, when Usk was sitting on the bench beside Helene, holding her in his arms, and alternately kissing and scolding her, while she laughed and cried at once, a murmur of excited admiration drew their attention to the door, where they beheld the whole family gazing at them open-mouthed.

"Oh, shut the door!" cried Helene hysterically. "The whole village will be here in a moment, as they were last night. Oh, Nym, how white you look!"

"Considering that we have been riding all night, you can scarcely expect us to look very blooming. I think you've hurried us here on false pretences, Nell. We couldn't make head or tail of your telegram, but we gathered that you were in dire distress, so Hicks and I, with the landlord and Jakob, mounted and rode to your rescue at once, with William driving the buggy. We had an awful time of it in the dark, but we kept on; and now I find you comfortably asleep, and able to criticise our looks. Do you think that shows proper gratitude, Lady Usk?"

"You mustn't criticise mine," laughed Helene unsteadily, as she stood up with difficulty, a forlorn little figure with tumbled hair and dark-ringed eyes. "Oh, it was so dreadful, Nym! They nearly made me give them my wedding-ring to pay for the telegram. But they were very kind afterwards, and it's all right now."

"Well, suppose you put yourself to rights a bit. Hicks is seeing after breakfast. Will a pocket-comb be of any service to you? And when you feel quite equal to it—not before, mind, by any means—I should be interested to know what got you into this fix."

Helene, tugging at her hair with the comb, stopped suddenly, and turned upon him a face full of horror. "Nym, I had forgotten it for the moment, but it is almost as bad as the worst we have imagined. I have seen the dear Count twice, and he didn't know me. He is—mad."

"Do you mean that he's anywhere here?" cried Usk, springing up.

"No; I lost him again. It was in trying to trace him that I came to this place. He is under the care of a dreadful doctor, who has a number of

Dardanians to keep guard over him, and he thinks he is Prince Shishman Pelenko, and that people are plotting against his life."

"Be quick with your hair," said Usk, "and you can tell Hicks everything at the same time as me. He may think of something that ought to be done at once."

But when Helene told the story of her doings the day before at the open-air breakfast table, Mr Hicks was as much at a loss as Usk to know what to do next, and sat silent and meditative, even while devouring his food at his usual speed. His experience as a war-correspondent had taught him never to neglect the chance of a good meal, and his skill in foraging had succeeded in providing one even in this unpromising spot. The table, which he had requisitioned from the custom-house, was placed in the open space in front of the post-office, the only flat piece of ground in the whole village, apparently, and the villagers stood round and watched the meal with much interest. When it was over, Usk held an open-air court of justice, and prompted by Helene, paid the postmaster for the telegram, and his wife for the night's lodging—much to her distress, for she would only accept the money to buy something for her children. Petros the waggoner was less diffident, and received his silver with pride, saying he would give it to his sweetheart to sew on her cap; and the customs-officer was so anxious to press his own claims to a reward that Usk at last yielded, advising him to buy a German dictionary. When this was settled, the horses were brought out again, and the visitors departed, their hosts speeding them on their way with a *feu-de-joie* of revolver-shots, which was gratifying, if a little alarming. Usk was driving Helene in the buggy, and presently Mr Hicks rode up close beside them.

"Lady Usk," he said, "there's a question or two I'd like to have you answer if you don't mind. You said Count Mortimer was moving his hands in a queer sort of a way when he stood on the doorstep. Can you show me just how he did it?"

"Something like this," said Helene, imitating the movements as well as she could remember them.

"Is that so?" asked Mr Hicks, and nodded gravely.

"What is it?" asked Helene, alarmed by his tone.

"The deaf-and-dumb alphabet, I guess, and he's no more lost his mind than you and I have."

"But he didn't know me in the least. He could not be in his right mind."

"That's just his smartness, you bet. He made out to disarm the suspicions of the folks that have him in charge by pretending not to recognise you."

"Oh, and I didn't know the alphabet, and now we have lost him again!" cried Helene. "It's all my fault. He was trying to tell me something. Oh, if I had only known!" and she burst into tears. "Perhaps we shall never see him again."

Mr Hicks was thinking deeply. "I guess I'll ride on ahead," he said to Usk. "I don't see but the notion that's just come to me may be right. We know the carriage didn't pass along this road, and I'll go on to Klotsch, and see if it passed there. If not, I'll get another horse and ride to Novigrad all I'm worth, and have them give me a warrant, or police permit, or whatever they call it, to search the Pelenko house. For if the carriage has not been seen on the road, it seems clear to me that it just waited around in the woods somewhere while Lady Usk was got out of the way, and then went right back to the house. And if the Count is there yet, why——"

"Underground!" cried Helene. "He began to speak of passages, or something of that kind."

"We'll see. I'll ride on, anyway."

But Mr Hicks's haste was in vain. Police assistance was obtained, and the Pelenko mansion duly searched, the old servants left in charge showing even the subterranean rooms, which had been constructed in Roumi days as a refuge in case of need. They knew that the foreign doctor, and the mad gentleman who imagined himself to be Prince Shishman, and the Dardanian servants, had all left the day before, but they could not say where they had gone. They had travelled in their own carriage, but no one had seen it on the road. The mystery was as deep as ever.

CHAPTER XXI.
QUEEN AND KING.

THE fifth Neustrian Revolution was complete. The *plébiscite* had been taken, and by an overwhelming majority Prince Timoleon Lucanor Malasorte was requested to proclaim himself Emperor of the Neustrians. Such a request was naturally regarded as a command by the person most concerned, and the telegram which informed foreign countries of the result of the *plébiscite* contained also the first proclamation of the Emperor Timoleon V. A semi-official *communiqué* accompanying the intelligence announced that the betrothal of the new monarch to the Grand-Duchess Sonya Eugenovna, cousin of the Emperor of Scythia, would take place almost immediately, and that this union would cement a closer alliance between the two countries than could ever have subsisted while the government of one was an autocracy and of the other a republic. These items of news were received without surprise by Europe generally, but in one distant corner of the continent they resulted in a wholly unexpected series of events.

It happened that there was a luncheon-party at the Palace at Bellaviste, to which the Premier, who had but just received the message from Neustria, came late, bringing the telegram with him. He said nothing until the meal was over, but then asked for an immediate audience of the King. Displeased by the breaking-up of her party, and no more disposed than she had been as Miss Steinherz to accept meekly anything that interfered with her wishes, Queen Félicia sent her equerry to ask her husband and Prince Mirkovics what the news was. The King, who had learnt by experience that his bride was quite capable of pursuing him and assisting at the interview unless her request was complied with, sent her a copy of the telegram, which she read as she moved about among her guests.

"Logan, come right here. I want you this instant!" were the words that startled the room, and made Baroness Radnika, who had accompanied the new Queen as her mistress of the household, look round in distress. She had thought Félicia cured of her Americanisms, but at the first moment of excitement the old habits revived. A covert glance of amusement passed between the ladies of the British and United States legations, and the Baroness threw herself bravely into the breach by trying to start a fresh subject of conversation as Maimie responded to Félicia's summons.

"Read that, now. I might have been an empress to-day," said the Queen, putting the telegram into her friend's hand.

"Well, I guess it isn't my fault you are not," was the swift answer, given in an undertone, for Félicia's words had been distinctly audible.

"That is so. And we can't alter things now, any way."

"No; you'll just have to make the best of them."

That was all, but Félicia remained pensive for the rest of the day, and there were those at hand who watched her every look and treasured up any incautious word. One of these was King Michael's aide-de-camp, Captain Andreivics, to whom his master had recently intimated that he might make himself useful by marrying Maimie, so that, while still about the Court, she might be removed from her position of paramount influence with Félicia. Somewhat against his will, so far as his personal feelings were concerned, but with a keen sense of the direction in which his material interests pointed, the aide-de-camp had done his best to obey, only to find himself smartly refused by Maimie, and to become, as he shrewdly suspected, a never-failing subject of amusement to his lady-love and the Queen. To-day he saw his opportunity for a neat little revenge on both of them, for even at this early date the married life of the royal couple was by no means a path of roses. The King's marriage had been extremely popular in Thracia, on account of the reputed wealth of the bride, which was expected to descend in a golden shower on all classes of the community. But it had proved rather to resemble the grants made to deserving objects by certain philanthropic bodies, which require as a condition of their reception that at least an equal amount shall be raised by the locality benefited. Moreover, the thrifty Thracians, already disturbed in their minds by the cost of the festivities incident upon the state entry of the King and Queen into their capital, found that their new sovereign had no intention of serving the country at the cost of her own wishes. Addresses presented by impassioned patriots implored her to adopt the national costume, which it was quickly known she had pronounced hideous, and to encourage local manufactures by wearing no materials but those made in Thracia, which she flatly refused to do. King Michael had never shown himself particularly amenable to the wishes of his people in the past, but he had a lively sense of the value of popularity, and felt that it would be an excellent thing for Félicia to make a few little sacrifices in the interests of the nation and the dynasty. Unfortunately, however, Félicia did not take this view of things. The King had already become aware that to be her husband meant chiefly that he was responsible for providing her with a "good time" generally, and that any attempt to coerce her would be either ignored or laughed aside. He had sufficient self-control to behave as if his forced acquiescence was due to a natural willingness to indulge his bride as far as possible, but he was keenly on the look-out for some means of inflicting an exemplary defeat upon her. It was unfortunate for him that in the first fall he tried with her, he himself was the defeated party. Félicia's yacht, the Bluebird, in which they had spent the honeymoon, was about to convey them on a series of visits to various foreign Courts. King Michael wished to arm the vessel and change her status to that of a warship, thus doubling the numerical strength of the Thracian navy at one stroke; but Félicia not only refused her assent to the change, but persisted in continuing to sail the ship under the Stars and Stripes, and retaining her American crew. King Michael saw Maimie's hand in this, and lacking the wisdom which would have led him to wait for the moment when the crew would begin to grumble at serving so far from home, argued the matter with Félicia on every possible occasion. His only hope of success lay in winning her over to his side, for her marriage-contract secured to her the absolute control of the vessel, but he could not bring himself to let the subject drop, and begin again when she had forgiven his persistence, and things were thus ripe for a quarrel between the two.

As for Félicia, she had obtained her ambition, and it wholly failed to satisfy her. Considered as the capital of a Balkan state, Bellaviste was wonderfully advanced, but to her it seemed dull, behind the times, and above all, provincial. The Thracians, who had so sturdily resisted Queen Ernestine's efforts to Europeanise them, were not more ready to succumb to the fascinations of Queen Félicia, even when these were backed by the prestige of her wealth, and she was beginning to see that her intention of gathering a gay society around her was not likely to become a reality. People who were accustomed to Lutetia and Vindobona might pay a flying visit to this far corner of Europe if a series of special festivities was in progress, but they would not make a long stay, and most emphatically they would never regard Bellaviste seriously as a spot which must be visited once a year. Thus disillusioned, Félicia found herself suddenly face to face with the fact that by her own action, or inaction, long ago she had thrown away the chance of reigning as the supreme arbitress of taste and fashion in the city which to her, as to all good Americans, was the actual centre of the world. Instead of setting the fashions, all she could now do was to be allowed, by the special favour of the great *couturiers* she patronised, to follow them at secondhand, and her taste could only be imposed upon the small and often recalcitrant circle of Thracian officialdom, instead of upon an admiring world.

Left to herself, Félicia would doubtless have followed Maimie's prudent advice, and, with the common-sense on which she prided herself, have determined to make the best of her position, but she had gained too many enemies to be allowed to do this. Captain Andreivics found an ally in one of the many ladies to whom King Michael's unguarded attentions in past years had given hopes of sharing his throne, hopes doomed to be blighted by a sudden and somewhat tardy recollection on his part of the duty he owed to his house. Félicia's remark to Maimie, her obvious depression during the rest of the day, offered abundant material for disturbing the mind of a husband who was already notoriously prone to jealousy, and almost without knowing it, the conspirators added a touch here, and deepened a shadow there, until the least that could be imagined was that Félicia had played off Prince Timoleon Malasorte and himself against one another until her very marriage-day, and had only chosen him at last because she distrusted his rival's prospects of establishing himself on the Neustrian throne. Whispers followed as to a certain mysterious cabinet in the inner boudoir which was sacred to her Majesty and Miss Logan. This cabinet had never been seen open, but ladies on duty in the outer rooms had heard it closed and locked, after the Queen and her favourite had sat for a long time rustling papers and talking in low tones. What more likely than that the cabinet contained love-letters, which would prove to King Michael that he had been cruelly duped by his bride, and in which she took a stolen pleasure even now?

There was this amount of inherent probability in the suggestions which Captain Andreivics ventured, somewhat gingerly at first, to throw out, that King Michael was very well aware Félicia had played off Usk and himself against one another in the manner described, so that she might quite conceivably have treated a third unfortunate in the same way without their knowledge. He had viewed her treatment of Usk with a fine indifference, but he was the last man to submit meekly to similar usage himself. Moreover, if there was any foundation for the aide-de-camp's hints, Maimie also had deceived him in the most barefaced way, which demanded condign punishment. A strong man would have taxed both women openly with the alleged deception, but King Michael preferred to work on different lines. Armed with various bunches of keys, he made his way that evening by a private passage from his rooms to Félicia's. The door opening into the passage from the inner boudoir was locked, but he opened it with a master-key, after listening to make sure that Félicia and Maimie were not talking inside. The room was empty, and switching on the electric light, he began to try the lock of the cabinet—a fanciful thing of old French workmanship, but well made and in excellent repair—with one key after another. To his disgust, there was not one that would open it, though he found two that seemed to fit. Striking a match, and examining the lock closely by its light, he saw where the difficulty lay, and that it was easily overcome. The blade of his knife, inserted where the doors met, forced back the bolt at once, and the secrets of the cabinet lay open before him. Moreover, the cabinet was packed with them; the mass of evidence was enormous. But as he took out one thing after another at random, he grew more and more perplexed. There were ball-programmes, bouquet-holders, *bonbonnières*, cotillon gifts and favours, a few valentines or Christmas cards of a specially flattering character, some invitations to important or exclusive gatherings. It was an interesting social museum, but it was not what he wanted. He pulled out the drawer at the top. Photographs!—he clutched them eagerly. But they were all of Félicia herself, in every possible variety of dress and attitude, and each marked with the date and place of its taking. More angry than ever, he drew out the deep drawer at the bottom. It was very full, and the rustling of paper rewarded him as he plunged his hand into it. But it was all newspaper—a collection of cuttings from all sorts and conditions of American journals, forming Félicia's social biography, from her school "graduation" and coming-out ball to her marriage, over which the journalistic mind appeared to have run riot. There were interviews with her of various dates, accompanied by unrecognisable portraits of herself and of "J. Bertram Steinherz, father of Miss Steinherz," and of "the late Mrs Constance L. Steinherz," and interior and exterior views of the family abode. Some of the accounts had a small piece of dress-material carefully pinned to them, evidently that of the gown worn at the ball or theatre-party in question, and all were neatly arranged and docketed.

King Michael stood before the rifled cabinet in a towering rage. He was in no mood for the consolation, of which the examination of his wife's dearest treasures might have assured him, that she loved no one but herself; all he felt was that he was in an absurd and ungraceful position. To put everything back as he had found it was almost an impossibility, even if he could get the cabinet-door to lock again. If he could not, Félicia and that American woman would guess the truth at once. Only one person would tamper with the cabinet so clumsily if he ventured to do it all. He was beginning to lay the papers in the drawer as smoothly as he could, trusting that Félicia might not remember the exact order in which she had left them, when he was horrified by the sound of voices in the next room.

"I just wish that Paris store would hurry up with those albums, Maime," said Félicia, and her voice was coming closer. "When one has them make things to one's own design, they're so awfully long about it."

"I'd have them send one at a time, just as they're finished," Maimie answered. "Then we can start on your graduation right away."

"I guess I will," said Félicia, as she drew the curtain aside. "Say!" she cried shrilly, "and what are you doing here, Michael?"

She seemed to grow taller as he looked at her, and towered above him so magnificently that he was conscious of actual fear. He tried to bluster the matter out.

"And if I am here, madame, has not your husband a right to—to——"

"To go through my private papers?" with deadly quietness.

"Exactly. I claim that right, and I exercise it."

"And to break into my bureau?" Her quick eye had caught sight of the knife, and she took possession of it before he could prevent her. "Thanks for the warning. You may claim your right just as much as ever you want to, but you've exercised it for the last time."

"In that you will find yourself mistaken, madame."

"You are pretty much mistaken if you think you'll have the chance of doing it again. Why, you little miserable——" she stopped suddenly. "But I won't call you names. You'll hear plenty before long from other people."

"In your present rank of life, madame, it is not the custom to make the world a sharer in family disputes."

"It is unavoidable at times," drawled Félicia—"when a separation is to be arranged, for instance."

"This is preposterous. You have no grounds for anything of the kind."

"Just wait until I go way back to the States and ask for one."

"Do you imagine that you will be permitted to visit America for any such purpose? No, madame, let us look at this affair in a sensible light. If I have damaged your cabinet, I will replace it. Your interesting records you will find untouched, and I shall be happy to add some article of value to your collection—" he waved his hand towards the drawers of nicknacks— "to show my regret for this slight misunderstanding. You will be so good as to make your own choice."

"And you think you can bribe an American woman to overlook an insult like this?" demanded Félicia, but Maimie was at her side.

"Don't fuss over it any more to-night, Fay. Leave things till morning."

"Miss Logan's advice is excellent. I trust I shall find you in a more accommodating temper in the morning, madame. I wish you a very good night," and King Michael left the room with what dignity he could muster. At a sign from Félicia, Maimie locked the door after him.

"Maime, what about the Bluebird's steam launch?" asked Félicia quickly.

"It was to wait around at the steps up to midnight to see if there was any change in the orders for to-morrow. Are you real set on it, Fay?"

"Dead set," responded Félicia through her teeth. "Send those girls to bed. Let them know I'm just pining for a walk on the terrace."

While Maimie went obediently to dismiss the dressers, Félicia threw on a cloak, and pulled the hood over her head. She had another cloak ready for

Maimie when she returned, but close upon her heels came Baroness Radnika, with an anxious face.

"You will not walk on the terrace to-night, madame?" she said uneasily. "It is cold, and the damp is rising from the river. I thought I would venture to speak when I heard Miss Logan telling your dressers."

"I am going out," said Félicia. "I can't stay indoors to-night."

"It is something more," said the Baroness, coming closer, and laying her hands on Félicia's shoulders. "Forgive me, madame, but I see it in your face. You will not gratify your slanderers by giving them such a handle against you? Ah, dear child, I loved your father; bear with me, and listen to me now. Don't take this step, whatever it may be. You are excited—agitated——"

"Feel of my hand, Baroness. There's no excitement there—not much! I'm real fond of you, but I can't have you delay me this way. The step I am going to take is due to myself, and nobody will blame me when they know the reason. If you'll sort these things here, I'll be grateful, for I may send for them soon, and I'm sorry that you'll just have to stay here till morning."

She withdrew herself from the clinging hands as she spoke, and before the Baroness knew what she was going to do, she had passed under the curtain Maimie was holding, and locked the door of the larger boudoir. This portion of the palace was now deserted for the night, and the Baroness could not make up her mind to attract the attention of any of the sentries in the garden to her position. Perhaps she had misjudged Félicia; she might only be intending to walk on the terrace, as she had said, but the Baroness's heart misgave her as she remembered that the Bluebird was lying at the mouth of the river, with her fires banked, in case the King and Queen should be able to make a start early on the morrow. She would have been more anxious still if she had known that the yacht's steam-launch was waiting off the palace itself for orders, and that those orders were conveyed to it by Félicia in person. But when the astonishing news arrived in the morning that the Queen was missing, and that her yacht had steamed out to sea in the night, it was the Baroness, released after a weary vigil, who undertook to face the King in the first fury of his wrath. He would send his gunboat to pursue the Bluebird, he would telegraph to every port that she was to be detained, he would enlist the help of every government in Europe to restore his truant wife, and he would—he would—words failed to express the punishment that should be meted out to every one concerned in the affair. But the Baroness held her ground, and fought Félicia's battle with a courage which was absolutely regardless of the King's frantic displeasure. To prevent a scandal, and leave the way open for the two to be brought together again, was her only aim, and she had her reward, when she left the King's presence at last, in the brief announcement which was to be added to the daily Court Circular:—

"Her Majesty the Queen, attended by Miss Logan, left Bellaviste last night on board the royal yacht Bluebird for a short cruise. His Majesty the King, who had intended to accompany her Majesty, is detained some time longer by the course of public affairs."

"For real genuine slave-driving commend me to a pretty woman who knows her own value—as all pretty women ought to," added Mr Hicks gallantly, repenting, apparently, of his opening complaint.

"Who is the lady?" asked Usk.

"No less a person than her Majesty Queen Félicia, sir. She is lying off Paranati in the Bluebird, and has had the mate come over the mountains on horseback at the risk of his life, with a message for me that she has no use for matrimony just now, and I may as well fix up a separation."

"What, already?" cried Usk, with unintentional irony.

"Why, certainly. The King has insulted her unpardonably, so she says, and I guess there isn't anything to be done but eliminate him for the future."

"Then you will be obliged to go to her at Paranati?"

"That's so, and it makes me real mad. I had concluded to wander around in these parts some, and try and solve the mystery of this last disappearance of the Count's, and now I don't see but you'll have to do what you can without me. What riles me is the way things seem to work for the other side all the time. It's that which is telling on Lady Usk too, I guess."

Usk nodded gravely, for it seemed as if Helene could not forgive herself for her failure to rescue Cyril. In vain her husband and Mr Hicks pointed out that she could not in any case have saved him by herself, and that the circumstances made it impossible for her to get together a band of helpers. She was convinced that there was something she might have done if she had had more presence of mind, or even—to go back to the beginning of her misfortunes—that she would have done far better not to approach the Pelenko mansion at all, rather than give the alarm by her sudden appearance there, and thus enable Dr Gregorescu to remove his patient. That there was some truth in this could not be denied, and Helene brooded over it until she was at times persuaded that Usk must hate her for her disastrous interference, and she made herself miserable over an alienation which was quite imaginary. To Usk such a state of mind was utterly incomprehensible. Helene was tired after her adventures and inclined to be morbid, he thought, and he dragged her out into the fresh air, and scolded her good-humouredly, never dreaming that she took his scoldings seriously to heart, and believed that he invited her out with him as a matter of duty.

"It's a real misfortune that your mother is set fast at Geneva, and Queen Ernestine at Vindobona," Mr Hicks went on. "You and I, Lord Usk, we don't know just the way to get hold of a little sensitive girl like that, and put things so's she must take a cheerful view of them. We can't seem to fix it that she should have a good cry, and feel better, which is what she wants."

Usk was silent. His private opinion was that Helene cried a great deal without feeling any better, but he was not going to say this to Mr Hicks, although he did not resent his curious assumption of a share in the charge of her, knowing that any woman in trouble imposed a responsibility upon the American to see that she was comforted or righted.

"Did you try suggesting to her that her mother should come here?" Mr Hicks asked.

"Yes; but it was no good. She said at once that her mother couldn't leave her father, and that the Grand-Duke wouldn't like this place at all."

"No; I guess he'd raise Cain a few dozen times a day, which wouldn't be soothing to his daughter's nerves. And did you propose that she should take a fortnight's vacation, and go right home to them?"

"Yes; and it made her perfectly miserable. She thought I wanted to send her away from me, and she was so unhappy I had to promise never to suggest such a thing again."

"Well, well!" remarked Mr Hicks soothingly, "things will pan out all right yet. You know the pay-dirt's there, and by and bye you'll get down to the bed-rock, and find you're come upon a real Bonanza. That'll be when you understand her all through, see? And for the present you'll do your level best to be father and mother to her as well as husband. That starched stone image of a maid of hers is worse than no one. And I wouldn't wonder if things will all go smooth when once we start finding the Count, any way. That little lady of yours has so much grit that it only needs an emergency to bring her along smiling."

"Pity the emergency doesn't hurry up!" said Usk. "Why, Hicks, there must be a countryman of yours inside there," as a slow voice of extraordinary solemnity, speaking in English, made itself audible on the terrace where they sat.

"That's the mate of the Bluebird," responded Mr Hicks. "I told him come out here when he was finished stoking. Is that you, Mr Bradwell? Come right out. Did the folks give you a good square meal?"

"According to their lights, sir, according to their lights." The sailor, a gaunt middle-aged man, emerged from the doorway and bowed to Usk. "They don't know to fix that sort of thing properly here."

"Nor anywhere out of the States," agreed Mr Hicks heartily. "I don't wonder her Majesty is tired of these one-horse countries. Did I hear you say she didn't incline to go back to Thracia alive?"

"Won't trust herself on shore, not even to visit the Prince and Princess," was the reply. "Ship prepared for action, rifles got up and ball ammunition served out. Boats patrolling around all night, watch on deck forbidden to snooze."

"Ah, she knows her way about!" said Mr Hicks admiringly. For a few minutes they smoked in silence, and then the sailor inquired suddenly—

"Is there any sort of a State asylum in these parts?"

"Not much there isn't—not near here, any way. What's the racket?"

"What would be your candid opinion of a man that located one in the mountains, just over the Dardanian frontier there?"

"Either that he was the worst kind of a fool, or that he had concluded it was safer to keep himself out of sight."

"Well," pursued the sailor slowly, "there's one of our firemen taken to hurling chunks of coal at the other men instead of into the furnaces. It ain't only his fun, but the rest of the boys object to it. It seemed sort of suitable when I asked that guide of mine this afternoon what a certain house was, and he gave me to understand it was a lunatic asylum. I don't see but a week or two way up there while we're lying off Paranati might set this nigger right."

"You didn't go so far as make any inquiries?" asked Mr Hicks.

"Well, I just did, as we were giving the horses a rest in the village. Saw the doctor chap, ain't been long at the business, only one patient at present, old fellow who's forgotten his own name, but looks smart enough."

"What's the doctor's name?" broke from Usk and Mr Hicks together.

"Gregory? no, something sort of foreign-sounding—Gregorescu, here it is. I said I would have him hear from me."

"So you shall, to-morrow morning," said Mr Hicks, "and I'll go along there with you."

"The doctor would as lief be rid of this old fellow, I guess. He told me he was quite safe to be allowed out, but he didn't know where to find his friends."

"Then his friends will find him. Did you say you were coming here?"

"Well, yes, I guess I did."

"I don't just see this," murmured Mr Hicks, "but we will look into it to-morrow."

CHAPTER XXII.
OPENING THE PRISON DOORS.

WHEN Mr Bradwell started the next morning on his return journey to the Dardanian port, Mr Hicks accompanied him, not without strong opposition from Usk and Helene. Dr Gregorescu's extraordinary change of front, as exhibited in his interview with the mate, seemed to them to show that the only thing that needed to be done was to go in a body and demand and obtain Cyril's release, but Mr Hicks could not satisfy himself that the matter was so simple. The utmost he would concede was that four hours after he had started, they might drive out as far as the bend of the road where Helene had first lost her way, and wait there in case he sent back a message by Jakob, whom he would take with him, and William could ride out with the carriage, as it might be an advantage to have another man at hand. But when Usk asked scoffingly what was the object of all these warlike preparations, Mr Hicks confessed that he didn't know. It was simply that he couldn't seem to see such an elaborate plot peter out without some sort of a surprise for somebody.

The two Americans and Jakob accomplished their journey to the village without mishap, although Mr Bradwell, who had seldom ridden any distance until the day before, was glad to adopt one of the high native saddles, well padded with sheep-skins, instead of the European one he had used. Arrived at the village, the horses were left in Jakob's care, and Mr Hicks and his friend turned into the rough track which led to the asylum. This track branched off from the village street at its upper end, where the road, now fairly in Dardania, became little better than a bridle-path, and the house stood on an isolated hill about a mile away. It had been a kind of watch-tower or rude fort in the Roumi times, but of late years had been enlarged and adapted to the purposes of an ordinary dwelling by a wealthy merchant of Paranati, who thought it would prove a pleasant summer retreat. He had made the winding path leading up the hill passable for the rough vehicles of the country, even if it could not justly be called a carriage-road, and he was proceeding to plant the bare hillside and lay out gardens, when a disastrous speculation plunged him into poverty, and left the place to its old isolation. It seemed admirably fitted for Dr Gregorescu's ostensible purpose. The situation was airy and commanded splendid views, there was space for moderate exercise within the outer circle of the old fortifications, and any patient who succeeded in escaping over the walls would be in view from the gateway almost as far as the foot of the hill.

Mr Hicks noted the possibilities of the place with a jealous eye as he and his companion climbed the path. There were one or two points where it might be possible to effect an entrance, but there was no way of descending the hill but by this path, which wound in zigzag fashion up the slope, with a steep cliff above it on one side and below it on the other. There were turns at which the passenger would be invisible from the gate for a moment or two, but he could not reach the foot without coming into view again. If Dr Gregorescu were really willing to surrender his patient peaceably, it was a most extraordinary piece of good fortune, but why should he establish himself in a place of such natural advantages if he had no intention of making use of them?

Mr Hicks was on the look out for suspicious circumstances, and when he met Dr Gregorescu face to face the interview seemed to justify him in the belief that the doctor was a party to the whole of the plot. Mr Bradwell was despatched to view the building with a Greek attendant who spoke French, and to make arrangements for the reception of the unfortunate fireman, and Mr Hicks approached delicately the subject of Prince Shishman Pelenko. When he hinted that the patient thus styled might in reality be identical with a missing personage of importance in whose fate he took a deep interest, the doctor rose to the bait immediately, with every appearance of frankness. His story was that he had received the charge of the unfortunate man from a lady, whose name he was not at liberty to mention, but whom Mr Hicks understood at once to be Mlle. Garanine. This lady explained that while travelling with her, Prince Shishman had been seized suddenly with the distressing delusion that his life was perpetually threatened, which was accompanied by an entire loss of memory, and almost of the sense of personal identity. There was no reason why Dr Gregorescu should doubt her statement as to his patient's name at the time, for when they arrived at the Pelenko mansion they were expected and welcomed. Moreover, the day after their arrival Prince Soudaroff called and had a long interview with the patient, endeavouring in vain to rouse him to any recollection of his former life. This account differed so totally from that given to Usk and Helene by Prince Soudaroff himself of his mission to Drinitza that Mr Hicks wondered for the moment whether the doctor had really been a dupe throughout, but in an instant he detected a false note. The evidence of the landlord of the Drinitza inn showed conclusively that the mysterious visitors had occupied the Pelenko mansion from the very evening on which Prince Valerian had left it, and when Cyril had disappeared; and the neighbourhood had been so strictly watched about the time of Prince Soudaroff's visit that the doctor, his patient, and their train of attendants could not have arrived unnoticed. But since the doctor must not be allowed to see that he had blundered, Mr Hicks repaid his confidence by imparting to him, under a pledge of secrecy, the history of Cyril's disappearance, and suggested that he should be allowed to see him without his knowledge. The doctor agreed to this at once, remarking that he had begun to be doubtful as to the identity of his patient of late, since Prince Valerian paid no attention whatever to the detailed reports and other documents he forwarded to him, and no other member of the family had shown the slightest interest. He took the visitor up to one of the flat roofs of the building, which commanded a view of a lower roof. On this lower roof Cyril was sitting idle, as Helene had seen him in the garden, his hair and moustache white, his expression perfectly vacant, except when he rolled a cigarette with great care and neatness. A dreadful misgiving began to creep into Mr Hicks's mind.

"If he's not mad, it's just about the finest imitation I ever saw," he thought, and then suggested to the doctor that they should show themselves and speak to him.

"Not from this distance," was the reply, "but I shall be delighted to take you to him and present you formally. The case is a most interesting one, and I shall be glad to see whether there is any return of memory at the sight of you. I suppose you still think this is the person of whom you are in search?"

The question was asked hastily, as if Dr Gregorescu feared he might have aroused suspicion by taking for granted that the visitor would know his patient, and Mr Hicks was also conscious that there might be danger in a sudden meeting; but he remembered Cyril's apparent non-recognition of Helene, and took comfort as he accepted the doctor's offer. They passed through various passages, and at last came out upon the roof where they had seen Cyril. He was sitting in a kind of stone summer-house, open in front, with a bench running round the three sides, and a rough wooden table in the middle.

"May I be allowed to present to your Highness Mr Hicks, who is travelling in this neighbourhood?" said Dr Gregorescu, appearing round the corner of the summer-house with a suddenness which the visitor felt sure was intentional.

"How you startle one, Gregorescu!" said Cyril in French, rising and bowing languidly. "This is not the first time I have had to speak to you about your roughness. A man in my unfortunate position has at least the right to expect consideration from his physician. Monsieur," he turned to Mr Hicks, "pardon the irritability of my nerves. It is difficult for the young"—he waved his hand towards the doctor—"to realise how the knowledge that death may be lurking at any corner tends to unman one. You are an Englishman, I presume? My good doctor will be able to air his linguistic attainments. He is a most accomplished person."

"No, sir, an American," said Mr Hicks laconically. "I understood from you just now that you did not speak English?" he added sharply to Dr Gregorescu.

"His Highness is too kind. I speak a few words, just enough to make English people laugh," was the reply, and another black mark went down against the doctor in Mr Hicks's mind.

"Mr Hicks is anxious to take your Highness away with him," the doctor went on.

Cyril raised his eyebrows. "It is really very kind of Mr Hicks, but I don't quite see why I should go away with him," he remarked.

"If you remember the conversation we had a day or two ago, Highness——"

"Ah, I see." Cyril turned frankly to Mr Hicks. "You must understand, monsieur, that I make no complaints against Dr Gregorescu, but—and I say this to his face—I am not altogether satisfied with his arrangements. I can quite believe that it was advisable to remove from my brother's house, since my enemies had tracked me there, and I only escaped assassination by a secret and hasty departure, but I do not care for the situation of this place. It is isolated—exposed. I have the sensation of being set up to be shot at. Moreover, I understand that the doctor intends to take other patients, which is a very different thing from being my private physician, as I intended when I placed myself under his care. Hence I should not refuse to consider—merely to consider—proposals for a change."

"Count, you are colossal!" was the exclamation Mr Hicks only just restrained himself from uttering. He looked inquiringly at the doctor.

"His Highness's remarks compel me to enter upon a rather awkward subject," was the response. "The money entrusted to me for his Highness's support by—the lady I mentioned to you, monsieur, is—is very nearly exhausted, and——"

"And you think his Highness's friends might prefer to make their own arrangements in future?" asked Mr Hicks. "Quite so."

"Oh, monsieur, why should we continue this farce?" cried the doctor excitedly. "I see you have no doubt that my patient is in reality your friend, Count Mortimer——"

Cyril bowed smilingly. "You are very kind, to endow me with a new name," he said.

"And nothing would please me better than to resign him to your care at once," the doctor went on; "but how could I reconcile it with my conscience? You have no authority—you are not a relation. If he had even recognised you"—his little black eyes were on Cyril's face—"but I cannot surrender him to a stranger."

"That is so," agreed Mr Hicks, wondering what this portended.

"If only you could bring his wife here; but you say she is dangerously ill at Vindobona——"

Mr Hicks saw Cyril start slightly, very slightly, and interposed hastily. "Not dangerously ill, doctor; you mistook me. In fact, when she hears I have found her husband, I think she will be well at once. As you say, the best thing will be to bring her here. But she could scarcely arrive in less than a week, for she must travel slowly."

"If his Excellency will continue to put up with our poor quarters here for that time——"

"By all means," said Cyril, with a whimsical smile. "But you place me in a curious position, gentlemen. You propose to bring a charming lady—of course she is charming—who is good enough to say that she is my wife, to take care of me. Well and good; the lady and I can but see one another, and the decision will lie with her, naturally. The state of affairs is quite interesting."

"Perhaps," said Mr Hicks, anxious to disarm any suspicion in the doctor's mind, "it might be well for the Queen to remain in this house for a day or two before taking her husband away. You would then see whether there was any hope of his recognising her——"

"Or any fear of a recurrence of violence," said the doctor.

"There is one important point which doesn't seem to have occurred to you," said Cyril, with languid impatience. "My personal safety must be provided for. Mr dear Mr Hicks, I like your countenance, but you must understand that I cannot consent to leave a place of comparative security in order to plunge into constant danger. You and the lady of whom you speak will be good enough to make adequate arrangements for protecting me from assassination when I am outside these walls. You will also, if you please, arrange to defray any sum that may be due to Dr Gregorescu for his services by that time. His mentioning money matters was quite unnecessary, but since he is so deeply concerned about them, pray let him feel himself secure. That is all I have to say. Please make your own arrangements. I shall be delighted to fall in with them, if these two points are remembered." He rolled himself another cigarette, and leaned back in his seat, tapping with his fingers on the table as if tired of the subject, while Mr Hicks and the doctor, the latter looking much subdued, entered into a discussion as to ways and means. It was while they were trying to arrange how Queen Ernestine could be accommodated in a house which contained no female inhabitants, that Mr Hicks was struck by the intentness of Cyril's gaze at the doctor.

"What can it mean?" he thought. "And that tapping—how he keeps it up! It might be Morse—Jehoshaphat! it *is* Morse. Four dots, two dots, dash dot dash dot, dash dot dash, three dots—*Hicks*! Hicks! Hicks! and he's been doing it five minutes already. I understand you perfectly," he said slowly to the doctor. "There is a difficulty. Perhaps the best plan will be for Lady Usk to drive over here and see what can be done. A woman's notions often come in useful for circumventing a deadlock."

Dr Gregorescu welcomed the suggestion, and thought that it might be advisable to hire some furniture, either from Paranati or Novigrad, with a view to the Queen's visit. Paranati was nearer, but the absence of roads made it almost hopeless to send there. Decidedly Novigrad would be better, but then there was the difficulty of the frontier. Mr Hicks listened and agreed, while all the time, though his eyes were fixed on the doctor, he was interpreting the tapping on the table.

"*Hicks, get me out of this to-day, for heaven's sake! He suspects something. I shall be mad in real earnest if you leave me here another week.*"

To answer this appeal, Mr Hicks summoned to his aid all the fertility of invention which had made him famous in three continents. He dared not respond by tapping on the table, but from where he sat Cyril could see his knee, while it was hidden from the doctor. Tapping the knee smartly for a dot, and rubbing his finger along softly for a dash, he answered according to the code.

"*Be here this afternoon, and when you hear a row down below, watch out for a stone.*" Then he turned to the doctor and summed up. "If I can get a message to Lady Usk in time, she shall come up this afternoon, and you will settle with her what arrangements you can make. The Queen will arrive in a week, possibly sooner, and you will keep his Excellency under your care until then? My friend and I must go over to Paranati to bring that poor mad chap, for he ought to be in your charge as soon as possible, and I may be back here almost as soon as Lady Usk, but if I haven't arrived, you will explain things to her?"

The doctor agreed, and he and Mr Hicks parted with the utmost cordiality. The patient Mr Bradwell, reduced to utter silence from having exhausted every possible topic of conversation with his guide, was rescued from the bench in the porter's lodge where he was meekly smoking, and the two men walked down the hill together. No sooner were they out of earshot of the asylum than Mr Hicks said—

"Now, Eben Bradwell, buck up. You've got the very biggest order on hand to-day that you ever had, and don't you forget it."

"I guess this ain't the first time I've shepherded a lunatic gently into an asylum," was the reply, in a somewhat injured tone.

"Ebenezer," said Mr Hicks, "that isn't a circumstance to what I'm going to have you do to-day. You'll just make the journey to Paranati and back in the quickest time you ever travelled, and you'll bring along with you the smartest man on board the Bluebird."

"If you air alluding to that unfortunate darkey, I guess——"

"I am not alluding to him, but to a smart man that must take his place. I wouldn't hand over my worst enemy to that smooth-tongued Dago back of us, after the time we're going to give him to-day. No, sir; what that smart man of yours has to do is to try and give you the slip right at the foot of the hill here, and after a real hard fight, with as much yelling and general violence as he can get in for the money, to lead the chase way back into Dardania. You will have despatched a messenger as soon as he began to be ugly to entreat the doctor to come and try his influence on him, see?"

"You want the doctor out of the road for a bit, is that so? Well, sir, I like the notion, and I know the man that'll tumble to it. We'll make a real handsome nigger out of him."

"That's so, but there mustn't be any waste of time. You've just got to break the record getting to Paranati and back. Pour out the dollars like water if they're needed. I'll have Lady Usk's Dutchy go with you to do the talking, for I must stay and fix things up here, but I'll meet you in the village, and the patient needn't begin his star performances before then."

"And what about her Majesty's message that I brought you?"

"I guess her Majesty will just have to wait until this row is hoed. If she's so mad that she gets reconciled again, it won't hurt me, any way."

With this reckless defiance of Queen Félicia, Mr Hicks sped the mate and Jakob on their way, and himself returned along the road to meet Usk and Helene. He found them waiting faithfully, but fuming, at the appointed spot, and he unfolded the plan he had elaborated as he rode. To one point Usk objected strongly.

"I won't have Helene mixed up in the rescue," he said. "She can stay in the village, and we'll pick her up as we come back."

"I don't see but we must have her come with us," said Mr Hicks doubtfully, "or we won't be enough for the business. You, sir, will have your hands full getting the rope to your uncle and helping him down it, and Lady Usk will be wanted to hold the doctor in talk, for I must be way down the hill with Bradwell's outfit. Then when the doctor is sent for to help us, you must distract the janitor's attention while the Count slips past. If the charms of your conversation will do it, so much the better, but if not, then the six-shooter I warned you to bring will come into play. I must have Lady Usk wait with William and the buggy at the turn of the track out of sight of the gateway, for there's no other way of getting the Count down the hill without being seen. You have the waterproof apron on the buggy, Lady Usk, I hope? I guess you'll admire to take your part in saving the Count, won't you? Don't you go and have an upset down the hill; drive gently till you're through the village, but then just take it out of the horses until you're past the Pannonian frontier-post. I've had a word with the boss there. He can't do anything to help us, for fear of a frontier incident, but once you're safe across he'll see you're not followed."

"But supposing these Dardanian fellows fire—she may be hit!" cried Usk.

"Well, sir, there'll be your uncle and William, who won't have her get hurt if they can help it. And as I said, I wouldn't bring a woman into this if there was any other way of fixing things, but your wife has grit, and she'll take the risk."

"Oh, Usk, please, *please*!" entreated Helene, squeezing his arm very hard. "You know it was my fault he wasn't saved before. If I could really help to save him this time!"

Usk yielded, with a sufficiently bad grace, and they waited impatiently until Mr Hicks thought the mate's party would be on its way back from Paranati, and then started for the frontier. The Gendarmerie officer at the Pannonian post came out and wished them luck as they passed, and they crossed the frontier-line and began to climb the street of the village, which lay some few hundred yards beyond it. Several of Helene's old acquaintances came out to greet her, and while she talked to them through the imperfect medium of the customs-officer as interpreter, Mr Hicks and Usk went into the post-office for a moment. When they emerged, Usk looked noticeably stouter, a fact attributable to the length of thin, tough rope, knotted at intervals, which was wound round his body under his coat. This rope Mr Hicks had obtained in the morning through the postmaster, and ensuring his secrecy by a judicious gift and the promise of another, had employed him to make the knots. It would have been wholly inadequate had the asylum been a modern building, with smooth, well-finished walls, but the masonry had been rough when it was first laid, and was now so weather-beaten that a young and active man might almost have descended it without the aid of a rope at all.

Mr Hicks remained in the village to meet Mr Bradwell, and William, leaving his horse, took the driver's seat in the buggy. Usk walked up the hill by the side of the carriage, and loitered about the gateway, while Helene, with much outward dignity and inward shrinking, paid her call upon the doctor. It was almost more than her husband could endure to let her enter the place by herself. What if she should be kidnapped too! But she looked round and smiled at him bravely when she went in at the gate, and after he had fidgeted about for the prescribed three or four minutes, he began to take an interest in the masonry, and to cross-question the porter. The man knew nothing of the history of the place, but he intimated that the noble gentleman was quite at liberty to walk round the outside, as far as the cliff afforded a foothold, and see what the rest of the walls were like. Usk waited only until he was out of sight of the gateway to unwind himself from the rope, and fasten the end of it round a suitable stone. Then he went on, along a very narrow ledge, until it ended suddenly, and he caught sight of Cyril looking over the wall some ten feet farther on. At first his heart stood still as he realised that he could not get under the wall at the right spot, but in a moment he saw that this did not really signify. The ledge was so narrow that it would have been next to impossible to throw the stone up perpendicularly with any hope of its lodging on the wall, but from the spot where he stood he could throw it diagonally with some chance of success. Cyril held up a finger as a warning to him not to begin yet, and he gathered the rope in his left hand and waited. Then the sound of a sudden tumult, shouts, yells, expostulations, and blows, mounted to them from the foot of the hill. Cyril nodded, and Usk threw the stone. After two or three attempts which fell short, Cyril caught it, and began to draw up the rope.

In the meantime, William and the gatekeeper were startled by the appearance of Jakob, who dashed up hatless and dishevelled to entreat that Dr Gregorescu would come down the hill at once. The lunatic from the Bluebird had suddenly become violent, and refused to mount the hill. He was fighting with such strength that Mr Hicks and Mr Bradwell feared they could not restrain him much longer. It would take at least six men to carry him up the hill, they thought. The doctor came out promptly, making final arrangements hastily with Helene as he handed her into the buggy, then hurried down the hill with three or four of his Dardanian servants, while William started the horses on the steep descent with cautious deliberation. At the turn in the track they paused, William almost as much excited as his mistress, until the tones of Usk's voice as he asked the porter whether his wife had started without waiting for him reached their ears. Almost immediately there was the sound of hasty footsteps, and Cyril ran down the road. William had handed the reins to Helene, and was out of the carriage immediately, lifting the apron on the farther side, and in a moment Cyril was crouching in the vacant space and hidden under the apron.

"William, put up the hood, please," said Helene, in a quick hard voice, and the servant, alarmed by her tone, turned to see Dr Gregorescu hurrying breathlessly round the turn in front of them. He might have no suspicion at present, but he could not but be surprised to see the carriage stopping and William standing in the road. Helene's presence of mind saved the situation, and William obeyed at once.

"Surely you must find this place very windy?" said Helene, as the doctor passed them. "I feel quite cold. Will you kindly tell my husband that I have driven on, if you meet him? But don't let me keep you. William, you had better lead the horses down the hill."

"A thousand pardons!" ejaculated Dr Gregorescu. "I cannot stay, madame, for the poor fellow from the ship has escaped. We must organise a search at once. Pray excuse me."

A gracious bow from Helene, and she drove on, her face so white and her hands so powerless that William, at the horses' heads, feared the reins would be torn from her grasp. At the next turning he stopped.

"Excuse me, my lady, but if his lordship would change hats and coats with me, he might sit up aside of you and drive, and no one the wiser, without they looked close under the 'ood, if you'll forgive me offerin' advice."

"Excellent advice too, William," came in Cyril's voice, muffled by the apron, "but what will you do?"

"I'll go off in your things, my lord, as if I was tryin' to get to the frontier post by a short cut, without passin' through the village, and lead 'em a rare dance. If they come up with me, I have my fistes."

As he spoke, William was divesting himself of his livery coat and cockaded hat, and replacing them with the soft felt hat and light overcoat Cyril handed to him. Cyril made the change almost as quickly, and stepped in front of Helene to the driver's seat. She gave up the reins without a word, for she was incapable of speech, and they were just starting when Usk rushed headlong down the hill behind them.

"What's all this? Oh, good! Drive for your life, Uncle Cyril. Gregorescu's found out! Now, William, let's put them off the scent!" and Usk and the disguised William plunged into the wilderness of rocks and low bushes beside the track, where the carriage could not pass, as if intending to cut off the angle formed by the turns of the road.

"Don't be frightened, Helene, but hold tight!" said Cyril, with a smile at his companion, as he kept a firm hand on the reins.

"Oh, I don't mind. Go fast—oh, do go fast!" she cried, finding her voice.

"Not until we are down this hill," he answered, but when they came to the short stretch of level road leading to the village, the buggy seemed to fly along. When they reached the corner, and turned down into the village street, Helene screamed.

"Oh, they are taking the short cut too! They mean to catch us up before we can reach the frontier-line."

"Never mind. They're only after Usk and William, who don't mean to be caught. They won't lead them across our track, you may be sure."

"No, no!" cried Helene, in agony. "I caught sight of Usk just for a moment, and they must have seen him too, but they are not following. They are coming straight across."

"Well, they are after William, then," said Cyril shortly. "Keep quiet, Lenchen, and don't frighten the horses."

He was driving very carefully down the steep street, which in some places was almost as rough as a flight of steps, and the horses were picking their way with the greatest daintiness. Suddenly Helene screamed again.

"Oh, I saw them—between the houses! They will be there before us! Oh, do drive faster!"

Standing up with one hand on the rail, she snatched the whip from Cyril, and struck the horses wildly several times. They swerved across the road, and Cyril was almost dragged from his seat.

"Sit down, Lenchen!" he said angrily. "Do you want us both to be killed?"

He recovered the whip, but there was no holding the horses now. The buggy clattered down the stony street, dispersing pigs and fowls and goats as it came. Horrified mothers caught up their children from before the very feet of the horses, and village elders, leaning against their houses for a talk, drew back out of the road with an injured air as the wheels crashed close by their toes. By some miracle, as it seemed, the horses kept their feet, and the buggy was not overturned, and when the foot of the hill was in sight, Cyril drew a deep breath, and said to Helene—

"It's no use trying to pull up here. I'm going to rush them. Crouch. Get under the apron if you can."

Glancing ahead, Helene saw that the Dardanians were straining every nerve to reach the road and intercept them as soon as they were upon the level. She slipped down under the apron as far as she could, and Cyril urged the horses on. Only two men leaped into the road in time to stand and meet them, and though both shouted that they would fire, they were too much shaken by their run to take accurate aim. One sprang aside, and struck a futile blow at Cyril with the butt-end of his gun; the other was knocked down, and the horses, terrified by the discharge of his rifle as he fell, and by the shouts which arose from behind them, dashed on faster than ever. Two or three bullets struck the hood of the buggy harmlessly.

"Not much farther now, Lenchen," said Cyril. "Get back to your seat, at once, and if I say 'Jump!' do it immediately, do you hear?"

Why should she jump? What could he see that made him think such a thing might be necessary? Helene cowered on the seat beside him with parted lips and staring eyes. Suddenly she saw what it was. A Dardanian sprang from some bushes on the right of the road, and standing in front of the horses, waved his arms and shouted. They swerved aside, but Cyril brought them round again, and as the man tried to leap up on the step of the carriage as it passed him, struck at him with the whip. He fell back, but at the same moment a fusilade broke out from the bushes, and terrified the horses beyond control. The high pole which marked the frontier, bearing on this side the emblems of Dardania, on the other those of Pannonia, was only a little way in front, and just beyond it were the gendarmes and their officer, drawn up in line, with their rifles ready. Cyril made a last effort to direct the horses into the lane kept open for them between the two ranks of men, but they dashed violently to the left, where the ground sank into a kind of wooden glen.

"Jump, Lenchen, jump!" cried Cyril, but Helene was too much frightened to obey. She was conscious of a violent jolt, a crackling of branches, the sensation of falling. There were shouts and cries, then a great silence.

CHAPTER XXIII.
THE PRICE TO BE PAID.

IT was late at night, but the windows of the little inn at Drinitza were still ablaze with lights. In the sitting-room which was held sacred to Lord and Lady Usk, Cyril was lying upon a sofa, while Mr Hicks bandaged systematically and scientifically the various injuries he had received in being thrown out of the buggy. Usk was wandering in and out of the room, restless and savagely miserable, for Helene had not recovered consciousness since she was extricated from the wrecked carriage, and Hannele and the doctor from Novigrad were with her upstairs, and would not allow him even near her door.

"There, Count!" said Mr Hicks, tying a final knot; "I guess you're about fixed up now, and I incline to think a meal of some sort would be a judicious investment after all this mussing around. Lord Usk, if we might requisition the services of that excellent William of yours to forage for us——"

"Oh, tell him to do anything you like," said Usk wearily, stepping out on the terrace for the twentieth time. "I don't want him."

The others heard him tramping up and down outside while William removed the traces of Mr Hicks's surgical labours, and brought in a hastily prepared meal. Seeing that Cyril was helpless with a sprained wrist, the servant asked if he should cut up his meat for him, but the offer was declined. Presently Usk, finding the companionship of his own thoughts intolerable, came back into the room.

"Now, Lord Usk," said Mr Hicks cheerfully, "just sit down and eat something."

"No, no, I don't want anything," was the hasty answer.

"Do you really feel that you can't break bread with me, Usk?" asked Cyril, pausing in his efforts to feed himself with his left hand.

"It's not that, of course. Here, let me cut that up for you, uncle. It's simply that I can't eat."

"It is that. You feel that if it had not been for me that poor little girl upstairs would have been sitting here with you as usual. It's quite true, but do you need to hear me say that if I had known what was to happen I would never have stirred a step to escape—that I would go back and give myself up to Gregorescu this moment if it would do her any good?"

"It's not that," repeated Usk. "I know it wasn't your fault—or Hicks's or mine, except that we ought never to have let her come—but that we, all of us strong men, should have got through without a scratch, and a little delicate girl like her—oh, God! when we got her out from under the buggy——" his voice failed.

"Well, the Count has a good few scratches to show any way," said Mr Hicks judicially, "and so has that good fellow William, blubbering out that he wished he was killed and her ladyship not hurt. But if I were you, Lord Usk, I guess I'd find something else to do beyond tearing my hair and scarifying my soul with remorse that way. You'll be a fine washed-out article when they want you upstairs to give a hand with the nursing. Now, for your wife's sake!" he took Usk by the shoulders, and pushed him down into a chair, "I'll have you make some sort of a meal, or I'll warn the doctor that it'll only mean another patient on his hands if he lets you sit up."

"I can't hear what they are doing from here," objected Usk.

"Nor can any of us. But we can hear if they open the door, or come out in the upper hall, and that's just all you want. Now the Count is going to tell us something of what he's been through. Yes, sir," he added firmly, in response to a look of remonstrance from Cyril, "I guess I mean just that."

"You needn't think you're going to make any sensational discoveries, Hicks. We may suspect till all is blue, but the real movers in the plot have covered up their traces too well to be brought to book."

"Ah, I sort of suspicioned that they weren't taking any risks. But I'd as lief know the way they fixed things up, Count, from that very evening when you swam out of our ken, like a new kind of planet."

For a moment Cyril hesitated still. "It's not the kind of story to make a man altogether proud," he said, "for whenever I was outwitting our friends the enemy most completely, I seem to have been making it easier for them to keep a tight hold on me. But you shall hear. Of course our driver must have been drugged when we got to Klotsch that evening, and it had probably been made worth the landlord's while not to be in too great a hurry to supply his place. At any rate, poor Paschics and I walked on a good way, and at last, thinking that as we had paid for the carriage, it was not much good doing the journey on our own feet, sat down by the roadside to wait for it. I think it was the first time in our joint lives that we were ever caught napping, and we have paid dearly enough for it, both of us, Heaven knows! but who would ever have anticipated danger on that straight piece of high road? There were not even woods on each side— merely rocks, and those stunted shrubs the goats eat. We were just beyond the turning which leads to this road below you here, down into Dardania, sitting rather high up on the bank so as to be out of the dust. Suddenly we were seized from behind, and blindfolded with something thrown over our heads. We hadn't a chance to struggle. How many men there were against us I don't know, but they carried us off quite easily, and when they took the cloak off my head again I was in a carriage, which must have been waiting just out of sight in the side-road. There was a woman in it—Tania Garanine, the Scythian actress—and when I saw her I knew the true inwardness of the plot at once. She is a favourite tool of Soudaroff's; and the Princess of Dardania turned her on when she wanted to keep her son from marrying Princess Emilia of Magnagrecia. The young fellow was staunch, you know, which didn't make the fair Tania any more kindly disposed towards me, who had made up the match. She looked quite radiant when I found myself opposite her in the carriage, and made no bones about answering my questions. It was desirable that I should be out of the way for a time, she told me, but everything would be done to make the short seclusion as pleasant as possible, and if I would give my word not to attempt to escape, I should be allowed a considerable degree of freedom. Since my revolver was gone, and my feet were fastened together, and my hands tied in front of me, it seemed rather unnecessary to ask for my parole, and I refused it promptly. She didn't seem to mind, but the fellow who sat beside me immediately poked the muzzle of a revolver into my neck, and remarked that he would fire if I moved. There was another man opposite, also with a revolver, and poor Paschics was at the bottom of the carriage, apparently choking. I pointed out to the lady that if she didn't want him to die before her eyes, she had better have the thing taken off his head, and she gave the order with a sweet smile, as a personal favour to me, she said. Just at that moment we passed another carriage—an elaborate old-fashioned affair with Dardanian outriders—coming in the opposite direction, towards Europe, and the man in it bowed very impressively to Mlle. Garanine."

"Prince Valerian Pelenko!" cried Mr Hicks. "Then I guess he told the exact truth, after all, when he said he had seen you riding with that lady, and on the best of terms with her."

"Probably, since he could not see the revolver, and the carriage-rug was drawn up over my hands. Did—did my wife hear it?"

"We all heard it, Count, but no one believed a word of it. To us it was only one more attempt to take away your character."

"But she might have believed it!" cried Usk violently. "It might have pained her most awfully. Why didn't you cry out, Uncle Cyril, even if you were shot the next moment? At least she would have known that their whole story was a lie."

"Would she?" asked Cyril. "My dear Usk, do you think my enemies would not have been able to arrange things so as to give her greater pain still? As it happened, Prince Pelenko was able to do his part without departing from the apparent truth, but do you think he would have objected to go a little beyond it if necessary? Would it have been much consolation to my wife to learn that I had shot myself, whether accidentally or otherwise, when in Mlle. Garanine's company? You may say that it would have been no worse than to hear that I was in her company living, but you must remember that I fully expected to be able to escape with Paschics in two or three days at most. If I had thought I should be a prisoner for more than three months!—well, I may tell you that many and many a time I have wished I had called out as you suggest, and taken the consequences."

"I think I hear them moving upstairs," interrupted Usk, and he went to the door and listened, but came back almost immediately, sitting down at the table with the same gloomy face.

"Go ahead, Count!" said Mr Hicks. "I want to know right now what happened."

"Nothing happened for some time, except that Mlle. Garanine threw out hints which were evidently intended to make me believe that I was merely wanted out of the way for a day or two while a revolution was carried through in Thracia. It was an ingenious idea, for, of course, with Michael out of the kingdom, and most of the Ministers away at his wedding, the time would have been well chosen, but I knew I must have had some inkling of it if things had gone so far, and I was prepared to believe anything rather than what she told me. I felt pretty certain that it was the affairs of Palestine, and not of Thracia, which were concerned, and that I was wanted out of the way for a good deal longer than a day or two. I saw several ways in which they might try to manage it, but I reserved my judgment until we stopped at that accursed house down there——" he waved his hand towards the hill at the back of the inn. "If you knew what it has been to be certain that there were friends and safety within a mile of me, and yet to be unable to take a step towards them——! I should like to tear that house down stone by stone, and make it a desolation for ever——"

"And bury Dr Gregorescu and his Dardanians under the ruins?" asked Mr Hicks.

"No," said Cyril calmly. "That would be too good for them. That man has made me twenty years older in these three months. I saw the whole plot as soon as I was face to face with him and heard his name, and it was the very worst of the alternatives I had imagined. You will wonder how I knew.

Well, I don't think I am a coward generally. Hicks, you and I have been in some tight places together; what do you say?"

"No man less so, Count."

"Thanks. But there is one thing before which I am an abject coward, and that is poison. Not ordinary poison—just going to sleep and not waking up again—nor even the fancy kinds which twist you up into an arch before they've done with you, but one particular kind of poison, the thought of which used to give me the horrors whenever I let myself remember it while I was in Thracia. Taken in small quantities, it doesn't destroy life, only the mind—takes away a man's memory, leaves him a sort of perpetual child, do you see? The knowledge of it is hereditary in one family, but for generations it has been at the service of the Scythian Government, and occasionally it has been used—not too often, so as to awaken suspicion, but just to get rid effectually of some troublesome person whose death might cause remark. All those years when I was practically the only barrier between Ernestine and Michael and a Scythian protectorate, I went in deadly fear of this devilish stuff. Of course I took precautions. Paschics and Dietrich were staunch, if all the rest of my household were traitors, but there was always the danger of the thing's being administered in some one else's house. I inquired secretly into the subject, and got some interesting information by bribing disappointed Secret Service agents, so that I had some faint idea of the nature and properties of the drug. Then I had an exhaustive list made of the members of the family that prepared it, and their various marriages, so that if I found myself in the neighbourhood of any of them I might be on my guard. In the last generation, one of the daughters married a Dacian named Gregorescu. Now you see why I knew my fate as soon as I heard the doctor's name. He was at the house, waiting to receive me, and Mlle. Garanine delivered me over to him in the most matter-of-fact way. She herself returned into Dardania at once—on horseback, I presume, for the carriage could not cross the mountains, and was laid up in the Pelenko stables—and the two men with revolvers went with her. But we were no better off for that. The house was guarded by a small army of Dardanians, who kept watch day and night, though of course I didn't find this out at once. My idea was to disarm the doctor's suspicions by pretending to swallow whole the notion of the Thracian plot, and I harped on the subject till late at night. I pointed out that it could not possibly be successful, but that I would make it worth his while if he would release me at once. I appealed to his cupidity, his ambition, everything I could think of, and at last he thought it advisable to pretend to yield. He would think it over, and let me know in the morning, he said, and in any case I might be sure my captivity should be as pleasant as he could make it. I had refused supper, but would I drink a little glass of benedictine with him to show there was no ill-feeling? This was what I had been expecting, and I agreed at once, only thankful he had chosen liqueur and not coffee, which would have been much more difficult to manage. The benedictine looked just as usual, except that I could just distinguish a very slight—almost imperceptible—cloudiness about the glass at my end of the tray."

"But why not have taken the other, and so forced on an explanation?" demanded Usk, who had become interested in the recital in spite of himself.

"Because that was what I particularly wished not to do. My idea was to make Gregorescu think I had taken the poison, and so gull him into keeping a less strict watch on me. He would not venture to repeat the experiment unless he was quite sure I had tricked him, for a second dose would kill any man living, and I was pretty certain they did not want me to die on their hands. For one thing, it would look bad if the matter came out; for another, it would spoil the full effect of the Princess of Dardania's revenge. So I took up the glass and sipped it quite calmly, to all appearance—only, instead of swallowing any of the liqueur, I poured it down my sleeve a drop at a time, by a turn of the wrist, when I raised the glass to my lips. He did not dare to watch me very closely while I drank, lest I should suspect something, and I am thankful to say my nerve lasted until the glass was empty. I thought then it was about the stiffest piece of acting I had ever been driven to. If I had known that I had to carry it on for three months! Afterwards I spoke a little thickly, and let him help me to my room. He was watching for the symptoms, and was quite satisfied, but early in the morning he very nearly had me. Poor Paschics, of course, knew nothing of the whole affair. He was imprisoned somewhere by himself, but in the morning they left his door open, and he crept along the passage to find me. I saw him standing over me with his finger on his lips when I woke, and I was just going to explain things to him when it struck me that his being allowed to be there was suspicious, and I pretended not to know him. It was heartbreaking to see the state he was in, but I persisted, and it was well I did, for Gregorescu was spying on us the whole time. I found out his spy-hole afterwards. He thought it was all right then, and came and had poor Paschics taken away, apologising to me for his intrusion. I looked as puzzled as I could, and when I got up did my best to make it clear that my mind was a blank—that I did not know Gregorescu himself, or where I was, or who I was, or anything that had happened. For the first day or two he used to try to catch me out, starting subjects suddenly, or asking questions, and it's just a chance that the strain didn't make me as mad as he thought I was. But when he felt pretty sure of the vacuum, he began to fill it after a fashion by suggestion. I was Prince Shishman Pelenko, and I was gradually fitted with a past to match the name—all hinted most carefully, and wedged into my mind, so to speak, by leading questions. It was horribly cleverly done, and when Gregorescu thought his work was complete, he had it inspected—by Prince Soudaroff himself. It was a good thing that I had had fair practice in guile by that time, or I could never have held out, but I baffled even him. He also went away quite satisfied——"

"And met us on the hill here, and told us a whole lot of lies about Shishman Pelenko," said Usk savagely.

"Well," said Mr Hicks, with some complacency, "I guess the champion liar of Europe had met his match that time, any way."

"Thanks for the compliment!" said Cyril. "I believe now that his perfect satisfaction with what he had seen and heard must have made him less clear-sighted with regard to what was going on in Neustria. He thought that with me helpless and in safe custody he had nipped the Palestine scheme in the bud, but no doubt he intended to make things safe after a while by opening negotiations with Ernestine and Goldberg, and handing me over, as a hopeless idiot, in exchange for a promise that the existing state of affairs at Jerusalem should remain undisturbed. It has been about the only consolation I have had, to think that the real scheme would go on all the better because Soudaroff was congratulating himself on having put a stop to the bogus one. But I needed the consolation, for it was just about that time that I lost poor Paschics. We had been kept so strictly apart that I had never had a chance of conferring with him or explaining matters, but he seems to have had some idea that I was only shamming madness. At any rate, one night, when there was a tremendous thunderstorm, I found him by my bed again. He did not utter a sound, simply took my hand in the darkness, and talked on it in the deaf-and-dumb alphabet. He said he believed he could escape under cover of the storm, for the Dardanians were all in a lively state of funk, taking shelter wherever they could, and he would bring back help and release me. I asked him in the same way why I should not come too, but he told me that the usual man—a rascally French-speaking Greek who posed as my personal attendant—was on guard at my door, and had only let him pass when he gave him all the money he had, under the pretext that I was always afraid of thunder. In fact, I saw the fellow inside the room by the next flash of lightning, listening jealously, but as he only saw Paschics holding my hand, he got nothing to tell his master. Well, as soon as the storm became less severe, Paschics departed, and the next thing I heard was that he was dead."

"And was he murdered?" asked Usk quickly.

"I believe not. As far as I could make out, he was trying to escape along the roof, intending to climb down one of the trees which grew near the end of the house, when Gregorescu discovered his absence and turned out the Dardanians. When he saw they were after him, he turned off to the edge of the roof, intending to drop from it to the back verandah, and so to the ground; but the parapet was rotten all along, and a great piece of it fell with him. He struggled up and threw himself over the edge of the verandah, and actually ran a few steps; then they saw him give a convulsive leap and fall to the ground. When they got to him he was dead. The shock and the fall together were too much for him, after the excitement and anxiety of the past weeks. That was Gregorescu's account, and I have no reason to doubt it."

"No; it's in accordance with the medical evidence," said Mr Hicks. "Death due to shock, bruises inflicted before death; that was all."

"But it doesn't explain our finding the body in the river," said Usk.

"That was to throw you off the scent," said Cyril quickly. "Didn't you all go off to some place on the Mœsian frontier, miles away, to see whether I was in that neighbourhood? But you didn't rise to the occasion as they hoped. You were quite expected to leave Drinitza, and take up your quarters at Bagnanera."

"Then you heard something of our movements?"

"Oh yes; they talked quite openly before me, at first to try and catch me off my guard, and afterwards, when they were quite sure the drug had taken effect, because there was no reason why they shouldn't. They had one more try to make me betray myself when they found Paschics was dead, telling me of it suddenly, and I had to affect ignorance and mystification, and go through the whole sickening show over again. It was so long before Gregorescu was really convinced of my madness that I suppose, in spite of all my care, I must have failed in some points, but he seems to have satisfied himself at last that it was more likely the drug should produce slightly different effects on different people than that a man should carry on such a deception for so long. Then came the news of the Neustrian revolution and Malasorte's dictatorship, and Soudaroff must have seen immediately that his plans for making use of me were foiled. In a sense, all that had been done was useless, except as a matter of personal revenge, and he could not hope to do any successful trading with me in the future, since his Emperor had gone behind him and was in league with Malasorte, and Malasorte was in league with the Jews. I gathered that the plan now was to smuggle me into Pannonia and leave me in a lunatic asylum there, to be discovered or not by my friends, as circumstances might determine——"

"No, sir," said Mr Hicks quickly; "you were to be discovered. Mlle. Garanine took the trouble to come here on purpose to give the plan away to us."

"That was to get us out of the way, as I said at the time," remarked Usk. "We were keeping too strict a watch on the neighbourhood to please them."

"No doubt," said Cyril; "and we must also remember that nothing would satisfy the Princess of Dardania but to restore to my wife a husband who could not even recognise her. The woman's malice had to be consulted as well as Soudaroff's statecraft, you see. Well, you may imagine my state of feeling, with such a prospect before me—a pauper lunatic asylum, from which I might or might not be released before I was driven really mad. Then there came poor Helene's sudden incursion." Usk moved restlessly. "It was almost more than I could do to keep up my pretence of not recognising her; but if I hadn't done it, I don't believe she would have got away alive. As it was, I saw her to the gate myself, and watched her out of sight, for those bloodthirsty Dardanians were capable of anything, but I had disarmed their suspicions so completely by that time that they all obeyed me in ordinary matters as if I had really been Shishman Pelenko himself. But Gregorescu was not going to risk Helene's bringing back help. The last thing he wished was to be caught on Pannonian soil, and to be identified with my disappearance, so we prepared for a flitting at once. The idea which he had so carefully 'suggested' to me, that my life was in danger from unknown enemies, was worked again, and I was warned I must escape at once. And I had to fall in with it, for I couldn't throw off the mask until help was actually at hand. When I saw Helene again, alone, hiding in the bushes, just as we were starting, I almost lost hope, for I couldn't make her understand what I wanted, and I could only trust no one else had seen her. If they hadn't found out who she was since the morning, by sending a spy to track her back here, I haven't a doubt she would have been killed, but they were afraid of meddling with her further than by sending an old woman to guide her astray while we got off."

"But how did you get off, any way, and what happened to the carriage, Count?" cried Mr Hicks.

"The carriage simply drove out of the gates and into the wood, where it was left, while we went on with the horses alone," answered Cyril. "After your visit to the house the next day, it was restored to its usual place, but when you were wondering which way it could have gone without being seen, it was hidden in a thicket quite close to you. And ourselves? Oh, we crossed the road and plunged into the hills on the opposite side, and so made our way round by mountain-paths to the house above the village, which Gregorescu had had in his eye for some time in case he found it necessary to take the bull by the horns and negotiate for my surrender instead of dumping me down in Pannonia. You see, it was on Dardanian soil, and he knew you could not touch him without a long diplomatic difficulty which would involve just what you didn't want—waste of time. You know how he worked the thing through the mate of Queen Félicia's yacht, and you know, Hicks, how very close the shave was at last. I don't know quite how I gave myself away in that interview this morning—or yesterday morning now—my nerve is not what it was, and my face may have shown what I was feeling, or perhaps he merely put two and two together, but I swear I solemnly believe that if I had been in his power for another day, he would have forced me to take another dose of his drug, in some way that I could not evade. Even as it was, I was in terror lest he should do it before you came back, but he thought he had a week before him, and he didn't know I had seen what was in his mind. You were only just in time, Usk, but I would rather you had been too late than that this should have happened."

"It can't be helped," groaned Usk. "Oh, what are they doing with her all this time? Can she be dead, and they haven't told me?"

"No, no," said Mr Hicks. "They had a lot to do, and I guess no news is good news. If you could sleep a little, now——?"

A mute gesture of refusal from Usk answered him, and they waited on, until at last the door of the room upstairs was heard to open. Usk met the doctor half-way up the stairs. "Well?" he gasped. "How is she?"

The doctor, who was a German and disapproved of misalliances, looked him over severely before answering. "There is no sign of consciousness," he replied slowly. "It would be as well to summon her Highness's august parents as soon as possible, and there is a specialist at Vindobona I should be glad to have at hand. It is not likely he could suggest anything, but it is always a comfort to the patient's friends to feel that everything possible has been done."

The Grand-Duke and Duchess came from Molzau, Queen Ernestine from her sick-bed at Vindobona, Lord and Lady Caerleon from Geneva, where they had just laid in the grave the exiled Pauline Vassilievna, who had been more than a mother to Lady Caerleon. Never had the little inn at Drinitza been so full, or entertained such important guests, but the old landlord felt no desire to congratulate himself. The "little Princess" had won every heart during her stay, and now, to all appearance, she was dying. When her parents first arrived, she seemed to recognise them—Usk was certain that she did—but she relapsed immediately into a state in which she appeared to be conscious of nothing but pain. As if it had not been agony enough to see her suffer, Usk found very soon that the blame was supposed to be his. The Grand-Duchess could not forgive either him or Cyril for the accident. At least, she said resentfully, she thought she was securing a kind and thoughtful husband for her Lenchen when she gave her to him, but he had gone and sacrificed her to his uncle before they had been four months married. She would have kept him out of the sick-room altogether if she could, and when he insisted on taking part in the nursing, mounted guard over him the whole time to make sure that he did not disturb Helene by speaking to her. If Usk's heart had not been very sore, and a good deal troubled by remorse, for which no one but himself and the Grand-Duchess could see any reason, he would have rebelled; but he could not engage in a squabble over his wife's unconscious form, and his imperious mother-in-law rode roughshod over him. To his astonishment, it was the Grand-Duke who took his part. He also was banished from the sick-room, and he did not venture to dispute his wife's decision, but he made friends with Usk in a rough kind of way, and they would take long walks together almost in silence, finding a fellow-feeling in their common grief. The Grand-Duchess, in a fury of maternal anxiety so vehement as almost to be ludicrous, made no secret of the fact that she would have preferred to be left with only Queen Ernestine and Lady Caerleon to share her labours. True, she bore a grudge against the Queen because she was Cyril's wife, but she credited her with a genuine interest in Helene, which she denied to any of the men. They could talk of politics, she said with scorn, when Lenchen lay dying. The accusation had some colour, unreasonable though it sounded. The question of the relations between Michael and Félicia had reached an acute stage, and must speedily become common property if no solution could be devised for it.

Up to this point, chiefly by the assiduous efforts of Baroness Radnika, the fiction that Félicia was merely taking a short cruise, and that her husband had not found time to join her, had been kept up. Even the Pannonian Court had been willing to account for anything that seemed strange in the arrangement by remembering Félicia's American education, but she had no mind to leave things in this state. When the Grand-Duke and Duchess paid her a hurried visit on board the yacht on their way to Drinitza, she told them the facts of the case with the greatest frankness, and refused to hear of a reconciliation. A separation she wanted, and a separation she would have, and the Grand-Duke saw no way of avoiding a scandal. He took counsel with Cyril and Mr Hicks (these conversations it was which aroused the Grand-Duchess's ire), and they beat their brains for some means of bringing Félicia back to Bellaviste. King Michael was far from implacable. He admired Félicia intensely, and was really as much in love with her as it was possible to him to be, and he had the grace to be heartily ashamed of his own part in the dispute. He saw it now through Félicia's eyes, and admired her secretly for resenting his conduct, and he was also painfully alive to the ridicule that would descend upon him if it came out that he had driven away his three months' bride by his groundless jealousy. He was willing to make promises and concessions for the future, but Félicia opposed a simple negative to all his proposals. Once more Cyril became the natural go-between, and travelled first to Bellaviste to interview the King, and then across the peninsula to Paranati to try to influence Félicia, but all in vain.

These journeys were not undertaken without strong remonstrance from Queen Ernestine, who never saw her husband depart without fearing that his enemies might contrive to get him again into their power. But he never travelled without either the Grand-Duke, Mr Hicks, or Lord Caerleon, and two or three armed servants, and with such precautions it was not likely that he would now incur danger. Dr Gregorescu had prudently disappeared, and his Dardanians were merged again in the general mass of their fellow-countrymen. It was in the highest degree unlikely that either Prince Soudaroff or the Princess of Dardania would attempt any further hostile move, when the victim was able to recount the whole history of the one that had just failed, although he had not at present chosen to make it public. Moreover, the political reasons which had induced the Scythian Chancellor to join in the plot existed no longer, and he recognised that he had been cleverly led aside by a false clue. Before the Emperor Timoleon V. had sat for a month upon the throne of Neustria, the world was startled by a rescript issued jointly by himself and his brother monarch of Scythia. From this document it appeared that the Scythian troops which had for three years occupied Jerusalem would be withdrawn immediately, and the city handed over to the representatives of the Jewish provisional government which had sat during that period at Nablus. Palestine would be neutralised, and the Jewish State guaranteed in its independence and privileges (nothing being said of the shadowy suzerainty of Roum) by Neustria, Scythia, and the United States of America.

There was little real opposition to the measure. The new alliance was immensely formidable, besides representing roughly the three Christian creeds which were wont to battle over the sacred soil. England had lost her opportunity of protesting when she acquiesced in the Scythian occupation of Jerusalem three years before, and Hercynia was quieted by receiving compensation elsewhere, as usual at the expense of Roum. There was a wild outcry from the mass of the poorer Jews that no provision was made for appointing a Prince of Palestine, but Cyril made it known that he should refuse to be nominated even if the post were constituted. As he had said, the agony of his captivity had made him an old man all at once, and he felt no temptation to mingle any longer in politics. It was typical of the change wrought in the man by the disastrous result of his last experience of the political arena, that he now desired nothing more than to return with his wife to the oasis in the Syrian desert, within whose narrow limits he had so often chafed, and there end his days in quietness.

And in the mean time, while the two Emperors were reorganising the map of the world, and Félicia was reiterating her undying defiance of her husband, Helene still lay unconscious in the inn at Drinitza. The agonies of pain had passed, but she did not recover. She had not sufficient vitality, the doctors said, to rally from the shock and the long suffering, and it was not unlikely that her life would flicker out without so much as a return to consciousness.

CHAPTER XXIV.
RISORGIMENTO.

AS to Helene herself, the days and weeks passed by without her knowledge. Once only since the accident had she waked to a brief interval of full consciousness, and that was when the old home voices first penetrated her dulled ear. Her father and mother were in the room as well as Usk, and she lay looking at them without their perceiving it, making no attempt to speak. But when the Grand-Duchess broke down and wept stormily, crying out to Usk, "You stole her away from us, and this is the way you take care of her!" the injustice of the speech moved her to protest. She tried to speak, but no words would come, and though Usk met her anguished eyes, and nodded reassuringly at her, she could not vindicate him. She saw her father lay his hand upon his shoulder, as though he felt he was unjustly accused, but the Grand-Duchess was evidently implacable. Helene still struggled to speak, but the effort was too great, and she relapsed into immobility, which yet was not complete unconsciousness, for she was very conscious of pain, although the outer world was a blank to her. To herself she seemed to be borne and buffeted on a sea of pain; she sounded its lowest depths, and was carried up to the height of its hugest waves. There was the pain which attacked her in a succession of violent shocks, like billows breaking over a helpless shipwrecked man on a rocky shore, and swept her away at last into such agony that she was forced to scream; and the pain which crept upwards slowly and gradually, like a gently rising tide, until her whole frame seemed nothing but one dull, paralysing ache, and all kinds and degrees of pain between these two extremes. She battled against this sea, she thought, although in some strange way the sound of the breakers and the throb of the rising waves was inside her head and not outside, as though she was playing the traitor to herself, but it attacked her persistently in fresh ways, and she felt that it must prove the stronger at last. But just when her strength was altogether at an end, and she knew that she could struggle no longer, the necessity for struggling ceased. There was no sea at all, either rough or smooth, and she was drifting gently down a broad calm river. Sometimes she had glimpses of scenes on the banks, sometimes she heard strange toneless voices speaking loudly, although she could not distinguish what they said, but she never saw any place or person or heard any voice that she knew. Most often, although the sensation of floating continued, the sights before her eyes were merely complicated patterns, endless in diversity and colour, which melted one into another like those of a kaleidoscope. It was very interesting to watch them, and she followed their changes eagerly, drifting down the river all the time.

There came disquieting interruptions to her enjoyment at last. Voices called to her—not the unknown voices of her visions, but voices that she knew—called to her earnestly, entreatingly, forcing themselves upon her attention when she desired only to watch the moving patterns. She felt a kind of resentment against these voices—a sort of malicious satisfaction in the fact that she could not answer their appeals, for there seemed to be a weight on her lips that kept them from moving. If only the voices would leave her in peace! There they were again, calling: "Lenchen, Lenchen! my little Lenchen! look at me, speak to me!" Before her eyes was a dun expanse flecked by splashes of colour that came and went, and against this background shadowy discs and half-discs appeared vaguely, took definite shape, became flaming and metallic, and vanished slowly away, as she watched them with breathless interest. She could not answer the cry that reached her, for the weight was still upon her lips, but it banished the vision, and in its place she saw a curious patchwork of many shapes and colours and patterns, something like the mosaic which industrious persons construct with small pieces of broken china sunk in cement. This also was interesting, although it had not the fascination of those advancing and receding discs, and she was watching the mosaic brighten and fade and re-group itself in new designs, when another voice broke in upon the dream, and made it vanish in its turn.

"Nell! Nell!" the voice cried, in tones of agony, and for the first time Helene felt an impulse to answer. But the weight was still upon her lips, and on the whole she was glad of it. Turning aside, as it were, petulantly from the call, she set herself joyfully to the contemplation of a myriad tiny bunches of pink-tipped daisies, floating in an atmosphere of dark dull green, which appealed to her almost more than all that had gone before. Nothing could be lovelier than this. Would it stay? would the daisy-buds unfold, or would they vanish into something else? Helene never knew, for into the midst of her vision came another sound, clear and distinct, the sound of a sob, before which the vision departed suddenly. She opened her eyes. There seemed to be no one in the room, but the sound of another sob guided her eyes to where Usk was kneeling beside the bed, his face hidden in the coverlid. The sight awoke Helene to pity and concern at once.

"Why, Nym!" she said, but her voice was the smallest, faintest whisper, and when she tried to stretch out her hand to lay it on the dark head just beyond her reach, she found that she could barely lift a finger. Usk heard the whisper, however, and as he lifted his head Helene had an odd feeling that the changes of which she had seen so many in her dreams were still going on, for his face was convulsed with pain when he raised it first, but as she looked at him she saw that he was smiling at her. It was most perplexing, but she smiled back at him, and then felt more perplexed still, for those warm drops that fell on her hand as he kissed it were certainly tears.

"Why, Nym!" she said again; and then suddenly, after a pause, "Nym, are you crying because I am going to die?"

"No—nonsense!—Of course not——" but his voice failed.

"I am so glad," said Helene, smiling radiantly, and Usk was cut to the heart. Had it come to this, that he had so utterly failed to make her happy that she was glad to die and leave him? But she was holding his hand fast.

"Sit beside me, Nym—close," she said eagerly, though her voice was so weak that he was obliged to lean over her to hear what she was saying, "and hold my hand. Don't let me drift down the river any more. If I do, I shall drift away, I know. Speak to me, call out to me, if you see me drifting, and hold my hand, so that you can pull me back."

"Are you afraid of going to sleep, dear?"

"No. I should like to sleep, but it is the river. It is pleasant—oh, so pleasant! but it will carry me away. Only you can keep me back, Nym. Your voice has driven the visions away. I think I could sleep safely if you put your arm round me, for I couldn't drift then. You won't let me go, will you?"

Not understanding in the least what she meant, and half inclined to think that she was still delirious, Usk passed his left arm under her head, still holding her right hand firmly in his own. Presently her eyes closed, but almost immediately they opened once more as she cried, "Oh, I was drifting again! Hold me, Nym; hold me!"

"I have got you quite safe," he answered, and at last she dropped asleep. Usk, trying to change his cramped position without waking her, happened to look towards the door, and saw the Grand-Duchess standing there, beckoning imperiously to him to come away. He shook his head, and tried to intimate that Helene must not be waked. His mother-in-law crept up to the bed.

"You have disturbed her!" she whispered angrily. "You have dared to move her! You may have killed my poor child!"

"No; I have saved her, I think," Usk whispered back. "She asked me to hold her."

"She asked you! She has spoken, then?"

"Yes. She seemed pleased to find me here, and as long as she wants me I shall stay." He could not bring himself to mention the words which had wounded him so sorely. He had taken his one small piece of revenge on the Grand-Duchess for the reproaches she had heaped upon him, and he would not put another weapon into her hand immediately.

"And after all, she turns to you instead of to me!" said Helene's mother, desolately; and Usk forbore to say that he could not conscientiously see any reason why she should not. He maintained his position, despite cramp and stiffness, until Helene awoke, and recognised her mother, and in the joy of that fact he and the Grand-Duchess buried their enmity. It would be long before Helene could return to her old active life,—there were weary months of pain and languor before her; but at least she would not slip out of life through sheer lack of interest in it, as she had been doing when Usk's voice recalled her. And yet, while the Grand-Duchess was unfeignedly grateful for her daughter's hope of recovery, and really glad she was happy with her husband, a curious maternal jealousy made it impossible for her ever to forget that it was Usk's voice, and not her own, which had brought Helene back from death.

"Nym," said Helene to her husband one day, in a puzzled tone, "why does mamma think you are not kind to me?"

"I'm sure I don't know, unless you have told her so. I haven't done anything particularly brutal just lately, have I?"

"Nym! as if I could be so wicked as to say things against you! But she seems to think the accident was your fault, and I have told her over and over again that it was mine for laying hold of the whip. And she blames the dear Count too, and nothing I can say will put it right."

"Well, perhaps you made shocking revelations in your delirium. I know you nearly broke my heart one day by something you said."

"Something I said? What was it?"

"You said you were glad to be going to die."

"I didn't! I couldn't! To leave you!"

"I'll take my oath of it. You asked me if that was why I was crying."

"Of course! I knew it! It was because you were crying that I was glad— to think you were so sorry to lose me."

"Well, this is startling and gratifying, I must say, after all my heroic determination to make you glad that you were alive, after all."

"Did you determine to make me glad I was alive, Nym? What were you going to do? Tell me."

"Why, I thought I would take you home—to England, I mean—by sea, before the winter gales begin, and that we would stay at Llandiarmid for a bit. I meant to get a low pony-carriage to drive you about in, and I thought we would spend whole days in the woods as long as it was warm enough. You don't know what the Llandiarmid woods are in autumn, Nell—how black the yew-trees look among the oaks and beeches on the river-cliff, and how pretty the golden birches are against the Scotch firs. And I thought we would take long drives, and stop at the farmhouses, and the tenants' wives would come out to be introduced to you, and tell you what a wretch of a husband you had got hold of, and ask if you wouldn't have a sup of new milk to bring some colour into your cheeks. And my mother would pet you, of course, and get so fond of you that I should have to forbid your going into the village with her, lest I should see nothing of you myself. And then perhaps you might be well enough about the end of November to come up to Southumberland with me, if the General Election was on then—not to canvass, of course, but just to go about with me and attract votes by looking so miserably pale, as if I ill-treated you, you know. That's just what I thought, you see."

"And now?" asked Helene breathlessly, smiling and flushing.

"Oh, now it's unnecessary, isn't it?"

"Couldn't you pretend it was necessary, Nym?"

"Oh, you like the programme, do you? Then we will pretend it's necessary, Nell. Every evening I shall ask you, 'Are you glad yet that you're alive?' and you will be hard-hearted, and say, 'Not yet.'"

"No, I shan't," said Helene, growing pink again. "I am glad because you are—because you don't repent. You don't, do you?"

"Repent what? Nell, don't be a baby."

"Oh, I have made you angry!—but you know what I mean. You don't mind having married me instead of Félicia, do you? I just want to hear you say it—only that."

"I'm not angry, but I should be if you were not such a child. Have I deserved this, Nell? I can't say that I have never thought of Félicia since I married you, but I can say that I never think of her without being thankful I didn't marry her. And you have been treasuring up that old piece of foolishness against me all this time!"

"I haven't! I haven't! It came over me suddenly that I wanted to hear you say it, though I knew it quite well. And I had a reason, Nym. You don't mind my not telling you what it is, do you? You will know very soon. I want to ask Aunt Ernestine something first."

"Shall I ask her to come and see you?"

"Oh, please do. And you are not really angry, Nym?"

"No, I am not. But it would serve you right if I said I was, you little mischief-maker!" But Helene's blissful smile did not look as though the epithet troubled her.

"Well, Lenchen darling?" asked the Queen as she came in; "what is it you want me to do?"

"It isn't anything for myself," said Helene, somewhat timidly. "It's—it's just that I have been thinking so much about Michael and Félicia, and I wondered why you didn't go and speak to her yourself."

"Why, what good could I do, Lenchen? My husband has tried, your father has tried, Mr Hicks has tried, and she won't listen to any of them."

"Yes, I know. But you see, Aunt Ernestine, I don't think they have any of them taken her the right way. Papa tells her that she will create a European scandal, and disgrace all her relations, and she doesn't mind that a bit. The dear Count reminds her that people will say horrid things about her, and that she won't be received at Vindobona, and she rather glories in it. Mr Hicks tells her that her money is invested in Thracia, and she may lose a good deal of it, and she says she doesn't care. When they told her even that the Thracian Legislature would dissolve the marriage if she wouldn't come back, she was startled at first, but she only said she would chance it. Oh, I know exactly what they would each say. I make mamma tell me all about it. But no one has gone to her yet simply as a woman. There must be some way of reaching her and working on her feelings, you know, and you are Michael's mother, you love them both—why don't you do it?"

"My little Lenchen, I am afraid I have only thought how wicked it was of her to leave Michael, and it wouldn't soften her much to hear that."

"Ah, but you will think of her side of it too?" asked Helene earnestly. "I think she must be terribly miserable all this time. Just imagine if I had run away from Usk, how I should feel!"

"I fear there isn't much likeness between you and Félicia, Lenchen," said the Queen, kissing her. "But I have always intended to see what I could do if all other means failed, and I will try now instead of waiting any longer. And I will try to look at the matter from her point of view."

Thus it was that when Cyril made his next journey across the mountains to Paranati, his wife accompanied him. She was slightly nervous as to her reception on board the Bluebird, for her conscience told her that Helene's words were true. In her horror at Félicia's unheard-of behaviour, she had forgotten to inquire whether Félicia might seem to herself to have sufficient reason for it. What Cyril thought of her sudden determination to go with him she did not know, for he refused to discuss the situation with her, lest Félicia should suspect her of having been primed by him. Maimie, who had come on shore to meet them, looked at her keenly, but was equally reticent. Of her Queen Ernestine was a little afraid, not knowing whether to regard her as Félicia's evil genius or as a moderating influence, and she did not like to question her as to Félicia's feelings. Félicia herself looked thinner and a little worn, and the Queen wondered whether it was *ennui* that was telling upon her, or a sense of her equivocal position, as impressed upon her by Cyril and the Grand-Duke. She rebuked herself immediately for lack of charity, and wondered why she could not simply believe that Félicia really cared for Michael, and was regretting the step she had taken. But this she found impossible, which was a bad beginning to her mission.

"Well," said Félicia suddenly, when they were alone together, "why are you come? I guess it wasn't just for your health. Did Mr Hicks send you?"

"No; certainly not," answered Queen Ernestine, taken aback by the tone and accent of the question as much as by its drift, "but I should have been very glad to come sooner if I had known you would like to see me."

Félicia laughed scornfully. "Mr Hicks thought he would get you here and have you talk me over, but I told him if he said a single word to you I wouldn't see you when you came. But why did you come, any way?"

"It was not Mr Hicks who sent me. It was my niece Helene, Usk's wife."

"Do tell! Is she so happy that she wants to see every one else happy too?"

"I think that was her feeling."

"Oh, it wasn't because if I remained unattached I might attract her husband away from her?"

"I am quite certain she had no thought of the kind. She has no fear for her husband, and she need have none." The Queen spoke strongly, for the suggestion had made her angry, but it occurred to her that this was not a very propitious opening to the interview. She drew nearer to her daughter-in-law. "Félicia," she said, "you believe I wish you well, don't you? My only desire is to see you and Michael living happily together. Do you feel it quite impossible"—she hesitated a little over the form of the question—"to return to him."

"Quite," answered Félicia calmly. "The insult was too great. He had absolutely no excuse for his conduct."

"I don't want to palliate it, but—had he any reason to think you would listen patiently if he spoke to you first? Was there such confidence between you that his jealousy was palpably unreasonable?"

"I don't know what you mean," said Félicia, sitting up in her chair, her eyes flashing. "If you are trying to shift the blame on to me——"

"I am not, believe me. All I mean is that you and Michael together had treated Usk very cruelly. Had Michael any guarantee that you would not treat him in the same way if you could?"

"I don't know," with a superb gesture of disdain. "I just expect to be trusted without any question of guarantees. Your son has had to learn that, and I guess the world will know it too before long."

"But, Félicia, you must make allowances for Michael. I don't defend his action, but will you not forgive it? I believe he really loves you, and I think he must have had some idea of satisfying his mind without entering on a disagreeable subject with you."

"But he broke open my bureau to read my letters," Félicia persisted.

"I know—but he has been punished for it. And he is anxious for your forgiveness, and has done all he could to shield your name."

"Oh, that's the Baroness's doing," said Félicia lazily.

"You make it very hard for me to plead for him. Surely, Félicia, you must have a little kindness left for him—the man you promised to love and honour?"

"I thought it was generally understood that those promises were made because one couldn't get married without them," said Félicia. "How has he kept his?"

"You must have some slight feeling for him, or you could not be so bitter. See, Félicia, I am his mother, and for his sake I lay aside my pride, and entreat you to forgive him. It is well that he should know how a woman regards such an insult as he offered you; but what will be the effect on him if his penitence brings him no pardon? You have a great opportunity before you now. He admires you, loves you, feels that he has misjudged you shamefully. If you return to him, you may exert such an influence over him as may change his whole character. I don't mean that he will ever be a husband on whose strength you can lean, but if you choose to—to fascinate him, as you can fascinate any man if you will, you may be of the greatest service both to him and the kingdom——"

"Yes; it's all right for Michael and the kingdom, but where do I come in?" cried Félicia shrilly. "I want to have a good time."

"I think that is what you have always aimed at," suggested Queen Ernestine, with unintentional irony, "and it has never yet——"

"Materialised," supplied Félicia. "That is so, but I don't expect now to find it in a little no-account State way back in the Balkans."

"Perhaps if you don't think so much about the good time it will be more likely to come to you. Think of your duty, instead, both as wife and as queen. Ah, Félicia, you can do so much for the kingdom. I tried, and failed. For the sake of the kingdom, I put aside my life's happiness for thirteen years—and at the end of those years it seemed that I had lost it for ever. I don't pretend that I made the sacrifice with a good grace—my husband could tell you quite the contrary—but at least I tried. You have none of my disadvantages. I was much younger than you are, and very soon made myself unpopular by listening to unwise advice, and I was foolishly jealous of the king's wisest and most trusted adviser. You are beautiful, rich, fascinating, and you are not afraid of taking your own line. I think you have a shrewd adviser in Miss Logan. I know you have a faithful one in Baroness Radnika——"

"I guess you don't know that Maimie and I don't speak now," interrupted Félicia. "We've quarrelled about this. She would like to have me accept Michael's apology, and go right back."

"And you have quarrelled with her? Oh, Félicia, she may have given you unwise advice at other times, but she is right now. I looked forward to your doing so much in Thracia in raising the condition of the women. They are so despised, so badly treated by the men—almost as badly as the Roumi women. And if the men take your doings as a sample of what is to be expected from civilised womanhood——"

"It will put back the clock in the Balkans a century at least?" suggested Félicia. "And to prevent that you'd have me take Michael back into favour?"

"No," said the Queen, wincing slightly, "to prevent your both leading soured, loveless lives apart from each other, always in search of pleasure and never finding it. If Michael were not penitent, I would not ask you to return to him. But you will understand each other better, you will grow nearer to each other after this separation, will you not?"

"I guess Michael will understand me better, any way. But I don't incline to go nearer to him than now—not much!"

"Félicia!" cried Queen Ernestine, in bitter disappointment, "is there nothing that will move you? Have you no regard for any one or anything?"

"That I have,—a real strong regard for one woman that no other person seems to think of at all. All of you come and talk to me about the kingdom, and Michael, and my own august relations, and political exigencies, and you yourself try to work upon my feelings for everything all round, but I myself count for just nothing. I have to watch out for my own interests, and I mean to do it. There isn't one of you cares a cent for me——"

"Indeed we do, Félicia," protested her mother-in-law feebly.

"As Michael's recalcitrant wife, maybe—not for myself. But I have one adviser that's shrewd enough, as you say, and she don't care a cent for any of you—just for me alone, though I was awfully ugly to her last time we spoke, and if I listen to any one, it'll be to her. Maime," she raised her voice, "come right in. I didn't feel like listening to you last time we talked, but now you may just state what you think. What good would it do me to go back to Michael?"

"Why, just this," said Maimie promptly, advancing into the cabin, and speaking with entire disregard of Queen Ernestine and her feelings, "you've staked out your claim, and you've got to work it."

"You had me do it," objected Félicia.

"And if I did, I'll help you see the thing through. It's not what you expected, maybe, but it's payable gold, and you won't do better any other place."

"Now that's what I don't see."

"Well, just listen. Put it you act the way you want to, and go right back to the States. Michael will get a divorce, and you'll have to stick over there, for you won't be received at any Court in Europe."

"Well, I guess America's good enough for me," but the tone was less resolute. Maimie seized upon the hint of wavering.

"*Is* that so? How will you feel to go back to old times after what you've got accustomed to these days? Félicia Steinherz, you can't do it. Just at present you're a queen, whatever that's worth, and I'd advise you stick to the position. Maybe you'll choose to do all of the nice things you've been hearing about, maybe not, but any way, you're much more likely to have a good time than if you take your separation."

"Well," said Félicia meditatively, "that is so. I'll go back to Bellaviste right away."

"Now? at once?" cried Queen Ernestine, bewildered by this sudden success. "But not quite so suddenly," she pleaded, after a moment's astonished pause. "It would excite remark, and deprive Michael of the pleasure he would feel in coming to welcome you. Come back with us to Drinitza, and let him meet you there."

"I guess I will. I'd like to meet that little Helene of yours, too, and have her see what a happy couple Michael and I are."

"Félicia, you will not go back to him in this spirit? What possible hope of future happiness can there be——?"

"Why, just this. Your son has had his lesson, and unless he's a fool he won't need any more. If he does, the Bluebird will be on hand yet."

"I hoped you might be going to yield to his wishes in the matter of the yacht. It would be a very graceful concession, and he could not help being touched by it. It would show your confidence in him——"

"Confidence?" repeated Félicia. "I don't confide in him worth a cent. You say he can't trust me because I tricked Usk? Well, he helped me do it, so I can't trust him. I shall continue to run the Bluebird myself, and I'll have Mr Hicks get a relief crew ready for me when this one wants to go home. And after all, you can just take it from me that this will be the best thing for Michael too. He would trample on a woman that couldn't defend herself, but one who's as strong as he is he will respect. And I guess I'll have him know that he can't trample on me."

A few weeks later, and the gathering at Drinitza had dispersed to the four winds of heaven. The Grand-Duke and Duchess had returned to Molzau, and Michael and Félicia to Bellaviste. Lord and Lady Caerleon were on their way to Pavelsburg, where they were to meet Prince Soudaroff (purely on a business footing) and arrange with him for the fulfilment of his sister-in-law's dying wishes; and Usk and Helene, with their diminished retinue, were on board a leisurely, old-fashioned steamer, which was supposed to be likely to reach England before the end of the year. Cyril and his wife were at Trieste, whence they intended to sail for Syria, but before leaving they were to meet the Chevalier Goldberg, who had entreated them mysteriously not to sail before seeing something that he had to show them. They drove down to a wharf belonging to a private firm, at which a large steamer was loading, and here the Chevalier met them, joyful, alert, elated, almost inspired.

"Well, Chevalier, and where is this wonderful sight?" asked Cyril, looking round at the crates and boxes which were ready to be shipped. At present, what looked like a number of huge blocks of stone were being swung on board.

"Dis iss it," was the proud reply, as the Chevalier waved his hand to include all the bustle around, "de crown off your worrk, Count—de consummation off de freeink off Issrael."

"But what are all these things? and what are they for?"

"Dey are de stones off de Temple which iss to be built in de Holy City."

"You are actually going to rebuild the Temple! Why, you never told me."

"It wass a secret hope, not to be told efen to de Chentile det hed done so much for Zion. But de stones hef been preparink for a cheneration, maybe lonker. See, here are de great blocks off marble for buildink—all squared and dressed, so det dere may be no sound off iron on de sacred site. Dere iss only one small part off dem on board dis ship; oders will follow. In dese boxes and cases are many oder thinks—rare marble off many colours for de linink off de walls, carfed by de greatest artists, wonderful metal-work, mosaic off precious stones, holy fessels off golt and silfer, embroideries such ess queens and sultans might lonk for in fain. All dose det are wise-hearted hef gifen, men and women alike—de poor woman her silfer clasp, de rich woman her diamonds. De glory off dis letter House shell be greater den any since de first."

"And you mean literally to revive the Temple ritual and everything connected with it?"

"Why not? We hef de priests, de sons off Aaron, we hef de secrifices in abundance, we hef de silfer and de golt, we hef at last de right to our own land. How could we dare delay, lest punishment come upon us for our sleckness?"

Cyril shook his head. "You are frightfully ill-advised," he said. "A temple, with sacrifices and all the other accompaniments of ancient Jewish worship, in the very midst of the holy places of Christendom, will revolt the world. It will unite all your enemies against you, and give them a tremendous power for mischief."

"How long hef we been refolted by de idols set up in de midst off our holy places? Let de Chentiles taste a little off de treatment dey hef gifen us. We are not afraid off what dey can do. We hef our rights guaranteed to us by de man raised up to help us. We are not dependent on de goodwill off Christendom."

"You would find it safer to be dependent upon a number of powers than on one despot. Their mutual jealousies might hinder their uniting against you, but he has only himself to please."

"Gif us only our guaranteed sefen years, and we shell be too stronk for any despot on earth to attack us."

"Only seven years? I didn't know your guarantee was limited. Well, if Malasorte leaves you undisturbed for the full seven years, he is not the man I think him."

"Count! Count! after all your noble worrk for our great cause, are you become a prophet off efil against us?"

"*Buona sorte, mala fede,*" quoted Cyril. "Even supposing that Timoleon V. has the best will in the world towards you, he has to think of his other friends. The Vatican and the Jesuits have got nothing yet for their support, and you think it a good opportunity to outrage their tenderest susceptibilities and exhibit an alien religion, possessing immense wealth, established at Jerusalem!"

"But why should det signify to dem?"

"Need you ask? Well, my wife and sister-in-law would probably be able to tell you, from the study of prophecy, the exact year or day you may expect the explosion, but I, as a practical man, will merely say that I shall be very much surprised if you are still at Jerusalem when your seven years are over. The Pope may be established there, and your temple turned into a second St Peter's, for all I can say."

"Ah, we shell worrk wid de Orthodox against dem."

"Don't be too sure. Neustria and Scythia united against us three years ago, you know. The two Emperors are very friendly, and there is time for their respective Churches to become friendly too. Well, there will always be a welcome for you at Sitt Zeynab, Chevalier, if you are driven out."

"Nefer! nefer! Wid all Issrael, I will die fightink in de Temple courts before Yerushalem shell fall again into de hends off de Chentiles. No, Count, we hef receifed our punishment, efen double, for all our sins. You hef lost your name. De Keptifity iss ofer for efer."

He bowed them off the wharf, and returned to his self-imposed task of superintending the loading of the ship, as if opposition had made him only the more determined to go on with it. Cyril and his wife walked some way in silence, and when he spoke, it was not of the Chevalier or his scheme.

"When we left Sitt Zeynab, I little thought I should be glad to return to it," he said at last.

"I know; you have always felt you were in exile there. But to me it is a haven of peace. I can't feel that you are safe anywhere else."

"Do you know, Ernestine, that when we left it last winter I was brimming over with ambition, though I didn't say so to you? I had an idea that my old powers might return if I plunged suddenly into the midst of the old life."

"Yes, I thought so when you were so determined to answer Michael's appeal for your help in person."

"And you never said so? Wise woman! Well, here I am returning meekly, quite shorn of my aspirations. Michael is safely married, but to the very last person we should have thought of for him then. Usk is married too, not at all to the girl who seemed obviously suitable. The Thracian finances are placed on a sound footing, but thanks far more to Félicia's money than to any skill of mine. Scythia is out of Palestine, but Malasorte's the friend, not Mortimer. And as for myself, instead of juggling with crowns, I am thankful to be rescued from a lunatic asylum. I not only did no good, but gave a great deal of trouble to other people. In future we will take our politics quietly, looking on at them from a distance."

"And living happily among our own people, doing what we can for them. You think you can be happy, Cyril?"

"Don't ask me to make rash declarations. At least I can say that, in view of ending my days at Sitt Zeynab, I am—content."

THE END.

Milton Keynes UK
Ingram Content Group UK Ltd.
UKHW040818051024
449151UK00004B/307